OUR SECRET CONSTITUTION

OTHER BOOKS BY GEORGE P. FLETCHER

Rethinking Criminal Law (1978)
A Crime of Self-Defense: Bernhard Goetz and the Law on Trial (1988)
Loyalty: An Essay on the Morality of Relationships (1992)
With Justice for Some: Victims' Rights in Criminal Trials (1995)
Basic Concepts of Legal Thought (1996)
Basic Concepts of Criminal Law (1998)

OUR SECRET CONSTITUTION

*How Lincoln Redefined
American Democracy*

GEORGE P. FLETCHER

OXFORD
UNIVERSITY PRESS
2001

149503

OXFORD
UNIVERSITY PRESS

Oxford New York
Athens Auckland Bangkok Bogotá
Buenos Aires Calcutta Cape Town Chennai Dar es Salaam
Delhi Florence Hong Kong Istanbul Karachi
Kuala Lumpur Madrid Melbourne
Mexico City Mumbai Nairobi Paris São Paulo Shanghai
Singapore Taipei Tokyo Toronto Warsaw

and associated companies in
Berlin Ibadan

Published by Oxford University Press, Inc.
198 Madison Avenue, New York, New York 10016

Oxford is a registered trademark of Oxford University Press

Library of Congress Cataloging-in-Publication Data
Fletcher, George P.
Our secret constitution: how Lincoln redefined
American democracy / George P. Fletcher.
p. cm. Includes bibliographical references and index.
ISBN 0-19-514142-3
1. Lincoln, Abraham, 1809–1865—Political and social views.
2. Constitutional history—United States.
3. Constitutional amendments—United States.
4. United States Constitution. 13–15th Amendments.
5. United States—Politics and government—1861–1865.
I. Title.
E457.2.F57 2001 320.1'0973'09034—dc21 00-057495

1 3 5 7 9 8 6 4 2

Printed in the United States of America
on acid-free paper

In memory of two teachers,
my father, Miklós, and my uncle Alex,
both immigrants and Americans,
both lovers of freedom and of equality

CONTENTS

PREFACE

About five years ago I was asked to give a lecture in Moscow on the question: Why do Europeans and Americans take distinctively different approaches to the scope of free speech; in particular, why are Europeans—but not Americans—willing to ban hate speech? This puzzle started me thinking about the systemic differences between the European and American constitutional traditions. I formulated a few claims for the lecture, which touched upon some of the arguments in this book. Bruce Ackerman paid me the compliment of saying, in his inimitable fashion, that I had "an idea." This was all the encouragement I needed to begin an extended exploration of American constitutional history. I was in the midst of these studies when Timothy McVeigh was charged with killing 168 people by planting a bomb in the federal building in Oklahoma City, allegedly a terrorist action and mass murder on behalf of the Republic as McVeigh thought the founders intended it.

Something was awry. How could the noble American dream of 1787 end up as homicidal terror in Oklahoma City? And how could we Americans who prosecute criminals, teach law, and write books—we the guardians of revolutionary myths—not recognize our complicity in the twisting of McVeigh's mind? We nurture a culture of fantasy about the basic freedoms established in the American Revolution and then we seek the death penalty against someone who takes these fantasies seriously.

There must be, I concluded, another side of the story. We must be hiding something—something that most of us know but that right-wing fanatics like McVeigh never comprehend. This hidden understanding, as I eventually formulated it, is Our Secret Constitution. How this hidden constitution came about and how it shapes our lives became a story worth telling.

My first cut at this new interpretation of constitutional history appeared in an article, "Unsound Constitution" in the June 1997 issue of *The New Republic*. Reactions to that article convinced me that there was an audience for a more elaborate rendition of the tale. Fortunately, my agent Angela Miller and my editor at Oxford Cynthia Read agreed and encouraged the project. I am indebted to both of these loyal readers and advisors.

When I started presenting my ideas to colleagues in law schools, I was pleasantly surprised by their willingness to hear and consider novel ideas about our constitutional history. I recall and appreciate warm nods of encouragement from Robert Post, Ken Karst, Akhil Amar, Kent Greenawalt, Anthony Dillof, David Richards, Sanford Levinson, Arthur Jacobson, Mark Tushnet, Andrzej Rapaczynski and, of course, Bruce Ackerman. The telling of the story of Gettysburg and the Civil War would hardly have been interesting—either for the reader or for myself—had I not been willing to think about the war from the Southern point of view. I am deeply indebted to my friend Steve Sheppard, a faithful son of Mississippi, for patiently bringing me to understand that in the "house divided"—as in most controversies—there were two angles of vision. Sheppard's understanding of the historical detail far exceeded my own, and he helped inordinately in trying to get the facts right.

The distinguished American historians at Columbia proved to be surprisingly generous in their counsel. Anders Stephanson and Eric Foner read the manuscript and offered me several helpful suggestions. I recognize that as a lawyer, I relate history with an interpretive edge that professional historians might not share. Yet I am pleased to have found a common language with those who are the curators of our American self-understanding.

Many of my ideas about religion and redemption found a sound testing in a seminar I offered to the political theory group at Yale in April 1999. I recall with appreciation the helpful comments of Steven Smith, John McCormick, and Robert Adams.

I want to express my appreciation to Ekow Yankah, Jeremy Pam, David Alexander, Margaret Garnett, and other students in my seminars, all of whom participated in various stages of the jelling of these ideas. Frank Lossy gave me a valuable critique of the Afterword. Above all, I am grateful to Russell Christopher, who, on this as on many other books, worked with me as my trusted associate.

Mentioning all these friends and colleagues reminds me of the pleasures and intellectual adventures enjoyed in writing these pages. One can only hope that the joy of these ideas will be infectious and that many of my readers will be moved to express themselves on these themes. Those who are so inclined may post their views and read the reactions of others on the website: *http://www.LegalDiscourse.org*.

May these pages and the ensuing discussion contribute to a new and better understanding of the Civil War and the American constitutional vision.

New York   George P. Fletcher
December 2000

THE ARGUMENT
FOR THE SECRET
CONSTITUTION

"We dance round in a ring and suppose,
But the Secret sits in the middle and knows."
—*Robert Frost*

Y ou are about to confront, my dear reader, a subtle and unusual argument. I will ask you to put aside your conventional assumptions about the law and the Constitution. I
invite you to think about the American legal system in the way you
might think about the psychological makeup of a person. We all know
that beneath the manifest behavior of an individual there lies a deep
structure of understanding that guides our actions more than we realize. We call this bedrock of the personality the "unconscious." Or, we
could call this underlying dimension of the legal personality the "deep
structure" of the legal culture. The term comes from the field of grammar. Noam Chomsky conceptualized the rules that guide our sense of
correct usage as the "deep structure" of language.[1] Therefore, the first
idea that I ask you to imagine is that there is an analogous bedrock of
our legal culture that influences and shapes the decisions of courts and
lawyers the way the unconscious influences behavior or the deep grammar shapes our sense of proper syntax.

In the same way that experience shapes our individual unconscious,
the historical experience of the American legal culture defines the deep
structure of the legal system. The most significant event in American

1

legal history, I will argue, is the Civil War that ravaged the country from April 1861 to April 1865. This war began with one set of purposes and ended with another. The original motive for resisting Southern secession was preserving the Union. The resulting and final idea was to abolish slavery and reinvent the United States on the basis of a new set of principles.

ORIGINS OF OUR SECOND AND SECRET CONSTITUTION

The Civil War called forth a new constitutional order. At the heart of this postbellum legal order lay the Reconstruction Amendments—the Thirteenth, Fourteenth, and Fifteenth Amendments, ratified in the years 1865 to 1870. The principles of this new legal regime are so radically different from our original Constitution, drafted in 1787, that they deserve to be recognized as a second American constitution. The new constitution established, in fact, a second American Republic. The first Constitution was based on the principles of peoplehood as a voluntary association, individual freedom, and republican élitism. The guiding premises of the second constitution were, in contrast, organic nationhood, equality of all persons, and popular democracy. These are principles radically opposed to each other. That we may appreciate the sharp contrast between these two visions of America, let us rehearse the points of difference, with a modest explanation of each set of opposites:

Choice versus Self-Realization.   The preamble to the 1787 national charter begins with the words "We the People." The people come together, at least as imagined by their self-appointed representatives in Philadelphia, to form "a more perfect Union." The emphasis is on voluntary association. We the people *choose* our form of government. The key word that defines Americans in the fraternal war of the 1860s is not their voluntary association in a *people* but the bond that defines them as a single *nation*. Choice marks the people. History breeds the nation. In the face of dissolution, Abraham Lincoln and his generation realized the ties—"the bonds of affection" of Lincoln's first inaugural address[2]— that led men to fight for the Union. The 1787 Constitution stands, therefore, for the choice of the people. The Civil War constitution builds on a recognition of organic nationhood as the legacy of the American experience.

Freedom versus Equality. The Constitution of 1787 stands for a maximum expression of individual freedom, at least against the federal government. Not only does the Bill of Rights safeguard the basic freedoms of speech, religion, and assembly, but the charter of the first Republic stood as well for the right of white people to assert themselves freely to seize and control the lives of certain other people known as Negroes. The second constitution is dedicated to the proposition that all men are created equal. The individual rights sanctified in the Bill of Rights carved out a space for each person to stand alone, free of governmental interference. The postbellum constitution emphasized not freedom from government but equality under law. The state would have to do more than leave us alone. It would have to ensure the equal protection of the laws for all.

Elitism versus Popular Democracy. The Constitution of 1787 entrenched élitist government. The model was the New England town meeting. The virtuous few, basically the white propertied males of the community, would concern themselves about the issues of public life. If this was self-government, the "self" was very limited indeed. The notion of "government by the people" takes on different contours in the second constitution. Virtue gives way to preferences and politics. Rule by the few surrenders, slowly and progressively, to the rough and tumble of universal adult suffrage.

These, then, are the three themes that run through this book—nationhood, equality, and democracy. Together, they define a new constitutional order that has its roots not in the late-eighteenth-century war against England but in the mid-nineteenth-century war between North and South.

Besides these striking dualities, other differences between the first and second American constitutions present themselves. The first Constitution is an expression of secular will: We the people convene to "establish a more perfect Union." They recognize no power higher than their agreed-upon aims. They think of the future—not of their debt to the past. The second constitution rests on the recognition that "four score and seven years" of history had created an organic bond among Americans, a bond that was expressed by thinking of the nation as having a distinctive mission in history. Lincoln expressed this distinct mission by referring, in the Gettysburg Address, to the "nation under God." Thus, the movement from peoplehood to nationhood also represented a shift from a purely secular will to create a better government toward a philosophy of submission to historical obligation and the recognition of a divine mission in history.

All of these themes are signaled in the Gettysburg Address, Lincoln's famous two-minute speech, delivered on November 19, 1863 in the middle of the war, in the apparent belief that "the world will little note nor long remember what we say here." In fact, the nation did remember and cherish those words at Gettysburg as the articulation of a new vision for American society. The themes articulated at Gettysburg captured the American yearning for a postbellum order based on principles radically different from the ideas that founded the Republic in the Constitution that took force in 1789. These 268 words, repeated regularly in school assemblies and preserved in stone at the Lincoln Memorial in Washington, became the secular prayer of the postbellum American Republic. Every time they are intoned, they remind us of our collective commitment to nationhood, equality, and democracy.

The Gettysburg Address functions in our historical consciousness as the preamble of the second American constitution. The second constitution, as initially articulated and embodied in the Reconstruction Amendments, was bold and explicit. Yet, the pragmatic mood of government that seized the American mind in the wake of the Civil War, the yearning for compromise after years of confrontational rhetoric and bloodshed, eventually drove the new constitution underground. It became our Secret Constitution, influencing us in the persistent recesses of memory. To appreciate how this happened, we must grasp the ideological contradictions laid bare in the Civil War. On the surface, the problem was not only the epic conflict between Union and secession and, as Theodore Parker put it, between the "Slave Power" and the "Free Power." At a less fully articulated level, the conflict centered on competing versions of the rule of law.

According to the moralistic vision of the abolitionists, the law—to be law in full sense—must incorporate higher principles of right and wrong.[3] Constitutional rules have no vitality if they fail to resonate with our most basic perceptions of justice.[4] Because the first Constitution incorporated accommodation on the issue of slavery, William Lloyd Garrison labeled it a "covenant with death" and an "agreement with Hell."[5] In issuing the Emancipation Proclamation in September 1862 and at Gettysburg in November 1863, Lincoln showed that he, too, understood the impulse to ground the Union in principles of higher law.[6]

In contrast, there stood the philosophy of the CSA—the Confederate States of America—an ideology that stressed autonomy and sovereignty, regardless of content. The best version of the Southern cause would be that they did not fight for slavery per se but rather to uphold their local autonomy to decide for themselves whether to keep their "peculiar institution." For them, the rule of law was not the sword of justice but rather a shield that insulated them from criticism. By upholding the practice of slavery, the 1787 Constitution should have guaranteed their sovereignty over the issue. As the drafters in Philadelphia suspended judgment about the merits of slavery for the sake of accommodation and union, the South believed that they had the right to decide for themselves whether to follow the worldwide trend and abolish slavery.[7] This attitude toward the Constitution and local autonomy is aptly called "legalism," for it treats the observance of legal rules not as the pursuit of justice for all but rather as a bulwark against one group's imposing its sense of justice on another.

The faith in principles of higher law explains why Lincoln, in the aftermath of war, was committed to articulating a new foundation for the Union. It accounts as well for Lincoln's casual attitude toward formal constitutional institutions, such as the writ of habeas corpus.[8] It also explains why, after Lincoln's assassination, the radical Republicans in Congress used allegedly illegal means to coerce the South to accept the Fourteenth Amendment.[9] Faith in a higher law leads to the view: Truth and Justice must prevail over legalistic formalities.

Those who fight in the name of the higher law allow themselves to sidestep the rules. Lincoln himself had doubts about the niceties of constitutional rules protecting individual liberty. Suspending the writ of habeas corpus, he imprisoned thousands of suspected copperhead Southern sympathizers without trial.[10] The Union suppressed over a hundred newspapers. By contrast, the "legalistic" Confederacy held, according to Robert Penn Warren, closer to the principles of civil liberties than did the "virtuous" North. They suspended the writ of habeas corpus only on a few limited occasions and they suppressed no newspapers.[11] Perhaps they did not have to worry as much as did Northerners about dissent from within.

These two attitudes—faith in higher law principles and the kind of legalism that insulates against criticism—stake out the extreme poles in our recurrent debates about law and justice in the postbellum republic. We should keep them in mind as we recount the fate of Lincoln's vision for a new constitutional order based on nationhood, equality, and democracy.

The ethics of higher law inspired the politics of the radical Republicans in the initial stages of Reconstruction after the war. The faith in the cause was evident in the manner in which Congress adopted the Fourteenth Amendment; the postbellum 39th Congress excluded ten Southern states from voting until they ratified this cornerstone of the new constitutional order. Some scholars claim that the Congress was entitled to coerce the conquered states to submit to the terms of peace.[12] Others argue that the Fourteenth Amendment found legitimation in a de facto standard for amending the original Constitution without observing the rigors of Article V.[13] It is better, in my view, to think of the 39th Congress as setting the foundation for a new constitution based on faith in the higher principles of equality and national solidarity that motivated the Union cause.

Yet, the legalism of the Confederacy lived on in the attitudes of the postbellum judiciary. In the decades after the surrender at Appomattox, the values of "states' rights" and "local autonomy" of the first Constitution enjoyed new vigor in the courts. The recourse to these antebellum slogans came partly as an expression of yearning for continuity with the past. In the aftermath of the Civil War, we also witness a third way of legal analysis—a "pragmatic" middle road between the ethics of higher law and the resistance to criticism that cloaks itself in the language of rights and autonomy. Pragmatic legal thinking, with its suspicion of ideological extremes, comes into its own as a generation of soldiers sought to heal and overcome the experience of fighting against their brothers in the North and the South.[14]

The bold plan for Reconstruction, based on the principles of nationhood and equality, encountered resistance from entrenched attitudes that had taken root before the agony of war. The Supreme Court invalidated the first major civil rights bill designed to eliminate discrimination in the public sphere and the justices tried to cabin the "equal protection" provision of the Fourteenth Amendment so that it applied, at most, to state-sponsored racial apartheid laws.[15] Even official segregation eventually won approval in the temporary defeat of Lincoln's vision of a nation "conceived in liberty and dedicated to the proposition that all men are created equal."[16]

Judicial decisions can suppress principles of higher law, but they cannot destroy them. Even after the judges turned their backs on the new order, the second constitution, sanctified by the six hundred thousand who died in its gestation, remained a firm but minimally visible commitment of American political culture. The Civil War constitution became our alternative charter, our Secret Constitution, waiting in the wings for a more propitious time to step out on the stage of open judicial debate.

The principles of nationhood, equality, and democracy began to express themselves in arenas other than the courts. The most significant traces are found in the variety of amendments to the Constitution enacted since the Civil War. The fourteen official amendments adopted between 1865 and 1993 reveal a little-noticed pattern, a systematic effort to remake the United States in the image originally cast at Gettysburg. These amendments spread the franchise, strengthen the powers of government, and, as a political interpretation of what equality requires in practice, they express compassion for the weak. They serve the implicit purposes of the Secret Constitution. They were all designed to further the causes of nationhood, equality, and popular democracy.

Even amendments repeatedly proposed but not yet passed by the required majorities in Congress—for example, the popular proposals to protect the victims of crime and to protect the flag against desecration—express the commitments of the Civil War constitution. As the much maligned Prohibition amendment sought to protect the weak from their inclination to alcohol abuse, the victims' movement has generated interest in protecting those rendered weak and defenseless by criminal behavior. Victims of crime arguably require more compassion than acknowledged in the Bill of Rights, which focuses primarily on the rights of criminal suspects.

The controversial flag amendment also expresses the spirit of the Secret Constitution. The symbol of the nation requires protection in order to foster the value of nationhood. These are the messages of a constitution embedded in our consciousness but not yet fully realized in the politics of law making.

The concern for victims of crime signals a larger theme that we might call the politics of equality. These efforts to extend legal protection to the weak and defenseless have their roots in the postbellum thrust toward egalitarian jurisprudence. Equality means that the humble as well as the strong shall prosper in America. Social legislation comes forth in the aftermath of the Civil War, when Congress adopted welfare programs to care for the widows and orphans of the war and, in addition, took affirmative measures to support the future of the freed blacks.[17] After some setbacks in the courts, these policies eventually came to prevail in the welfare legislation of the late 1930s. They continue to unfold today in the form of federal initiatives designed to promote equality in the workplace and to secure the interests of those who are at a competitive disadvantage.

The roots of current policies lie in the constitutional order that should have emerged from the brutal crucible of the Civil War, but that, because of resistance from the courts, became instead our implicit commitments—our Secret Constitution—waiting to be realized in practice. The ideological groundwork for an activist government that would protect the weak and promote equality was forged in the suffering of both strong and weak in the killing fields of Gettysburg and Antietam.

In order to understand the Secret Constitution, we need to avoid the bias of lawyers preoccupied with the work of the courts. The legal system reaches deeper than the decisions and opinions of judges. It is expressed in our collective understanding of our historical debts and in the implicit commitments of our national experience. As Mark Tushnet has argued in his most recent book, we must now take the "constitution away from the courts."[18] We must think in broader terms of a constitution implicit in the basic political assumptions of our politics.

Like a rule of grammar that explains speaking behavior without itself being observable, the powerful principles of the suppressed postbellum constitutional vision reappear from time to time, in different forms, and with different purposes. The principle of equality, for example, now looms as the regulative principle for understanding many of the basic rights laid down in the Bill of Rights. With varying degrees of success, reformers invoke the principle of equality in debates over the proper scope of free speech, the right way to recognize freedom of religion, and the correct measure of procedural rights to be accorded criminal defendants. In all of these areas, the commitment to equality provides the source of values that weigh against unqualified rights of speech, of religion, and of criminal defense. Those who are hurt by racist speech, those discriminated against when the religious receive special privileges, the victims of crime who are forgotten in the rush to protect defendants—these other groups are now the beneficiaries of the politics of equality.

To summarize, there are three distinct stages in the emergence of our current constitutional framework of controversy. The first stage is the crystallization of higher law principles beginning with the Gettysburg Address and culminating, at the level of black-letter law, in the Reconstruction Amendments ratified between 1865 and 1870. The second stage is the rejection of this new order in the courts of the 1870s and 1880s. The judicial rejection drove the new higher law principles underground. Official rejection generated a Secret Constitution that would begin to rule us from its intended grave. The third phase of history begins with the reassertion of the Secret Constitution, first in constitutional amendments, then in academic discourse, and, finally, in the rhetoric and the decisions of the Supreme Court. In short, the Secret Constitution goes underground and then gradually reemerges to shape the thinking of lawyers, politicians, academics, and judges.

A fourth stage requires brief mention. The assertion of the equality principle in certain areas of our constitutional history, particularly in the field of free speech, called forth resistance in modern doctrines of free expression. Our commitment to freedom of speech and of the press supposedly dates back to the adoption of the First Amendment in 1791. But this historical rooting is largely rhetorical. As we shall see, the "new birth of freedom" in the fields of speech and press are of recent origin, and they stand as a counterweight to the new politics of equality. This summary of the four stages of the argument provides a roadmap for the detailed journey of this book.

My aim is to induce readers to think differently about both law and the American political experience. I recognize that it is a bit of rhetorical indulgence to claim that we have two constitutions instead of one. The rhetoric seeks to induce the realization that our history resembles the history of European nations more than we realize. As France has endured numerous republics and constitutions, holding fast always to the *Code civil* and the 1789 Declaration of the Rights of Man, we have undergone a major disruption in our constitutional history, which we try to camouflage as a single evolving constitution. It is more illuminating to think of ourselves as having two constitutions: one the outgrowth of the American Revolution and the other the product of the war sometimes called the Second American Revolution—the Civil War. The two coexist uneasily in our current consciousness.

ALTERNATIVE READINGS OF HISTORY

The interpretation of American history offered in this book differs greatly from other worthwhile accounts to be found in current literature on law and political theory. The idea of transformations in constitutional history trades heavily on the work of Bruce Ackerman, but Ackerman espouses a positivist, value-neutral conception of restructuring the constitutional order that pays little attention to the intrinsic merit of the values that triumphed after the Civil War. In his view, the legal principles of Reconstruction and of the New Deal represent a recurrence of the constitutional will that characterized the convention in 1787. "We the People" assert ourselves a second time and, indeed, a third time, to endorse an activist government during the "New Deal."

I argue, in contrast, that there is only one major rupture and restructuring in constitutional history and that it is brought on not by "We the People" but rather by rejecting the people and their Constitution in the throes of war.[19] The values of nationhood, equality, and democracy do not triumph in American consciousness by virtue of some constitutional convention's choosing them over those enshrined in the first Constitution. They are enacted in the suffering of a redemptive war. They crystallize not in the minds of officials but in the struggle of soldiers. They are forged not by election but the cleansing action of a war that Lincoln described, in the biblical language of his second inaugural address, as the "scourge" that the world must suffer because of its "offences." The emergence of a new postbellum legal order, the foundations of the Secret Constitution, was a historical necessity, and there is no turning back from the course we then adopted.

Other writers have taken a stand on these transformations in American history and they all see the patterns of history differently. Akhil Amar has developed an unusual thesis that is, in many respects, the opposite of my own. He holds that the antebellum constitution stressed communal participation; the postbellum legal order, in contrast, emphasized individual rights.[20] The values of nationhood and equality suffer in his account. Michael Sandel argues that a procedural republic, favoring rights as a neutral structure of society, developed out of the earlier period of republican élitism, which he claims was based on the cultivation of virtue as a necessary condition for the maintenance of a free society.[21] This view unduly glorifies the republican ethic, which supposedly cultivated public virtue in an élite group of white, propertied men who saw themselves as the custodians of society. Sandel thinks that this kind of élitist practice is properly called "self-government," and he writes nostalgically about this public-spirited commitment to politics.

I have little to say about virtue in my account of democracy in the postbellum legal order. Yet, it seems to me obvious that conditioning the franchise on finding in the potential voter some appropriate set of attitudes stands in clear contradiction to "government of the people, by the people, for the people." No serious democrat who believes that the people are entitled to rule themselves would speak so longingly of a republic based on virtue. Also, Sandel believes that the procedural republic has come to define the United States. Apparently, he thinks that the American legal system has taken a neutral position on the qualities of the good life. This claim is hardly borne out by the details of our legal and political experience. A little attention paid to our commitment to public education, our drug laws, and our eager acceptance of public religious rituals ("IN GOD WE TRUST" printed on every coin and bill) reveals how diligently the government seeks to induce certain values in the citizenry.

A more congenial book, to my mind, is Charles L. Black's last opus, which draws on the Declaration of Independence to develop a more robust conception of individual rights than those recognized under the current state of the law.[22] Black also draws heavily on the inspiration of the Gettysburg Address, which makes his effort the closest to mine in the literature.

Also, I have benefited greatly from the works of our talented Civil War and Reconstruction historians. It is hard to match Eric Foner in mastery of the period and his passion for racial justice,[23] or Garry Wills in his learned and imaginative style,[24] or James McPherson in his ability to synthesize the grand moments of postbellum America.[25] Yet, all of these writers understate two phenomena that I have found to be critical in understanding the emergence of the Secret Constitution. First, they pay too little attention to the religious fervor that motivated both the Civil War and the quest for justice after the war; and, second, more seriously, they overlook the consolidation of the United States as a nation in the mid-nineteenth-century European sense of the term.[26]

I write more as a lawyer interested in the history of ideas than as a historian required to look at the evolution of the law. Also, my thinking as a law professor, the reader will soon discover, is situated someplace in the mid-Atlantic, caught between the case-law style of the American constitutionalists and the European emphasis on the struggle for survival among the great ideas of our heritage. Both American lawyers and American historians suffer, in my mind, from the curse of American distinctiveness. We really think that in some deep, unarticulated way we are better than the fighting nations of the Old World. The historians fail to see that we, too, became a nation struggling for unity in the Civil War and that we, too, experienced a major rupture in our supposed two-hundred-plus years of continuity under the same legal order. The lawyers who rarely look beyond our own borders employ a methodology of "original intent" that can only make continental Europeans smile at our simple-mindedness. One purpose of my writing is try to overcome these intellectual divisions between the Old World and the New World, between the style of continental European legal thinking and the merits of the common law tradition.

The single work of American legal and historical scholarship that has inspired me the most is the late Robert Cover's classic essay, "Nomos and Narrative."[27] Cover brought to bear several sensibilities that I share. First, he wrote boldly about the influence of religious ideas, and particularly Jewish thought, in the grand struggle of ideas that animates American law. More important, he had a conception of law that went far deeper than the superficial decisions of courts and legislatures. Law flourishes, Cover argued, by mediating among the great ideas that arise spontaneously from our forms of social life. Legal decisions, by legislatures and courts, do not create the law but rather affirm the survival of some ideas ("jurisgenerative" rulings) and kill off other emergent strains ("jurispathic" verdicts). The law also creates a Nomos, a world in which we come to interpret and understand the political events that swirl around us. These basic qualities of a great essay inform my efforts in this book.

Cover would have readily understood the idea of a Secret Constitution — a hidden structure in our political and legal thinking — and he would have grasped that the Secret Constitution derived not from official decisions by lawmakers but from the historical experience of the nation. Now I invite you to join us in thinking about both law and history in this new and illuminating way.

CHAPTER 1

REDEMPTION
UNDER LAW

"Without the shedding of blood there is no remission of sins."

—*John Brown*

I n the Western experience with evil, we choose repeatedly to put our faith in law and the legal culture to redeem ourselves from sin. Over and over again, we find states indulging in total war, terror, genocide, and the mass killing of their own people, and then turning to the legal culture in the hope that they can atone for the iniquity and live once again as a civilized nation. This view—that the law shall make us clean—should give us pause. Faith in the law has not been an unqualified virtue in the Christian West. One might expect individuals influenced by Jesus's Sermon on the Mount to turn first to love and charity as the means of atonement. But nations—organized, organic societies—must take a different path. A nation must proceed collectively to find redemption.

I write in this chapter of religious ideas and their value in understanding our legal experience. This, admittedly, is an unusual take in our rigorously secular academic world. The American university world has distanced itself from the sensibilities of ordinary Americans who take the Bible seriously as a source of wisdom and who live their lives with devotion to values of faith and redemption. In this interpretation of law as the path to national redemption, I seek to find a middle way between Jewish and Christian thinking. There is no doubt that the nations whose struggles I describe—France, Germany, and the United States—think of themselves as Christian nations. Yet, the very idea of redemption of the entire nation through law resonates more with the older tradition of the Jewish national mission under the Torah revealed at Mount Sinai. My account seeks to unite the divergent strains of all religions that trace their roots to the original idea in Exodus of a nation living under God and under law.

To understand the phenomenon of communal redemption, we must turn to the Bible as our source. The model of the Hebrews' deliverance from servitude and their ensuing acceptance of God's law at Mount Sinai have repeatedly appealed to dominant powers of the West and often to opposite sides of the same conflict. In the rhetoric of the abolitionists, slavery in the United States made the country into "a House of Bondage." Both blacks and whites identified with the same story of liberation from this domain of oppression. Nat Turner thought he was recreating the biblical story when he led a slave revolt in 1831. The slaves whom Harriet Tubman led to freedom in the North called her Moses. Abraham Lincoln readily saw himself in the image of Moses leading his people out of bondage into the realm of freedom.

The Hebrews fled Egypt in order, eventually, to accept the law revealed at Mount Sinai: Delivery from servitude requires more than violent revolt. The message of Exodus is not simply liberation from slavery but the domesticating of violent sensibilities under the rule of law. Jews celebrate this submission to God's law in the holiday of *Shevuot*, which commemorates the revelation of the Torah at Mount Sinai and is celebrated fifty days after the night of the Exodus. Christians have reinterpreted this event as the descent of the Holy Spirit, celebrated in the analogous spring holiday of Pentecost.

The idea that freedom exists only under law is often understood as a Central European or German approach to the individual in society. Americans tend to subscribe rather to the myth of a Lockian state of nature, where individuals exist prior to the organization of society under a social contract. The Declaration of Independence relies heavily on the principle that the "consent of the governed" is indispensable to the legitimacy of government. Yet, in actual American practice, the law—particularly constitutional law—serves the same function of sanctifying the social order as it does in the European experience. Before turning to the details of the American appeal to law after the surrender at Appomattox Courthouse in April 1865, let us examine first two significant European efforts to domesticate tendencies toward violence under the rule of law.

REDEMPTION BY LAW IN FRANCE AND GERMANY

Think first about the way in which the French sought repose from postrevolutionary terror in their *Code civil.* The country passed through fifteen years of regicide, terror, and mass executions. Amidst voices clamoring for stability and security, Napoleon staged his *coup d'état* in late 1799. High on his agenda was revamping the legal system. In 1804, he charged a group of lawyers with the task of drafting a new civil code in language accessible to ordinary people. The committee produced the elegant *Code civil,* now a mainstay of French culture and a model for civil codification all over the world. The language is so refined that the novelist Henri Stendhal reportedly reviewed the style of ten code provisions every night before retiring. Today, when the Francophones in Quebec preach the distinctiveness of their culture, they never fail to mention their *Code civil,* modeled after Napoleon's effort to use the law as the means of restoring civilized order to France.

The *Code civil* has proved to be remarkably durable in French culture. Constitutions have come and gone and the French have endured recurrent changes of regime, including communes, dictatorships, and five distinct republics. Yet, through all this, the civil code has survived. It is the cultural monument that unites the French across history.

In its substantive content, the *Code civil* is strongly identified with the achievements of the 1789 Revolution against the *ancien regime.* The code sweeps away the vestiges of feudal influence in the law of property and in the law of evidence and proclaims a liberal legal order. The end of feudalism in the law of property meant that a single concept of ownership would replace the ancient system of embedded estates. The implication was that all land would be freely alienable, without being burdened by the residual control of lords higher in the feudal chain. The code thus provides the legal foundation for a market economy. The end of feudalism in the field of evidence means that the testimony of a nobleman is no longer worth more than the oath of a peasant. Thus the code institutionalizes the *égalité* of all citizens, as promised in the slogan of the Revolution.

Standing for these liberal values, incorporating the messages of revolution, and surviving all changes of political regimes, the *Code civil* functions like a constitution for the French. It is the bedrock of the legal culture. In their code, the French have found an enduring symbol of the rule of law, a conviction that the language, concepts, and rules of the legal order can hold back the impulses toward violence, terror, and reciprocal vengeance. Faith in the code has redeemed the nation from the nightmare of the guillotine.

The metaphor of redemption should not pass our lips lightly. In its original meaning, it has legal connotations; something on loan gets returned to its owner. The older Jewish law of homicide relied on the metaphor of the *Goel haDam*, "the redeemer of blood" to refer to the victim's next-of-kin who, under certain circumstances, could pursue the murderer and kill him. David Daube has interpreted this practice against the background assumption that at the time of a natural death, the life force—symbolized by blood—always returns to God.[1] If the death occurs at the hand of another, the manslayer unnaturally acquires control over the victim's "blood." The *Goel haDam*, the redeemer-of-blood, executes the manslayer in order to release the victim's blood, thus enabling it to return to its divine source. The notion that our life force belongs to God accounts for the views of virtually all secular liberal systems that no one can validly consent to his or her own killing at the hand of another.

It is tempting to extend this idea and to think of all humanity as enjoying a temporary privilege of life on earth. God somehow will redeem all of us at the end of history. In fact, the Jewish view, as it has evolved and matured, seems to have avoided this universalization of the idea that individual life stems from God. As the idea developed, the agent of redemption would be the Messiah, who would bring a reign of peace and harmony to life on earth. The redemption occurs in life as we know it. Orthodox Jewish culture takes the observance of God's commandments, living under the rule of revealed law as interpreted by the rabbis, as the way to hasten the Messiah's reign of harmony and order. The law, then, becomes the path toward redemption. Until the Prince of Peace comes to "fulfill the law," or until the Apocalypse at the end of days, the secular law of the nation is the only means we have to work toward the perfection of life on earth.

The place of "blood" in the religious tradition of redemption proves to be subtle and problematic. There are some strains in the Jewish tradition that link the letting of blood with returning the soul to God. The "redeemer of blood" reminds us of that connection, as does the popular view that the founding of Israel stood in some kind of organic relationship with the Holocaust. The connection between blood and salvation becomes much stronger, however, in the Christian interpretation of its Jewish legacy. The theme of blood spilling from the body becomes powerful in the crucifixion and reaches its apotheosis in the faith that a great battle, an Apocalypse, must precede the Second Coming of the Messiah. The spilling of blood in a great battle is understood instinctively as the suffering that must precede redemption. As John Brown was led to the gallows on the eve of the Civil War, having unsuccessfully sought to stimulate a slave revolt, he handed one of his guards a note, "I John Brown am now quite certain that the crimes of this guilty land will never be purged away but with blood."[2]

But blood alone does not save a nation from its sins. The argument here is that indulgence in evil—slavery, mass killing, persecution— must first issue in the suffering of the people. To overcome their sense of self-inflicted brutality, they turn to the law as the path of secular redemption. They search for stability after having succumbed to their baser instincts. The law provides a source of hope that the civil order can resist the recurrent slippage into violence and brutality. The important point is that the rule of law—not charity, not prayer, not animal sacrifice—should provide the means of secular redemption.

For nations as a whole to seek redemption, they must find a discipline that operates on them as a group, as a community. Individual acts of devotion will not suffice. Needed is the discipline represented by the law—the expression of communal cooperation, par excellence. The compromises and obligations of life under the law hardly makes sense to individuals standing alone, preoccupied by their own values and their own needs. The law redeems not the individual but the community or the nation as a whole.[3]

This view of the relationship between law and redemption finds expression in the Hebrew Bible, the Old Testament. It continues to inspire the law-based thinking of Judaism, Islam, the Catholic Church, and some Protestant theologians. The law given at Sinai, the law embedded in the covenant, is not the expression of individual aspiration but only of collective obligation. Seeking redemption or salvation through the church or through faith provides a way of cleansing ourselves of sin and, as it were, perfecting our individual creation.

Legal cultures, too, must seek to perfect themselves. They cannot exist simply as the product of will. When legal cultures lose sight of their natural end of bringing a reign of justice and harmony to human affairs, they decline into corruption and the arbitrariness of power. The German philosopher Gustav Radbruch defined the ideal of Law as the practice of establishing rules in the pursuit of justice.[4] Communal life seeks, through law, to perfect itself. This secular idea parallels the eschatological aim of perfecting the creation of the world under God's reign.

Seeking redemption under the law cannot simply be a desire for one's parochial values to triumph in the courts. It matters which values are in play. And it matters how these values are debated in the legal culture. Debate about legal issues must be open and robust, and the very process of legal argument must communicate respect for the opposition. At the end of a legal argument, both sides must have the sense that they have been listened to, and that the dignity of the losing party is affirmed in the process of decision. Here, as well, we have much to learn from the model provided by the Jewish tradition of Talmudic debate. When a rabbi questioned how two of the greatest sages, Rabbis Hillel and Shammai, could persistently disagree, the response was: "These and these are the words of the living God." Although Rabbi Hillel's views are generally followed, Rabbi Shammai is treated, in defeat, with the greatest respect.

It is not surprising that when the established authority's respect for the political opposition is debased, the legal culture invariably suffers. This is most noticeably clear in dictatorial societies where legal debate is reduced to little more than efforts to placate the powers that be. Although the National Socialists purported to rely on legal forms and administrative regularity, their contempt for free and mutually respectful discourse led to a corruption of the legal culture. The Nazis' conception of law fluctuated between two unpalatable extremes. Sometimes the slogan was that law was what Hitler wanted and commanded (*Recht is das, was der Führer will*). At other times, utility to the German people was the ultimate source of legitimacy (*Recht is das, was dem Volke nutzt*).[5] The National Socialist Party's manipulation of these slogans and their observance of legal forms served only to bring the culture to a deeper level of corruption.

It is an extraordinary feature of postwar German culture that a new generation of jurists managed to save, to redeem, their concept of law from its racist and Nazi associations. In the wake of their unforgettable crimes against humanity, the West Germans, too, sought redemption in the rule of law, in the *Rechtsstaat* that they have cultivated along with economic prosperity. Living by the law, and seeking justice within the law, redeems the humanistic side of German culture. It has suppressed the romantic will to break all restraints for the sake of glory in power.

The Germans, too, have a civil code that has united them, since 1900, through the transitions from Bismarck, to Weimar, to the Third Reich, to the present. Yet, under the National Socialists, the code, which contains the provisions on family law, became tainted with notions of racial purity. Jews and Aryans could not marry. Of course, this stain disappeared in the postwar reform, but the memory remains of a corrupted civil code. Not surprisingly, then, Germans have sought redemption by promoting both a new constitution, enacted in 1949, and the rule of law in a united Europe. More than any country seeking redemption under law, the Germans identified their new constitution, the *Grundgesetz*, as the focal point of state authority. The sanctity of the constitution—and not the personal head of state—became the interest protected under the reformed law of treason. When West Germans felt their infant postwar republic endangered by Communist subversion, they appointed an agency to protect the integrity of the government. The announced aim of the agency was to protect the constitution (*Verfassungsschutz*).

The preamble of this charter, called the Basic Law (*Grundgesetz*), repeatedly reminds Germans of the imperative to atone for the sins of the past:

> Conscious of its responsibility before God and humanity, possessed of the will to serve the peace of the world as an equal

member of a United Europe, the German nation [*Volk*] commits itself, by virtue of its inherent constitution-making authority, to the following Basic Law.[6]

No other constitution, so far as I know, stresses its sense of "responsibility" and declares as one of its primary purposes "to serve the peace of
the world." These gestures recall the descent of the German nation into
the evils of aggressive war and crimes against humanity.

The first article of the Basic Law invokes the humanistic Kantian un-
derpinnings of German culture: "Human dignity is inviolable. All state
power is obligated to protect it and respect it." This provision provides
the backdrop for interpreting all the basic rights guaranteed under the
constitution. The protection of human dignity is the fundamental value
suffusing the entire legal order. The highest virtue of the postwar German constitutional order, then, was precisely the greatest casualty of the
Nazi regime. The path to redemption lay in reclaiming the liberal and
humanistic values most systematically violated in their darkest hour.
The point is carried forward in the second article: "Everyone has the
right to flourishing of his or her personality. . . . Everyone has the right
to life."

These are provisions that enabled Germans to redefine their identities.
They would no longer be the people devoted to the *Volk* above all. They
would become the nation of human dignity that served the cause of human flourishing and the sanctity of human life. For the postwar Germans, then, the law, and particularly the Basic Law became the means for
suppressing evil impulses and returning to the promises of an earlier national self. This is what redemption means in a secular legal world.

The redemptive impulse leads national courts to place an emphasis on
values that resonate against past sins. The German Constitutional Court
has made a number of controversial decisions that make sense primarily
as efforts to resolve the burden of memory. The court decided to uphold
a law abolishing the twenty-year statute of limitations for concentration
camp murders.[7] It invoked the constitutional "right to life" to strike
down a liberal abortion law that permitted abortion on demand in the first
trimester.[8] And, more recently, the court rejected an East German statutory
justification for border guards who shot at their own citizens trying to flee
the country for the West.[9] All of these decisions brought to the fore funda-

mental values of protecting life and punishing those with contempt for life. Yet, the particular German emphasis on these values would probably not appeal in the same measure to other European courts.

The Germans themselves have coined a unique, hard-to-translate phrase to describe the controversies that have driven their system of justice for the last fifty years. They call it *Bewältigung der Vergangenheit*— "overcoming" or "coming to grips with" the past. Settling accounts with the past provides a critical perspective on the process of redemption from evil. We cannot avoid the past, for we are all prisoners of it. In real life, we cannot reenact the forty years of wandering in the desert that the Hebrews had to endure before they could shake off their ingrained ways and a new generation could seek redemption under the law. In the world of practical politics, we must act now, and criminal punishment often provides the mechanism for distancing ourselves from the past so that we can start anew.

CIVIL WAR AS THE PATH TO REDEMPTION

As France and Germany had their experiences of seeking redemption after reigns of terror, Americans, too, indulged in the mammoth bloodletting on the killing fields of the Civil War. When Lincoln sought to resupply Fort Sumter in Charleston harbor, and General Beauregard chose in response to fire on the federal fort, the long-simmering feud between North and South bled into brothers' killing each other at close range. They fired their canons on Fort Sumter, they fixed their bayonets at Little Round Top, they lobbed shells onto Vicksburg until troops could seize the forts reigning over the Mississippi, they burned down Atlanta, and under William Tecumseh Sherman they scorched the earth on their march to the sea. The blue and the gray fell everywhere. And they were not sure why. They only had abstract ideas in their heads— some died for the Union, others for their separate nation. Over six hundred thousand lives stained the ground, more than all the former and subsequent American wars put together.

Having barely won reelection midway in this slaughter, Abraham Lincoln could only say of the reign of terror, "Woe unto the world because of offences!" We had descended into the bloodiest war of our history without clear purposes and no understanding of how it might end. "For it must needs be that offences come; but woe to that man by whom the offence cometh!" The self-inflicted pogrom is seen as a "woe" and a "scourge" inflicted for the terrible "offence" of slavery. Lincoln's second inaugural address prayed for redemption. The nation had bled its sins onto its own soil and craved a rebirth of American civilization.

The survivors turned to law. One year into the war, after a string of Union defeats, Lincoln learned that the old Union could not possibly survive. "A new one had to be embraced."[10] And the new Union would have to be based on a new constitutional order. A nation of free Americans, including emancipated slaves, would bear responsibility for rebuilding the United States on the basis of a constitution acceptable to all. Formally speaking, the original charter of 1787 would remain in place, but it would be so radically transformed that it would stand to the *ancien* United States as the *Code civil* related to the French feudal order or, as any redeemed legal culture compares to the brutality and chaos that precedes it.

The American hope for a new beginning lay in the Reconstruction Amendments—the Thirteenth, Fourteenth, and Fifteenth—all enacted in quest of a new definition of freedom and equality under the law. The first clause of the Fourteenth Amendment specified who would be a member of the new polity: "All persons born or naturalized in the United States, and subject to the jurisdiction thereof, are citizens of the United States. . . ." With a single stroke the new constitution erased the effects of one of the worst scars in American constitutional history—the *Dred Scott* decision of 1857, which held that persons of African descent could never become citizens of the United States. In the new United States, there would be no discrimination based on blood. The only question that mattered was whether you were born within the polity and whether you were therefore likely to come to maturity with the language and consciousness of American culture.

With just boundaries of the new nation-state properly defined, the highest order of business was to define the basic rights of its citizens. The structure of these rights follows the pattern established in the Declaration of Independence: life, liberty, and the pursuit of happiness. Yet, there was a new recognition that the inalienable rights of all Americans were now to be realized not in the state of nature but under the rule of law. The naturalistic "pursuit of happiness," celebrated in the Declaration, gives way to the quintessential creature of the law's definition—property. Yet, the basic rights of life, liberty, and property are inalienable without being absolute. The ideal must be adapted to the practical demands of competing claims. The legal system would have to decide when individuals could fairly be deprived of liberty or property or even of life; thus, the coining of the famous and influential clause of the American Constitution, namely that no "State [shall] deprive any person of life, liberty, or Property, without due Process of law." The law would define the content and the limits of the inalienable rights celebrated in the Declaration of Independence.

Also, for the first time, the law would define duties incumbent on the states. The individual state governments must not only guarantee due process for all persons within their jurisdiction, they must also secure "the equal protection of the laws" for all to whom their power extends. True, the original Constitution places some limits on the legislative competence of the states. They must defer to the supremacy of federal law and recognize the privileges and immunities of the citizens of all other states.[11] And there were specific restrictions: They could not enact bills of attainder, ex-post facto laws, or any "law impairing the obligation of contracts."[12] In the postbellum constitutional order, however, the states acquired a pervasive duty to treat their residents—those subject to their jurisdiction—decently.

This was a revolutionary change. The states were no longer the autonomous sovereigns that they thought they were when they claimed the right of secession. They were now, in fact, servants of their people. Governments existed to guarantee due process and equal justice for all. The local law was no longer simply a creature of the states. The states themselves were enmeshed in the law and subordinate to it.

In addition to embedding the states in the rule of law, the new constitutional order embarked on an affirmative program to ensure equality among those citizens subject to the jurisdiction of the United States. The heart of the new consensus is that the federal government, victorious in warfare, must continue its aggressive intervention in the lives of its citizens. It must protect the weak against the risk that they would slip into states of subordination resembling the past from which they sought to escape. According to the Thirteenth Amendment, there could never again be relationships of slavery or involuntary servitude in the United States. The federal government would have to be ever watchful to insure that this kind of slippage would never occur in the private relationships among citizens. Furthermore, under the "equal protection clause," the states must recognize and promote the equality of those subject to their jurisdiction. To round out the commitment to equality, according to the Fifteenth Amendment ratified in 1870, the states could no longer deny voting rights to citizens on the grounds of their race, color, or previous condition of servitude.

These objectives and guarantees are insufficient in themselves to create a constitution, a framework of government. One needs, in addition, a definition of legislative empowerment that would enable the federal government to realize its commitments. This definition is laid down in all three of the postbellum amendments. All three grant the power to Congress to enforce the basic framework "with appropriate legislation." True, the new Congress takes as a given many of the provisions of the original Constitution. The new order inherits an operating Congress, Executive, and Judiciary. They would be recast in new functions, but the forms remained the same.

The argument, then, is that the three Reconstruction Amendments enacted a second American constitution. The terms of this constitution, as culled from the amendments—with some rearrangement and leaving out historically specific clauses—can be stated in a few words:

The Second American Constitution

§1. All persons born or naturalized in the United States, and subject to the jurisdiction thereof, are citizens of the United States and of the State wherein they reside.

§2. No State shall make or enforce any law which shall abridge the privileges or immunities of citizens of the United States.

§3. No State shall deprive any person of life, liberty, or property, without due process of law.

§4. No State shall deny to any person within its jurisdiction the equal protection of the laws.

§5. Neither slavery nor involuntary servitude, except as a punishment for crime whereof the party shall have been duly convicted, shall exist within the United States.

§6. The right of citizens of the United States to vote shall not be denied or abridged by the United States or by any State on account of race, color, or previous condition of servitude.

§7. The Congress shall have power to enforce the foregoing provisions by appropriate legislation.

These seven propositions summarize the enduring content of the Reconstruction Amendments.[13] The key provisions of these amendments define political membership, articulate basic rights, and provide an ambit of legislative competence. So reformed, the American system of government would be able to protect individual rights as well as promote the equality of all persons who survived the war. Of course, we must assume a set of institutions—a Congress, an Executive, and a Judiciary—that will continue to function according to the terms of their initial creation.

Still, there is something missing in this filtering off of the three Reconstruction Amendments and calling them a separate constitution. The missing factor is the consciousness of setting forth a new framework of government, a structure based on values fundamentally different from those that went before. To find that consciousness, we need to turn, I wish to argue, to the critical message of the Civil War, the address that would generate a new normative world in which to make sense of the epic war that consumed America from the firing on Fort Sumter to the surrender at Appomattox. The new Nomos, the new framework of values that necessitated a new constitution, comes forth in one of the great prayers of the American civil religion, the Gettysburg Address. It is worth recalling some of the enduring phrases of this civil prayer, the incantations that reverberated in American consciousness:

Four score and seven years ago our fathers brought forth on this continent a new nation. . . .

[This nation was] conceived in liberty and dedicated to the proposition that all men are created equal.

From these honored dead we take increased devotion to that cause for which they gave the last full measure of devotion.

We resolve that these dead shall not have died in vain, that this nation, under God, shall have a new birth of freedom. . . .

Government of the people, by the people, for the people shall not perish from the earth.

In the ensuing chapters, we will look at these words and the entire address in greater detail. For now, I wish to make the unusual claim that these revered words serve as the preamble for the constitutional order that emerged from the unification of the nation. They are a preamble in much the same sense that the language beginning "Conscious of our responsibility before God and humanity" provides the organizing principle of the new German constitution or the following words echo in memory as the convening of the Philadelphia Constitution:

> We the people of the United States, in order to form a more perfect Union, establish justice, insure domestic Tranquility, provide for the common defense, promote the general Welfare, and secure the Blessings of Liberty to ourselves and our Posterity, do ordain and establish this Constitution for the United States of America.

Constitutional preambles speak in prophecy. They set forth a vision of the future—for the broad purposes of the national charter that they introduce. And, most important, they define who the people are who share in the constitutional vision. The original preamble in the Philadelphia version stressed the position of "We the People" as the enactors of the Constitution. For Lincoln, the body politic expressing itself in the new constitution included the prior generations who "four score and seven years ago" adopted, with great courage, that proposition of equality that gave birth to the American nation. Those represented in the new order included the dead at Gettysburg and at all the battlefields of the war who, if the new order is realized, "shall not have died in vain." And, furthermore, because he avoided all partisan references in his address, he clearly meant to articulate a conception of the nation that included the South as well as the North, black as well as white. Ultimately, the beneficiaries of the new order would be the future generations of the nation, those who would flourish under "a new birth of freedom."

To say that the Gettysburg Address provides the preamble to a new constitutional order is, to say the least, a bold claim. When Lincoln took the train up to Gettysburg in November 1863, he had in mind only to comfort the mourners of those who died in the fierce four-day battle in early July. The bodies were being pulled together from the battlefield and spared further decay. The soil was turned and the dead laid to rest. The battle had turned the tide of the war—just barely, mind you—and it was time that the president began to articulate the meaning of the long suffering that culminated in the gruesome hand-to-hand fighting in the Gettysburg fields.

At the ceremony dedicating the Gettysburg cemetery, Lincoln was designated the second speaker. The renowned orator Edward Everett spoke for two hours before the president mounted the podium. He had a written text with him that amounted to about 268 words.[14] Perhaps Everett prepared the audience to absorb the poignancy of Lincoln's message. Perhaps the very brevity of Lincoln's words lent them additional power. The impact of the address was felt not only by the mourners gathered at the new cemetery but by an entire country yearning for a sense of meaning in the bloodshed.

True, the Gettysburg Address was not legally binding, but preambles are never meant to have the status of positive law. They are designed to explain why it is necessary for the government to bind itself to certain objectives. Lincoln's preamble, accepted in the hearts of the nation, explains the meaning of the war and provides a guide to the building of a constitutional order based on nationhood, equality, and democracy. The setting of clear goals in inspiring language—this is all one can expect of a constitutional preamble.

This constitutional order stands in radical contrast to the Constitution drafted in Philadelphia and amended by the Bill of Rights in 1791. It defines membership in the American nation, it brings the principle of equality to the fore, and it initiates the process of extending the franchise to virtually all adult citizens. The original Constitution did none of these things. It slighted the problems of nationality and citizenship, it sidestepped the problem of equality, and it minimized the significance of popular democracy.

THE IRRELEVANCE OF ORIGINAL INTENT

At the outset, I should be clear about the claims I am not making and the methods I am not using. Above all, I am not making an argument about the "original intent" that lay behind the Reconstruction Amendments. Nothing strikes me as intellectually and morally more impoverished than the current trend in constitutional scholarship to believe that the wishes, desires, and intentions of the founders should determine the content of our Constitution. There are two major hurdles that the advocates of this method have never negotiated. First, we need an argument about whose wishes, desires, and intentions really matter. If we think we are bound by a certain take on the world that prevailed in 1787, 1791, or 1868, then we should decide whose sentiments matter. Should we look to the people who wrote the document, to the majority who voted for it, to the states who ratified it, or to the "people" as a whole for whom these various democratic agents acted? Among all these possible sources of "original intent," there was intense conflict. I would imagine that even those who actually voted for and against various drafts suffered from doubt and changing sentiments. But even if each person voting had a concrete intention to support every sentence he or she endorsed, there is no coherent way of finding a common denominator among their divergent positions. A single intent cannot unify the inevitable cacophony of desires that stand behind every piece of legislation. But let us suppose there was a single intent of the group. We then encounter a more basic question: Why should we care what the founders actually thought?

The best political theory to support the relevance of original intent would be to think of the lawgiver as something like a military commander.[15] The commander wants us to do something, and has used the language of the law to move us toward action. We should try to figure out what these purposes are and execute them. And if we don't? Well, the commander cannot really punish us, but somehow we would be breaking faith with the framers if we don't act with the appropriate subservience or at least act as though we were submissive to the original intent of the founders. This, I regret to say, is the best reconstruction I can offer for a view that never seems to get articulated; namely, why we should pay so much attention to the wishes and desires of the agents who bequeathed to us the words we live by.

In great historical moments of law making as well as literature, writers choose words that resonate far beyond their original context. When the representatives of the colonies "pledged their sacred honor" in July

1776 to a document that included the words "All men are created equal," they may merely have intended to stress the equality of all "collective" peoples: the new Americans had as much right to choose their form of government as did the British. They also could have had the limited purpose of arguing that they were of the same moral status as King George III. If all men are created equal, then no one of them can claim to be anointed as ruler by divine right. The only source of legitimacy, as the Declaration argues, is the "consent of the governed." Whatever their intentions as individuals or as a group may have been, their words had lasting significance. They bequeathed a great maxim to the American people—a maxim that would in due course serve as the battle cry of emancipation.

When the drafters and ratifiers of the Fourteenth Amendment adopted a commitment to equality under the law, they did not think particularly about whether they wanted to bring about integrated schools. Yet, a vast literature has grown up around the question of whether the "original intent" of the Fourteenth Amendment was to integrate the schools—an event that the Court did not mandate until 1954 in Brown v Board of Education.[16] The dispute seems to be entirely irrelevant.[17] The complex body of national and state legislators who drafted, passed, and ratified the Fourteenth Amendment did not think about a single system of education for blacks and whites. There were too many other issues on their minds. We cannot attribute to them an intention to have all Americans study together in the same classroom, nor can we burden their memory with a commitment to keep black and white forever apart.

Those who frame constitutions and constitutional amendments obviously have some purpose in mind, but the purposes are typically abstract. If they want to bring about equality among all Americans, they do not want to be bothered with working out precisely what equality means at each stage of historical evolution. If you had asked them whether, ninety years later, the schools should be desegregated, they would have been nonplussed by the question. "Well, that is the reason we have courts," would have been the typical reply. The Fourteenth Amendment established an ideal, it affirmed an idea that has roots in the Declaration of Independence. The drafters implicitly endorsed the principle that all men are created equal and because they are created equal, they are entitled to equal treatment before the law. What this language should mean in practice was not their concern. Together with scholars who reflect on the ideas behind the law, the courts assume responsibility for the proper interpretation of the language that constitutes a shared heritage of government principles.

I never cease to be amazed that legal scholars, particularly in the United States, continue to be confused about the relevance of the framers' original intent. Secular legal systems could not possibly be more demanding, more deferential to authority, than religious cultures that believe that their binding legal principles were declared by God. Yet, a story from the Talmud beautifully illustrates the folly of invoking original intent in a dispute about the meaning of God's commandments. A group of rabbis were engaged in a debate about whether a particular earthenware oven was kosher or not. One of them, Rabbi Eliezer, said no; the other rabbis said yes. Rabbi Eliezer proceeded to invoke a variety of fantastic signs to support his view: at his command, a carob tree was uprooted and flew across the field, a stream flowed upstream, and the walls started to collapse before they were halted. The rabbis were not impressed by these signs. Then Rabbi Eliezer, desperate and alone, invoked the argument of original intent: "If I am right, let heaven be the proof." A heavenly voice then proclaimed: "How dare you oppose Rabbi Eliezer, whose views are everywhere the law." Rabbi Joshua arose and quoted Deuteronomy: "It is not in Heaven." Rabbi Jeremiah explained the reference: Ever since the Torah was given at Mount Sinai, "we pay no attention to heavenly voices, for God already wrote in the Torah at Mount Sinai."[18] The point is that once the language is released and given to jurists to fashion to the needs of their time, the task of lawgivers is finished. Their intentions and desires cannot rule—either from the grave or from heaven.

The intention of those who framed the Reconstruction Amendments should, therefore, not control their interpretation today. But what about the intention of Abraham Lincoln, when he mounted the podium on November 19, 1863? There are some who will say that if Lincoln did not intend specifically to articulate the preamble to a new constitution, then the words spoken at Gettysburg could not possibly be, as I claim, the preamble to the postbellum constitution. If Roosevelt did not intend to amend the Constitution with his court-packing plan, then the resulting changes in Supreme Court attitudes could not constitute a de facto amendment, a radical transformation of American law.

Here we take a page from British constitutional history to understand how a practice can be become part of the accumulated historical constitution without this being the purpose of those who initiated the practice. The British Constitution remains, as is well known, famously unwritten. Customary rules determine the role of the Crown in a system that has evolved as a constitutional monarchy. Only the accepted practice of generations prescribes that the queen must sign legislation for it to be binding as law or that the queen may intervene, under certain circumstances, to break a party deadlock and select a nominee for prime minister.[19] In all systems of customary law, the relevant perspective is not that of those who first engage in the practice but rather of those who witness the pattern of the past and adopt it as binding on themselves. So it is with the Gettysburg Address. The right question is not what Lincoln intended, but rather what the words meant to those who looked to them as the explanation of the war and as a charter for freedom and equality for all Americans. If the address had been ignored, it would not have mattered what Lincoln intended. But because these 268 words[20] were adopted into the civil religion of the United States—the secular meditation on who we were and what we were about—their life after formal recitation by the president determines their constitutional status. They are the preamble to the constitutional order because we came to understand them as nearly sacred. And although we did not until now think of this secular prayer as the preamble to a new order of nationhood, equality, and democracy, that is what they became.

These words are, in fact, better known in the United States than the preamble to the first Constitution. Schoolchildren routinely recite them and thereby imbibe the intuition that these words defined America after the Civil War. Yet, because we know these resonant phrases, we rarely stop to listen and ponder the meaning of each well-crafted line. Let us now put ourselves among the crowd of mourners at Gettysburg. Let us transport ourselves back into the frame of mind of those suffering losses, those looking for the meaning of brothers slaughtering brothers.

> Four score and seven years ago our fathers brought forth on this continent a new nation, conceived in liberty and dedicated to the proposition that all men are created equal. Now we are engaged in a great Civil War, testing whether that nation or any nation

so conceived and so dedicated can long endure. We are met on a great battlefield of that war. We have come to dedicate a portion of that field as a final resting place for those who here gave their lives that that nation might live. It is altogether fitting and proper that we should do this. But in a larger sense, we cannot dedicate—we cannot consecrate—we cannot hallow this ground. The brave men, living and dead, who struggled here have consecrated it far above our poor power to add or detract. The world will little note nor long remember what we say here, but it can never forget what they did here. It is for us the living, rather, to be dedicated here to the unfinished work which they who fought here have thus far so nobly advanced. It is rather for us to be here dedicated to the great task remaining before us— that from these honored dead we take increased devotion to that cause for which they gave the last full measure of devotion— that we here highly resolve that these dead shall not have died in vain, that this nation, under God, shall have a new birth of freedom, and that government of the people, by the people, for the people shall not perish from the earth.

CHAPTER 2

RADICAL
GETTYSBURG

"To many he [Lincoln] seemed like a minor prophet come back
to life out of the Old Testament."

—*John Dos Passos*

With his carefully crafted two-minute speech at Gettysburg, the best political address in the nation's history, Lincoln created a Nomos, a world of norms and meaning, for comprehending the mass slaughter on American soil. The new understanding of why we were in mourning pointed to a resolution of the conflict and the beginnings of a new constitutional order. Rereading the speech now as the preamble to that new order, we can begin to understand the significance of the phrases so carefully chosen. The words of the Gettysburg Address are too powerful, they represent too much concentrated energy and wisdom, to be absorbed in the two minutes that it takes to read them slowly. I suggest that we proceed and listen, sentence by sentence, phrase by phrase, to these words heard so often.

The first sentence states the heart of the matter and sums up the past, present, and future of the American commitment. *Four score and seven years ago our fathers brought forth on this continent a new nation, conceived in liberty and dedicated to the proposition that all men are created equal.* This sentence alone was enough to formulate the preamble to the new constitution. It harbingers the themes that follow in the address and that will come to dominate American life for the rest of the

1860s. Let us read each of these phrases as elements in the preamble to the postbellum constitutional order.

Four score and seven years ago... By 1863, a historical consciousness had taken hold in American thinking. Rooting ourselves in the past stands in sharp contrast to the preamble of the 1787 Constitution, which begins simply, without setting the context: "We the people of the United States, in order to form a more perfect Union. . . ." There is no reference in the 1787 document to the first settlement dating back some 160 years, no sense that the new country was the outgrowth of an English-speaking culture across the seas. In 1863 the nation still desired to create "a more perfect Union," but it had in addition a past that both inspired and troubled the newly indigenous psyche.

The particular past that Lincoln cultivates retains its ability to surprise and to make us take notice. One would expect the president to root his address in the Constitution that created his office, but the great address is defiantly silent about the initial Constitution. As the 1787 document was silent about its great embarrassment, slavery, Lincoln passes over a national charter that carried within it the seeds of war. In this preamble for a new order, the original Constitution is nowhere mentioned. Lincoln locates the birth of the nation four score and seven (eighty-seven) years prior to 1863. Until you do the arithmetic, you do not realize that, in Lincoln's mind, the critical moment of the founding was 1776, the signing of the Declaration of Independence. For those who knew Lincoln well, this might not have been a surprise, for he had said two years before: "I never had a feeling politically that did not spring from the sentiments embodied in the Declaration of Independence."[1]

The historical retreat to the Declaration of Independence left Lincoln with a major paradox. He claims to be speaking as president, and his office owed its existence to Article II of the Constitution of 1787. Yet, he thought himself back prior to the Philadelphia convention and the creation of the presidency. He pulled the rug of legitimacy out from under his own office. To be able to advocate the principle that all men are created equal, that a nation was born committed to this principle, he had to speak from a time prior to the creation of the government for which the Union troops died.

The precursor to this unusual mode of dating comes in an unexpected place—in the final paragraph of the Emancipation Proclamation, which went into effect on January 1, 1863:

Done at the City of Washington, this first day of
January, in the year of our Lord one thousand eight
hundred and sixty three, and of the Independence of the
United States of America the eighty-seventh.
By the President: ABRAHAM LINCOLN

It did not occur to Lincoln that there might be some dissonance between his relying on 1776 as the beginning of the American nation and
his acting in an office constituted by a document drafted in 1787. When
he returned to the same figure of "eighty-seven years" in November of
the same year, he meant to stress the continuity of the nation. In Lincoln's vision, the men who died at Gettysburg gave their lives not for a
government, not for a constitution, but to realize the peculiarly American blend of nationhood and a set of ideas, particularly the idea that the
nation was "conceived in freedom." There might be some disagreement
about the moment of national coalescing, but to be sure, the nation was
at war by 1775. A year later, American patriots exposed themselves to
great risk by appearing to have committed treason. It is with some appropriate fear of reprisal that they conclude the Declaration of Independence: "We mutually pledge to each other our lives, our fortunes and
our sacred honor."

Lincoln's posture toward the 1787 Constitution was less than reverent.
He treated the founding charter of the government more as a guideline
to action than as a set of absolute restrictions on his actions. His decisions, particularly in the early stages of the war, suggest a willingness to
assert extraconstitutional executive power and, thus, to permit the exigencies of war to restructure the government. In April 1861, in the immediate shadow of the shelling of Fort Sumter, he declared a blockade
on Southern ports. Whether the Union forces could properly seize ships
without congressional approval became one of the early legal controversies of the war.[2] And then came the dispute about Lincoln's authorizing
his generals in the field to suspend the writ of habeas corpus—the great
writ by which the courts retain the power to supervise the arrest and detention of criminal suspects. The Constitution permits suspension of this
protection in times of civil unrest—but fails to specify whether the president may act unilaterally in ordering suspension. Sitting alone as a circuit judge, Chief Justice Taney interpreted the constitutional provision
to require congressional authorization for suspending the writ.[3] In light

of Taney's notorious opinion in the *Dred Scott* case,[4] his views hardly
carried much weight in the White House. In a move widely regarded as
authoritarian, Lincoln simply disregarded Taney's opinion. Lincoln justified his unilateral action with a famous claim of necessity, articulated
in a message to Congress on July 4, 1861:

> The whole of the laws which were required to be faithfully ex-
> ecuted were being resisted . . . in nearly one third of the States.
> Must they be allowed to finally fail of execution, even had it
> been perfectly clear that by the use of the means necessary to
> their execution some single law, made in such extreme tender-
> ness of the citizen's liberty that, practically, it relieves more of
> the guilty than of the innocent, should to a very limited extent
> be violated? . . . Are all the laws but one to go unexecuted, and
> the government itself go to pieces lest that one be violated?[5]

Read with our current sensitivity to civil liberties, these are embarrassing words. Lincoln argues, in effect, that he can justify violating a
constitutional prescription by appealing to the necessity of the moment.
Of course, if the stark option were posed—violating this "one law" or
letting the government "go to pieces"—most of us would agree that the
government should survive the emergency, even by transgressing the
Constitution. Yet, there is no evidence that the country's circumstances
were anywhere near this flashpoint of imminent destruction. And Lincoln's casual disdain for the writ of habeas corpus ("it relieves more of
the guilty than of the innocent") reveals a lack of appreciation for the
point of constitutional protections in criminal procedure. My own reading is that Lincoln's suspending the writ on his own initiative and disre-
garding Taney's supposed invalidation of the decision testifies to an
altered state of constitutional thinking. The Constitution of 1787 lay
suspended in the fires of battle. A new constitutional order would arise
from the war, but no one quite knew what shape it would take.

Of course, during the war, the 1787 Constitution remained nominally
in force. There was little suggestion of a "military dictatorship," though
some Northern critics of the government invoked the phrase. Lincoln's
elected term came to an end in March 1865. In the midst of the war,
therefore, he was constitutionally required to stand for reelection. This

event in itself warranted the stability of American institutions, but still ambiguity reigned on the shape of the postbellum constitutional order. The confusion came to a head in 1868 when the House impeached Lincoln's successor, President Andrew Johnson, for arguably asserting excessive executive power in firing his Secretary of War Edwin Stanton. The outcome of that impeachment trial is well known: Johnson avoided conviction by one vote. Less well known is the outcome of the struggle to develop a new constitutional order, the struggle that is signaled in Lincoln's address commemorating the dead at Gettysburg.

... our fathers brought forth on this continent... The biblical cadence of these words resonates in memory. We know that we have encountered it someplace before. They remind us of the way God introduces himself to Moses in the Book of Exodus: "I am the God of your *father* . . . So I have *come down* to rescue [my people] from the hand of Egypt, *to bring it up* from that land to a land, goodly and spacious, to a land flowing with milk and honey. . . ." It is not surprising that Lincoln would evoke the style of Exodus. Even the introductory phrase "four score and seven" has a prophetic ring. The Bible, after all, was one of Lincoln's favorite books—along with the works of Shakespeare and Aesop's Fables.

Garry Wills makes much of the Greek influence in shaping Lincoln's style at Gettysburg.[6] But of the biblical influence on the Gettysburg Address, Wills has almost nothing to say. This is a rather curious twist in seeking to understand the president whose thinking and rhetoric were probably more influenced by the biblical idiom than the writings of any other president. Lincoln's second inaugural address is replete with references to the Bible, including, notably, the latter part of Psalm 19, 10: "The fear of the Lord is clean, enduring forever; the judgments of the Lord are true and righteous altogether." Lincoln saw the entire Civil War as a righteous judgment of the Divine. It is almost inconceivable that he would seek to formulate a framework for understanding the war's place in American history without relying on biblical imagery.

Of all the biblical themes that shaped Lincoln's thinking, the Hebrews' Exodus from Egypt was the most compelling. In a speech he gave in Trenton, New Jersey in 1861, he referred to the American people as "His almost chosen people." The "His" refers, of course, to God. The Americans stand, one almost dares to say, in the place of the Jews in a covenantal relationship with God. The idea that some institution or some people replaced the Jews in their covenantal relationship was a familiar Christian theme. The Pilgrims brought the idea with them as they founded their first settlements. Now Lincoln comes close to repeating the Puritan idea. This accounts, I believe, for the apparent redundancy in "brought forth *on this continent.*" His audience would surely have understood that Lincoln was talking about the United States "four score and seven years ago" without locating the events "on this continent." But *this continent* was the locus of the new covenant. The Pilgrims had made a journey to a new land, and the new land promised a partnership with God that was not possible without an exodus from the old world. The single word "continent," reminding us of the journey, invokes an entire theology.

We should remember that although the Declaration of Independence overflows with references to the Creator and the imprint of the Divine in American destiny, the Constitution of 1787 is a totally secular document. In style as well as substance, Lincoln returns to the religiosity of the 1776 Declaration.

. . . brought forth on this continent a new nation. . . The use of the word "nation" signals a major theme of the address. In the remaining 252 words, it will appear four more times.[7] By accentuating the term "nation," Lincoln sets himself at odds with the first preamble's invocation of "We the People" as the source of all legitimacy. Now, in place of the people appears the nation, a term that with its connection to birth (*nasci,* Latin for "to be born") suggests a conception of the American people that extends over generations—reaching back to the founding eighty-seven years before and encompassing those who will survive the war and flourish in its aftermath.

"We the People" are sovereign in every generation. A single cohort can found a constitution and another can presumably decide to withdraw from the commitment. Thus some scholars have argued that the people of every generation retain the authority both to transform the Constitution or, if they so choose, to repeal it entirely.[8] I disagree. If the American people are understood as a nation including the dead and the unborn, then no single generation can undo the work of the past or renege on its implicit promise to the future. There is no way that those who happened to be alive in the 1860s could overrule the confirmation by preceding generations of the American union. Thus, by extending themselves out over history, Americans became a nation in the European sense, in the same sense as had already been realized in England and in France and was then making itself felt in the unification movements in Italy and Germany.

The mid-nineteenth century was a time in which the nations of the West, tracing their lineage to common linguistic and historical roots, built political movements grounded in a shared national identity. In the same year that the Civil War broke out, Italy's *Risorgimento*, or nationalist awakening, entered its critical phase. Thanks to the political leadership of Camillo Benso di Cavour in the north and the military prowess of Giuseppe Garibaldi in the south, Italy achieved a unification of diverse states, including Piedmont, Sicily, the papal states, and Sardinia. Victor Emmanuel II of Sardinia became the first king of the united nation. In 1871, by a combination of military annexation, diplomacy and bribery, Otto von Bismarck was able to unify the northern and southern German states in the Imperial Reich, with Prussia as its central power. There followed, in the same year, the enactment of the first pan-German criminal code.

This process of unifying the European nations and, at the same time, establishing a state to govern the nation had given us the idea of the nation-state. The nation as a prepolitical reality finds its embodiment in the apparatus of state power. The traditional view is that the United States was different, that Americans were not a nation in the European sense. I beg to differ.

My claim is that Lincoln's address expresses the same idea that was then current in Europe. Each people of common history and language constitutes a nation, and the natural form for the nation's survival was in a state structure. The idea that Americans constituted an organic national unit explained, implicitly, why the eleven Southern states could not go their own way. As he assumed the presidency, Lincoln still spoke of the Union rather than a nation; but in the course of the debates in the decades immediately preceding, the notion of union had acquired the metaphysical qualities of nationhood. In his first inaugural address, Lincoln invoked the "bonds of affection," and even before shots were fired on Fort Sumter in Charleston Harbor, he stressed the unbreakable ties of historical struggle:

> The mystical chords of memory, stretching from every battle-field, and patriot grate, to every living heart and hearth-stone, all over this broad land, will yet swell the chorus of the Union. . . .

The nation was bound together by historical experience and by its destiny, its "manifest destiny," in the phrase used to explain the push westward that occurred in the decades leading up to the Civil War.

Lincoln's purpose on November 19, 1863, was not to intensify but to transcend the war effort. Significantly, the "nation" of which he speaks includes the South as well as the North. He was speaking at the dedication of a Union cemetery, but there is hardly a partisan word to be heard in the entire address.[9]

My sense of the literature of American history is that our scholars not only ignore the biblical influences on Lincoln's thinking at Gettysburg but also fail to understand the significance of the "nation" that "our fathers brought forth on this continent." The common mistake, particularly of lawyers, is to read the "nation" in this context as equivalent to the national government, as opposed to states, or to the national territory as opposed to local geographical units. In this limited sense, the "nation" is constituted by a federal government in Washington or by a physical space staked out on maps and recognized by other countries. The nation is then equivalent to the Union or the federal government. But the issue is *not* the authority of the "national" government in contrast to states' rights. The derivative sense of nationhood as denoting "unified at a federal level" is surely present as a subsidiary meaning in Lincoln's invocation of the term, but this could not possibly be all that he meant to say.

The American nation, as it existed in 1863, was a nation in the European sense. The assumption that drove the movements of national unification on the continent was that each nation should be able to govern itself. And self-government requires that each nation should be able to constitute itself as a state. If this was the thrust of mid-century European history, the same was to be expected of the immigrant nation of the United States.

. . . a new nation, conceived in liberty and dedicated to the proposition that all men are created equal. Thus ends the remarkable first sentence of the address. The nation of which we speak is immediately qualified. This is not simply a nation of common lineage—an extension of tribal identity. We are indeed different from the European nations, for our nation is born of an idea. It is conceived in liberty and dedicated to an aspiration of equality.

What exactly does it mean to be "conceived in liberty?" This phrase is so redolent with meaning that we simply savor it without reflection. Does it mean that the nation is conceived free, as if it were in a state of nature? Is it only after its conception that the nation binds itself by the strictures of government? It could mean these things. Or it could simply mean that our first constitutional commitment was to freedom, which, as we shall see, was certainly true. Yet, somehow the glorification of freedom of speech, freedom of religion, the right to bear arms— among the freedoms sanctified in the Bill of Rights—fails to capture the measure of being "conceived in liberty." Our liberty persists as our birthright, even as we search for the proper way to build a democratic nation of equal citizens.

A stylistic point should intrigue us. It is hardly an accident that in this phrase "conceived in liberty," Lincoln chose the Latin-based "liberty" rather than the Germanic "freedom." "Conceived in freedom" might have had roughly the same meaning, but it would have lacked the lyrical ring. The reason, I believe, is that both "conceived" and "liberty" derive from Latin as opposed to Germanic sources. We return to this point later in the address, when Lincoln links "freedom" rather than "liberty" with the image of a new birth.

What, then, is the relationship between liberty and equality in Lincoln's vision of a new order? We are conceived in liberty and dedicated to the proposition of human equality. That was the way it was then, and it is the way it is now. The realization of equality in practical affairs will always elude us. Even after this aspiration was incorporated into the Fourteenth Amendment, the ideal of equality remained a distant point on the spectrum of political possibilities. Eventually, women would be rendered politically equal and receive the franchise; eventually, the schools would be integrated and the laws against mixed marriages would, with a sense of shame that they ever existed, be struck down. None of this was obvious in 1863 or 1868 or even in 1900. Yet, the commitment Lincoln made at Gettysburg—all men and women, as individuals, are created equal—became a moral lodestar testifying to the equal dignity of all human beings, whether the legal culture had validated that equality or not.

Implicit in this structure—conceived in one value, dedicated to another—lies a conception of an ordered legal culture. Some values are stated in rules that are capable of immediate realization; others are stated as principles of aspiration. The latter are ideals to be pursued, opportunities for self-improvement. Liberty is a given. Equality remains the promise.

Some stylists have objected to Lincoln's labeling the great maxim of the Declaration of Independence as a "proposition." Encountering this word in the first sentence, the great English poet Matthew Arnold reportedly stopped reading in literary disgust.[10] "Proposition" was too legalistic for his taste. But it was critical for Lincoln to restate his understanding of the Declaration's vision of equality. As he said in his Springfield speech in June 1857:

> They [framers of the Declaration] meant simply to declare the *right*, so that the enforcement of it might follow as fast as circumstances should permit. They meant to set up a standard maxim for a free society, which should be familiar to all, and revered by all, constantly looked to, constantly labored for, and even though never perfectly attained, constantly approximated, and thereby constantly spreading and deepening its influence. . . .

Immediately following the victory in Gettysburg, in an informal talk at the White House on July 4, 1863, Lincoln began the process of looking to and reiterating the "standard maxim" of 1776. Thinking of equality as a "proposition" gives it a reality, an ontological presence in our lives, not quite captured by alternative terms like "ideal" or "vision." We are conceived in one value and live anchored to another proposition, not yet instantiated in our daily practices.

In structural terms, this means that the Constitution of 1787 and, notably, the Bill of Rights represent the baseline. They enshrine the liberty in which we are conceived. But the ideals toward which we yearn are incorporated in a charter morally superior to the Constitution, namely the Declaration of 1776. The Declaration served both as a legal brief for the War of Independence and as the standard for criticizing the compromise represented by the Constitution of 1787. The freedom achieved in the war against the English necessitated another war in 1861 to redeem us from tolerating the South's "peculiar institution."[11]

In this magisterial first sentence of the Gettysburg Address, there lurks ammunition for both sides in the great conflict that surrounded the calm of November 19, 1863. The forces of the Union could draw sustenance, as I have suggested, from the reconceptualization of the American people as an organic nation. But so far as the address also validates the case for separation from England, it also provides an argument for secession from the Union. What, after all, was the difference between America's seceding from England and the South's leaving the Union? The Confederate loyalists could well argue that as their grandfathers had consented to the Union, they were entitled to withdraw their consent. They as a group were equal to the people of the North, and, therefore, they could choose which form of the social contract would work for them.

We sometimes forget the context in the Declaration of Independence in which we find the phrase: All men are created equal. The claim of equality prepares the reader for the more important thesis that all men, as equals, possess certain inalienable rights, "that among these are life, liberty and the pursuit of happiness." The purpose of government is to secure these rights. The people consent to government as their agent to realize these ends. But if "any form of government" should be perceived as "destructive" toward these ends, then the people that originally gave their consent are entitled to withdraw it. They are entitled to "alter or abolish" a government that departs radically from the one to which had given their consent. It follows, supposedly, that the colonists were entitled to withdraw their consent to the government of King George III.

When fully stated in this fashion, the argument of 1776 invites several observations. First, the colonists never officially gave their consent to the government of George III. They grew up under the tutelage of the English monarchy and their adhering to the government of the Crown was something like a child's joining its family. The most that one could say is that they never consented and that therefore when they matured and reached the age of consent they were entitled to say no. By contrast, the Confederate states did join the Union by signing the Declaration of Independence as states and ratifying the Constitution as states. If they gave their consent to a form of government, they—by the logic of 1776—should be able to withdraw from the pact. Paradoxically, it

seems, the logic of the Declaration of Independence applies more co-
gently to the claim of the Confederacy against the Union than to the arguments of the Americans against the British.

Note further that in the structure of the argument, the premise of
equality plays a curious role. All men are created equal. So what? How
does that strengthen the case against the Crown? The cornerstone of
that case is that governments derive their legitimacy from the consent
of their governed. If a people has not consented to their form of government, the government is not legitimate. This would be true even if
within the society, human beings were not all of equal dignity and status. Whether some people were intrinsically superior to others or not,
they could all enjoy a collective right to withhold consent from a repres-
sive regime.

What, then, is the point of the Declaration's claim that all men are
created equal? The answer is twofold. First, there is an implicit claim
that as a people the Americans are equal to the British and to all other
peoples. If any people should be able to consent to their government,
then the Americans, too, enjoyed that fundamental right. That they
were a colony—nurtured as the metaphoric child of the Crown—did
not mean that they could not assume the posture of an equal people. If
this is the meaning of equality in the Declaration, then it provides little
support for Lincoln's claim that the nation was dedicated to a proposition that implicitly required the abolition of slavery.

A more compelling reading of "All men are created equal" would be
that all human beings are equal among themselves as well as being equal
as collective entities. They are equal among themselves precisely in that
they possess inalienable rights—the same inalienable rights to "life, liberty, and the pursuit of happiness" possessed by everyone else. Reading
the document in this way enables us better to understand Lincoln's posture toward abolition. There is ample evidence that Lincoln regarded
blacks as morally and socially inferior to whites. He said so in numerous
speeches in the 1850s. But despite these "racist" assumptions that were
common to his time, he fervently regarded slavery as an evil. It was an
evil precisely because it deprived blacks of their inalienable rights to life,
liberty, and the pursuit of happiness. They could not enjoy the fruit of
their own labor. Slavery was a system under which slaveholders were
"wringing their bread from the sweat of other men's faces."[12]

The nation is born dedicated to this proposition that all men are equal with regard to their basic human rights. This idea is extracted from the Declaration of Independence, but the rest of its argument is discarded as outdated. There is no mention at Gettysburg of the requirement that the people consent to their government and that they should have the right to withdraw consent when unsatisfied. Nor, in light of the argument's utility to the Confederacy, would Lincoln have acceded to the language of 1776. He would have little reason to argue that every generation had the right to consent or withhold consent to its government. Now the *nation* was in place, and the *nation* made claims across time. No particular generation could undo the work laid so carefully in the past.

The address continues with a second sentence that locates us in the present. *Now we are engaged in a great Civil War, testing whether that nation or any nation so conceived and so dedicated can long endure.* Thus begins the internal portion of the address, which is devoted to the war and its dead. Lincoln repeats the conventional label for the four-year indulgence in bloodletting—the "civil" war. The word has the connotation of the private or domestic (*Code civil*) or of a phenomenon arising spontaneously up from the citizenry (civil society). The South preferred the expression the "War between the States," by which they hoped for recognition that the war was more than a rebellion and that the Confederacy had full legal status as a belligerent under international law. Lincoln's choice of the favored Northern expression is his only partisan word in the address.

I prefer the unconventional label: "The War between Brothers" or the "Brothers' War." That is indeed what it was. Brothers met and fought each other in the field. But even more significant, the slaying of 620,000 men should be understood as an offering on the altar of fraternity. For every seven slaves who were liberated, at least one man had to die. They gave their lives so that the nation "might endure." Significantly, in this sentence, Lincoln repeats the claim of nationhood and stresses that the great evil of the war is not that it threatens the federal government, the Constitution, or the Union. The great danger is that the Civil War threatens the survival of the nation. The nation, of course, includes both sides in the conflict.

This conception of a single American nation accounts for Lincoln's religious language in his second inaugural address delivered, as victory seemed near, on March 4, 1865. Here Lincoln thinks of North and South as bound together in their religious devotion: "Both read the same Bible, and pray to the same God; and each invokes His aid against the other. . . . The prayers of both could not be answered." The massive bloodletting of the four-year war is seen as a divine response to evil in the American founding.

The Almighty has his own purposes. "Woe unto the world because of offences! For it must needs be that offences come; but woe to that man by whom the offence cometh!" The terrible war is seen as a "woe" and a "scourge" inflicted for the terrible "offence" of slavery. The offense was committed by all—those who were active and those who were passive. The nation suffered punishment for its collective sin. But it could return to normalcy with the same sense of collective compassion, and thus Lincoln extends his hand: "With malice toward none, with charity for all; with firmness in the right, as God gives us to see the right." The president ends his second inaugural address in the expectation of peaceful reconstruction and with a gesture of solidarity toward the widows and other victims of the killing fields.

The policy of "malice toward none, charity toward all" is anticipated in the affirmation at Gettysburg of a single nation enduring, as it were, a calamity imposed for its sins. Yet, there was a deep contradiction between this charity expressed toward the enemy and the military objectives that were becoming obvious in the fall of 1863. In order to achieve the newly set goal of emancipation, to achieve the end that in 1865 he calls the "right, as God gives us to see the right," Lincoln would send his generals to wage total war against the civilian population. Philip Sheridan's destruction of the Shenandoah crops, William Tecumseh Sherman's conquest of Atlanta, and then his march to the Atlantic all anticipate the terror that became commonplace some eighty years later in the bombings of Hiroshima and Dresden. From Gettysburg to Appomattox, Lincoln will maintain a political policy of charity and reconciliation, coupled with a military posture that would leave no doubts about the right in the minds of the defeated.

The choice of the words "Civil War" to describe the conflict also expresses charity toward the rebellious Confederacy. They are not treated as criminals attacking federal installations and killing federal troops. Rather they are in a joint effort with their fellow countrymen to determine the future of the nation.

There follow seven sentences in which Lincoln ties together the mourning of the moment with our commitment to higher ideals:

> *We are met on a great battle-field of that war.*
>
> *We have come to dedicate a portion of that field as a final resting place for those who here gave their lives that that nation might live.*
>
> *It is altogether fitting and proper that we should do this.*
>
> *But in a larger sense, we cannot dedicate—we cannot conse-crate—we cannot hallow this ground.*
>
> *The brave men, living and dead, who struggled here have conse-crated it far above our poor power to add or detract.*
>
> *The world will little note nor long remember what we say here, but it can never forget what they did here.*
>
> *It is for us the living, rather, to be dedicated here to the unfinished work which they who fought here have thus far so nobly ad-vanced.*
>
> *It is rather for us to be here dedicated to the great task remaining before us—that from these honored dead we take increased de-votion to that cause for which they gave the last full measure of devotion—that we here highly resolve that these dead shall not have died in vain. . . .*

Let us leave this sentence in the middle and reserve the final perora-tion for a closer look. Here, in the heart of the address, it becomes clear that the key themes of the preamble for the postbellum legal order are three: *nation, death, and dedication.* And the three ideas conveyed by these words are intimately connected. The notion of the nation and the fact of death root us in the past. These are irreversible facts. The nation is born of history; the dead link us to time past. The fantasies of power, the aspira-tions of "We the People" cannot undo the defining power of history. The nation is implanted in time, and the dead are interred in the plots that lie before the speaker's dais. Yet, the dead can live, and the nation can live, if these shadows of the past are transformed into memory, and memory is nourished by dedication to the values that define the nation.

Lincoln remains ambiguous about the "great task" to which we should be dedicated so that "these dead shall not have died in vain." The long-range objective is the redemption of the nation from its "offences"—from its original sin of having tolerated entrenched inequality in the very framework of its original Constitution. The immediate task is finishing the war and reuniting the nation. We are not informed of the task that matters until the concluding two clauses of the address: *that this nation, under God, shall have a new birth of freedom, and that government of the people, by the people, for the people shall not perish from the earth.* Along with the first sentence, these words have taken on a nearly sacred quality in America's conception of itself and its mission in the world. They retrace the three themes of *nation, death,* and *dedication.* The "nation" is present, now in conjunction with God. The nation shall defeat "death:" it shall have "a new birth" and it "shall not perish." The nation will surmount death with its new dedication—to freedom for all.

These words have entered into the civil religion of the United States. They are better known than the preamble to the Constitution of 1787. Let us pause and take a closer look.

> *. . . that this nation, under God, . . .*

The invocation of the Divine signals a major departure from the resolutely secular nature of the Philadelphia Constitution. The Declaration of Independence itself repeatedly refers to the Creator. Yet, the Constitution of 1787 studiously avoids any word suggestive of a power higher than the will of the people. The purpose of the 1787 national charter is to serve the goals enumerated in its preamble (justice, domestic tranquility, the common defense, the general welfare, and securing liberty), and its legitimation lies exclusively in the possibility that a federal government will advance these worldly goals. This was fitting for a Constitution that sought to distance itself from countries that had established churches at the national level and that relied on religious tests for public office. There would be none of that in the United States.[13]

Significantly, the abolitionist movement in the 1830s, 1840s, and 1850s brought a passion for religious truth in American politics that had not previously existed. Theodore Parker, among other devout leaders of the movement, preached against "the Slave Power" in tones that made one think that the devil was marching into the new territories. The recognition that slaves, too, were "made in the image of God" provided a powerful rallying point for a crusade to correct the original mistake of 1787. Of course, various biblical passages served the other side as well, but the ardor for abolition drew heavily and indispensably on the sense of a higher law.

The Gettysburg Address, as written, apparently did not contain the reference to "this nation, under God." As he spoke, Lincoln spontaneously broke with his prepared text. The reference to God appears in neither of the drafts that his assistants, John Hay and John Nicolay, said were the prepared texts. Yet, the four journalists who were present reported hearing the divine invocation, though some observers have Lincoln saying "this nation shall under God have a new birth" rather than the word order that has come to be accepted "this nation, under God, shall have a new birth."[14]

The reference to "this nation under God" reinforces the conception of the nation as an organic entity, a single subject that could, like the Jews, enter into a covenant with a God. The substitution of the Americans for the covenanted Jews—however sacrilegious the idea may sound—landed in the New World with the Puritans and became a standard item of Protestant theology. Thus, we can understand Lincoln referring at Trenton to the Americans as "His [God's] almost chosen people."[15]

The Civil War was not only a war to establish the unbreakable bond that unites all Americans. It was also a war understood by many, Lincoln included, to have theological significance. It drew its power from religious claims about the humanity of all human beings, and its leaders found their solace in psalms and prayers. To close his second inaugural address, Lincoln expressed the faith: "The judgments of the Law are true and righteous altogether."[16]

We can date the advent of civil religion in the United States to this period of theological ferment in American politics. It was at this time, 1864, that the government initiated the practice of printing "IN GOD WE TRUST" on our coins and currency. It is hard to imagine that any other country in the Western world would permit their money—the currency of secular commerce—to advertise a religious message. Yet, nondenominational expressions of faith have become normal in the rituals of the American people. Opening sessions of Congress with a prayer, using the Bible in swearing-in ceremonies, recognizing Christmas and Easter as national holidays—all of these rituals testify to an abiding nondenominational religiosity. Americans are virtually united in their willingness to advertise a widespread faith in God. For some reason, this is not generally understood as contradicting the principle of separation of church and state laid down in the First Amendment.

The phrase "nation under God" has acquired an almost casual banality. A generation after the end of the Civil War, in 1892, the practice of reciting the Pledge of Allegiance spontaneously swept the country. In the original version of the pledge, we swore allegiance to "one nation indivisible. . . ." In 1954, the sense that something was missing persuaded President Dwight Eisenhower to return to the formulation that crossed Lincoln's lips at Gettysburg: "One nation, under God, indivisible, with liberty and justice for all."

As a "nation under God," Americans have been both blessed and cursed by a sense of mission in the world. Covenanted with higher powers, the nation has a destiny—a "manifest destiny" as journalist John L. O'Sullivan dubbed our policy of westward expansion in the mid-1840s. The phrase took hold and gave American politicians a sense of national purpose as they annexed Texas in 1845, negotiated a division of the Oregon territory with England, and led the country into war with Mexico a year later.[17] This was territorial aggrandizement in the name of the "nation under God." These were the aggressive moves that established most of the boundaries of the western United States as they are today.

The firm belief in "manifest destiny" and territorial expansion led ineluctably to the Civil War. As long as the Union was fixed at a certain number of slave states and a certain number of free, both sides could calculate the future. The South could count on the continuation of its "peculiar institution" despite fierce opposition in the North. But the westward expansion and the absorption of new territories led to intrigue and suspicion about whether slavery would be permissible in the new states that would eventually develop out of these territories. The acceptance of slavery in the original Constitution might have been an unholy compromise. With manifest destiny and the occupation of new territories, the compromise became not only unholy but unstable.

. . . *shall have a new birth of freedom,* . . . Here, near his peroration, Lincoln reaffirms the foundational value of the Bill of Rights. Freedom of speech, of the press, of the right to bear arms in a "free" state—these were the motivating values of the original constitutional order. They

would be cherished in the new order as well, but for the first time freedom would be available to all. There would be no scar in its connotations,
as there was in the three-fifths compromise, which for purposes of representation in Congress counted "the whole number of free persons" and
three-fifths "of all other persons."[18] That distinction between the free and
the unfree would disappear in the birth of a new constitutional order.

Our stylistic question recurs. Why did it seem more natural for Lincoln to use the word freedom in this context than liberty? Somehow it
would not do to speak of "a new birth of liberty." The opposition of
"conceived in liberty" and "new birth of freedom" convinces me that
the Latin origins of the first (*conçue en liberté* in modern French) and
the Germanic roots of the second (*eine neue Geburt der Freiheit* in modern German) lends internal harmony to these phrases. It is almost more
than one can expect of Lincoln, the great stylist, that in forging a new
nation of black and white he should recall for us the melding of the
English language from Latin and Germanic sources.

*. . . and that government of the people, by the people, for the people shall
not perish from the earth.* In this final phrase that, along with the opening
"four score and seven years ago" has become the most familiar cadence of
the address, Lincoln formulates an additional commitment of the postbellum era. The government should be elected "by the people," it should be
"of the people" and exist "for the people." The entire nation would vote
at the polls. And government would serve the entire nation. At least, this
was the aspiration. It would take several more generations for the nation
of voters to absorb not only black men but also women of all races.

The hypnotic cadence "of, by, for the people" did not originate with
Lincoln at Gettysburg. In an 1850 speech to an antislavery convention in
Boston, Theodore Parker had used similar language in explaining the
new American conception of democracy:

> That is, a government *of all the people, by all the people, for all
> the people*; of course, a government of the principles of eternal
> justice, the unchanging law of God.[19]

There might be a strong link between thinking of the United States
as a single organic nation and bringing God into politics, but it is much
harder to make out Parker's view that a democratic government would

function "under the unchanging law of God." The democratic idea is that people remain free to change the law by majority vote. A more generous interpretation of this phrase is suggested, however, by Parker's linking the law of God to the "principles of eternal justice." As the law of judicial review would eventually develop in the United States Supreme Court, these "principles of eternal justice" provide the bedrock for testing the constitutionality of state and federal justice under the "due process" clause of the Fourteenth Amendment. One could well accept, then, the idea of a universal popular franchise exercising its authority to make and change the law under the check provided by "eternal principles of justice."

Parker's and Lincoln's commitment to popular democracy represents a clean break with the limited forms of indirect democracy recognized under the Philadelphia document drafted in 1787. According to the élitist republican scheme envisioned at the founding, the only institution that would be popularly elected would be the House of Representatives, and that body would be chosen by the group that was qualified to elect "the most numerous Branch of the State Legislature."[20] Two delegates to the Senate would be elected by each state legislature.[21] The president was, and still is, to be elected by an electoral college chosen by the voters in each state.[22] The original Constitution was silent not only about who was entitled to be a citizen but also on the questions of whether only citizens and which citizens should be entitled to vote. All this was left to state law and the states generally limited the franchise to white male adult citizens who owned the requisite amount of property. The word "democracy" is not even mentioned in either the Constitution of 1787 or the Bill of Rights.

War has a democratizing influence. Men fight side by side and when they lay down their arms they expect to be able to rule side by side. It is not surprising, then, that in the aftermath of the Civil War we find a new commitment to government by all the people. The postbellum constitutional order takes the expansion of the franchise as one of its first priorities. In 1870, the Fifteenth Amendment secured the right to vote regardless of "race, color, or previous condition of servitude." Of the ten succeeding amendments from the Sixteenth to the Twenty-Seventh (leaving aside the Eighteenth on Prohibition and the Twenty-First repealing the Eighteenth), seven have addressed the extension of the power of the people to choose their government.[23] In short, the securing of Lincoln's promise of universal popular suffrage became the primary focus of the new constitutional order.

The Gettysburg Address, understood as the preamble to a new constitutional order, underscores four values that stand in radical relief to the motivating concerns of the Constitution as it stood, with the Bill of Rights, in 1791. In outline form these are the constitutional structures:

REVOLUTIONARY CONSTITUTION	CIVIL WAR CONSTITUTION
Dates:	**Dates:**
Proposed 1787, ratified 1787, went into force 1789, amended by the Bill of Rights 1791	Preamble in 1863, Reconstruction amendments in 1865, 1868, and 1870
Source of authority:	**Source of authority:**
We the People	The Nation as Defined by History
Primary value:	**Primary value:**
Freedom	Equality
Mode of government:	**Mode of government:**
Republic	Democracy
Highest power:	**Highest powers:**
Will of the living	Command of history, divine mission

The contrast could not be stronger. And, most significantly, the four new points of reference were all articulated in the Gettysburg Address.

Each one of these groupings hangs together with internal coherence. It makes sense for a constitution that glorifies the will of the living also to take freedom as its highest value. Our Philadelphia charter was very much a document of eighteenth-century reason: it placed faith in the capacity of men to order their affairs as they saw fit. Four score years of history proved that their self-ordering led them, as Lincoln put it in the second inaugural, into committing "offences" for which they would pay with a "terrible war."

The new constitutional order begins more humbly with obeisance to both God and the finer strains in our own historical tradition. It partakes of the historicist thinking that dominated German Romantic thought at the beginning of the century. The "spirit of the times"—the *Zeitgeist* in Savigny's classic phrase—was speaking in the triumph of the American nation and its commitment to the equality of all.

The new constitutional order cohered as a compelling ideological whole. The values of nationhood, equality, and democracy were interrelated and mutually supportive, precisely as was the original trilogy of 1787—peoplehood, freedom, and republican élitism. But Lincoln's vision of a new constitutional order may have been too radical for the jurists of the time. There emerged reactionary forces that sought to mystify and entrench the values of 1787. Before turning to the counter thrust of postbellum history, we need to understand more fully the internal coherence of the constitutional order signaled by the Gettysburg Address.

CHAPTER 3

NATIONHOOD

"It is war that turns a people into a nation."
—*Heinrich von Treitschke*

Gettysburg marked a major moral breakthrough in the political ideals of the United States. It prepared us for the postbellum struggle to realize the value of equal citizenship. It began the movement toward broadening the franchise and converting the United States into a popular democracy, a government "by all the people." The "second American revolution"—the felicitous phrase of James McPherson—established our primary political trilogy: *Nationalité, Égalité, et Démocratie*. Although these three are not as well remembered as the trilogy associated with the French Revolution, they became the guiding forces of American politics. They provided the bedrock for the new constitutional order erected in the Thirteenth, Fourteenth, and Fifteenth Amendments.

Of our three guiding values of the postbellum Republic, the least appreciated is our commitment to nationhood. We recognize, more or less, the values of equality and democracy. We acknowledge that the "equal protection" clause of the Fourteenth Amendment has served as the vehicle for some dramatic strides toward the equal dignity of black and white, men and women. And popular democracy has been on the ascendancy since the Civil War. Not only blacks but women, those who cannot

57

pay the poll tax, residents of the District of Columbia, and eighteen-year-olds all acquired the right to vote by constitutional amendment.[1] And the structure of government has been reformed as well. The people now elect their senators,[2] and we rely on the electoral college to function as a conduit for the popular vote.

Although we have made these advances in the fields of equality and democracy, we fail to acknowledge the ideological foundation that made these legal developments possible. Without the solid commitment to nationhood expressed at Gettysburg, we could not have achieved equality among the diverse groups that constitute the American polity and we would have had little faith in encouraging "government of the people, by the people, for the people." Lincoln and many of his contemporaries understood the "bonds of memory" that forged solidarity in the nation,[3] but the message has been lost to many in our current generation of lawyers, historians, and other contemporary observers.

The fact is that the concept of nationhood—like God—played well on both sides of the battle lines in the Brothers' War. The Confederacy, too, claimed to be a distinctive nation. English politician William E. Gladstone, elected prime minister in 1868, said that Jefferson Davis and his compatriots had created not only an army "but a nation." Loyal Southerners thought they, as well as the North, belonged to a distinctive organic entity and, as such, were entitled to embodiment in a separate state.[4] Yet, Lincoln was committed to the view that all Americans who traced their lineage to the Declaration of Independence constituted a single nation. "We are building a nation," Republican leader Charles Summer declared in the Senate at the end of the war. But the single nation had already been forged—in the blood of the blue and the gray.

Whether Americans constitute a single nation is always open to dispute. In his diary of the Civil War, George Templeton Strong wrote: "We have never been a nation, We are only an aggregate of communities, ready to fall apart at the first serious shock."[5] The debate over American nationhood falters in part because of the very ambiguity of the word. We should underscore the complexities of nationhood in the hope of avoiding misunderstanding. Three distinct uses of the term stand out. First, there is the use of nation in the phrase "national government"—a single government for the entire country. "National" in this sense simply refers to an organizational structure or indeed to any phenomenon that applies to the whole country, as in the expression "national bestseller." "National" in this geographic sense says nothing about the sentiments that bind the country together.

A second sense of "national" applies in the conduct of foreign affairs. A country that seeks to aggrandize itself by extending its laws, its policies, and its territorial claims is nationalistic. But any government, whether or not it represents a single nation, can be nationalistic in this sense. The former Soviet Union pursued a nationalist foreign policy, but it conceived of itself as consisting of many distinct nations.

The third sense of nationhood is the one that concerns us. "A nation" expresses solidarity as well as the bonds of collective identification with a particular history, language, and folklore. The nation exists across time. It includes the dead, the living, and the unborn. Geography—living together within a well-defined space— may be important in the crystallization of some nations, but fixed borders are hardly necessary for internal solidarity. The Jews, Palestinians, and Gypsies are all paradigmatic examples of nations in search of a homeland. The factors that bond people together in a nation are typically three: language, religion, and a shared sense of historical oppression. My claim is that the Civil War generated an American nation in this third sense of organic solidarity.

Misunderstandings arise because these three distinct senses of the term overlap and intersect. A nation in the historical, organic sense typically has as its goal the establishment of a state that expresses its collective yearnings. The Zionist politics that led to the founding of the state of Israel illustrate this phenomenon. Once established in a state, the nation may or may not find embodiment in a centralized national government and its foreign policy may or may not emphasize a nationalist spirit. The nation can coexist with a decentralized government. Indeed, many nations have existed over time without any government at all.

The cornerstone of my argument is that in the mid-nineteenth century, a conceptual shift coalesced in American self-understanding. A transformation, long in the making, reached a decisive stage. We had abandoned the language of the late eighteenth century, the language of the documents drafted in Philadelphia in 1776 and 1787, and begun to think of ourselves as a nation with a distinctive historical personality. We had become more than "We the People"—a collection of individuals with a political will. We had acquired an existence over time and a personality deeper than just the present generation and its yearnings.

The shift is evident in Walt Whitman's introduction to *Leaves of Grass* in 1855. The great American poet writes of America in the style of a psalm praising the supreme power of the universe. Implicit in his encomia for the land and the people is a recognition of the American nation:

> The Americans of all nations at any time upon the earth have probably the fullest poetical nature. The United States themselves are essentially the greatest poem . . . . Here is not merely a nation but a teeming nation of nations. . . .[6]
>
> Of all nations the United States with veins full of poetical stuff most need poets and will doubtless have the greatest and use them the greatest.[7]

Whitman attributes to Americans a distinctive appreciation for poetry. Perhaps this is correct, perhaps not. The most important point is the assumption that we, like other peoples with particular histories, and languages, constitute a nation. It is clear that the poet does not see the nation in its governmental structure, for as he says, "The genius of the United States is not best or most in its executives or legislatures . . . but always most in the common people."[8] Americans were a nation, and as a nation their greatness lay both in their poetic sensibility and in their mystical connection with their land.

Whitman is surely not the first to describe the American people as a nation. From the very beginning, there were voices that thought of Americans as a nation by analogy to the great European entities that, after the French glorification of their *nation*, sought also to express their distinctive organic selves. The question is one of degree. By the mid-nineteenth century, both Europeans and Americans had the assertion of national consciousness on their minds. In the early 1800s, the various newly constituted countries of South America had undergone the process of rebellion, the assertion of independence, and the self-definition of distinctive national entities. Now it was time for the United States to realize that it was a nation, as Lincoln argued. Its roots lay in a late-eighteenth-century struggle for independence, but now it had acquired a personality and an internal cohesion that made claims of loyalty on all its citizens.

The emergence of the United States as a nation carried great political significance. In the ensuing chapters, I shall argue that nationhood implied and supported the thrust toward treating all those subject to the jurisdiction of the states as equal under the law. It also drove the incipient movement, signaled in the Gettysburg Address, toward widespread diffusion of the democratic franchise. In the immediate aftermath of the Civil War, the self-understanding of the American nation provided the vantage point for criticizing and chastising the disloyalty of the rebels. These ideas—equality, democracy, and loyalty to the nation— dovetail as a single braided whole, and together they constitute the bedrock of the intended second constitution.

AMERICANS AS A SINGLE ORGANIC NATION

The transformation occurred gradually. The voluntarist group called "We the People" gradually became a historically bound, organic entity that transcended choice and time. Prior to the Civil War, Supreme Court justices adverted occasionally to the question of whether the American people constituted a nation. Yet, it is difficult to find the kind of discussion that becomes commonplace in the mid-nineteenth century. In a 1793 case, for example, we find the suggestive question: "Do the people of the United States form a nation?"[9] The answer is ultimately yes, but in this context the term "nation" has little to do with organic nationhood. As of the 1787 Constitution, the United States was a nation in the first sense of possessing a centralized government that ruled over a defined geographical area. Thus, the United States could become a subject of the "law of nations"—also known as international law. The United States was also a nation in the sense that the Supreme Court, as a *national* court, could bind the states. As the Court said in 1793: "The sovereignty of the nation is in the people of the nation, and the residuary sovereignty of each State in the people of each State. . . ." The point is that people of the United States are sovereign and prevail over the states.

These practical matters of determining the legal personality of the United States government do not require an answer to the question of whether the American people constitute an organic and inseparable nation. The impetus to think about an organic nation springs largely from the romantic urge to suppress our apparent divisions and to see ourselves as a new stream of historical consciousness. In every nationalist movement—in Germany, Italy, or the United States—there is always an element of faith, a leap from what one sees to an imagined unity. The abolitionists cultivated a sense of nationhood as they preached emancipation of their "brothers and sisters" in chains. In 1833, Lydia Maria Child published a popular nationalist tract entitled *An Appeal in Favor of That Class of Americans Called Africans.* She argued that, "Africa is no more their native country than England is ours,—nay, it is less so, because there is no community of language or habits. . . . "[10] Even Daniel Webster's famous invocation of unity, "Liberty and Union, now and forever, one and inseparable," can be understood as an appeal to organic nationhood.[11] These are typical of the many sources that issued in Lincoln's Gettysburg prayer for the nation's survival.

If only whites were moved by Lincoln's 1863 address, however, we would hardly speak of a single nation emerging from the war. But the impetus to identify with the newly conceptualized nation came from black as well as white voices. Emancipated slave Frederick Douglass poignantly wondered whether "the white and colored people of this country [can] be blended into a common nationality, and enjoy together . . . under the same flag, the inestimable blessings of life, liberty, and the pursuit of happiness, as neighborly citizens of a common country." "I believe they can," he affirmed.[12] It is not so easy to find this opinion replicated among black Americans of the time. Yet, it is hard to deny, even in the face of black separatist movements in the twentieth century, that many have shared the dream that Martin Luther King, Jr. articulated one hundred years after the Gettysburg Address:

> I have a dream that one day this nation will rise up and live out the true meaning of its creed: We hold these truths to be self-evident; that all men are created equal. I have a dream that one day on the red hills of Georgia the sons of former slaves and the sons of former slave owners will be able to sit down together at the table of brotherhood.[13]

To speak of the nation as an idea shared by both black and white is not to assume that this idea would be harmoniously realized within the lifetimes of those who endured the war, or indeed that the American nation would ever transcend its inherent conflicts. I do not disregard the virulent racism that sparked the antidraft riots in New York in the same month as the Union victory at Gettysburg or the pogroms against the freed blacks that took place in Memphis and then in New Orleans within two years of Appomattox. The line of spontaneous racial violence continues to this day. But violence on the ground can coexist with a shared dream of peace between the descendants of oppressors and the oppressed.

The freedmen had a dream of peace. Lincoln was their Moses and they had reached the promised land. They would find redemption in emancipation and in the law that would secure their rights as free Americans. Their patriotism did not go unnoticed. In 1869, in the debates leading to the Fifteenth Amendment, Senator Alonijah Welch argued eloquently that the emancipated African Americans had the virtue of patriotism and this qualified them for the franchise.[14] As time passes and our ranks are continually nourished by immigrants, the descendants of slaves constitute an increasing percentage of the "original Americans"— those whose forebears were here at the signing of the Declaration of Independence or at least to witness the surrender at Appomattox. Indeed, the time may come when a majority of Americans whose ancestors were present at the founding of the postbellum legal order will be the descendants of slaves. Historical struggle has shaped our sense of nationhood, and there is no doubt that this history has brought black and white together into the same narrative of national experience.

The poets and philosophers understood the romantic surge of American nationalism better, apparently, than did the lawyers. The poet James Russell Lowell could see the events of his time with the lens that then shaped the European view of national unification. Looking back to the role of Henry IV in France in the pacification of the religious wars of sixteenth-century France, Lowell wrote within a year of the Gettysburg Address:

> Henry (IV of France) went over to the nation; Mr. Lincoln has steadily drawn the nation over to him. One left a united France; the other, we hope and believe, will leave a reunited America.[15]

Lowell captured the national moment. But the literary monument of the Civil War was not a poem but Edward Everett Hale's short story, published in the year of the Gettysburg Address, "The Man Without a Country." Hale fittingly bore the surname of the famous martyr, his great-uncle Nathan Hale, as well as the given names of the famous Harvard orator who preceded Lincoln at Gettysburg. Edward Everett Hale's tale of Philip Nolan expresses the sense of organic nationhood that prevailed at the time. Nolan was an army lieutenant who fictitiously collaborates with Aaron Burr in his plot to wage war against the United States. At his trial for treason, Nolan curses the United States and intemperately says that he never again wants to see the country of his birth. This wish becomes his punishment. He is sentenced to spend his life at sea, never to see or hear of his native land. The author dwells on the suffering entailed in breaking the organic tie of nationhood and ends the tale, sentimentally, with Nolan's dying wish that his tombstone read: "In memory of Philip Nolan. Lieutenant in the Army of the United States. He loved his country as no other man has loved her; but no other man deserved less at her hands."

The popularity of "The Man without a Country" might be all that one needs to prove that, by the mid-nineteenth century, Americans had developed a new self-understanding. They were no longer simply a voluntary association called "We the People." They had become an organic nation from which separation was the greatest penalty that one could imagine. Yet this romantic idea of nationhood required a philosophical as well as a sentimental grounding. We must turn then to two writers who at mid-century tried to explain the theoretical grounding of the new American nation. The two—Orestes Brownson and Frances Lieber—are of different political leanings. In today's idiom, we would call Brownson a conservative and Lieber a liberal. Although they differed on many issues, they concurred on the concept of nationhood as it applied to the United States.

TWO PHILOSOPHERS: BROWNSON AND LIEBER

Orestes Brownson was born in Vermont in 1803 and educated himself under the influence of Emerson, Thoreau, and the transcendentalist school. A keen analyst of American politics, he wrote widely about the issues of the day. In *The American Republic*, published in the year the war ended, Brownson offered a set of arguments that lend philosophical grounding to Lincoln's effort to reconceptualize the American people as a nation consisting of the dead, the living, and those yet to be born as Americans.

The core of Brownson's thinking is his rejection of the idea of the United States as a voluntary association replicating, symbolically, the creation of civil society in a social contract. In opposition to hypothetically free choices made by individuals in a state of nature, Brownson makes the nation the centerpiece of his theory of society and government. It cannot be the case, he contends, that "Individuals create civil society and may uncreate it whenever they judge it advisable." Attributing these philosophical views to John Adams, Brownson argues that they lead to the Confederate argument for secession.

To support his view of nationhood, Brownson tries to transcend the conventional distinctions between nature and society, between individuals and their environment:

> Man in civil society is not of nature, but is in it—in his most natural state; for society is natural to him, and government is natural to society, and in some form inseparable from it.[16]

This communitarian thesis, which has recently become more fashionable in academic circles, underlies several assumptions that motivated both Lincoln's approach to preserving the Union and the policy of reconstructing the defeated South on the basis of a new constitutional order:

It explains why secession, even voluntary secession, from the United States was wrong and even conceptually impossible. The nation has a life of its own—a "spiritual" and "mystical" existence—which could not fall victim to the will of the states to proceed on their own path.

It leads to the conclusion that the leaders of the "secession" were acting disloyally toward the United States and were arguably guilty of treason.

It accounts for the necessity of a new constitution that would derive from the inherent power of a united nation to constitute itself as a state. "The nation must exist as a political community before it can give itself a constitution."[17]

Brownson thought it a mistake to think of a constitution as a piece of paper certified according to rules of voting and ratification. A constitution springs from the heart of the nation. It is not the product of negotiation among distinct parties within "We the People" but a declaration of the people or the nation acting as a collective whole. We find a similar idea endorsed in the preamble to the 1949 German Basic Law: The German nation presents the constitution to itself "by virtue of its inherent constitution-making authority."

Brownson's political philosophy drew on the romantic strains of nationalist thinking then current on the European continent, but he distinguished the American nation carefully from others then struggling for unity. The distinctive feature of the American nation was not blood but rather the role of territory as a constitutive factor in the definition of the political community that becomes a nation. Brownson regarded the German conception of the nation—based on blood and transcending conventional borders—as "barbaric."[18] The only civilized approach to nationhood, he claimed, acknowledges that all peoples are mixtures of different tribes and genetic sources: "A Frenchman, Italian, Spaniard, German, or Englishman may have the blood of a hundred different races coursing in his veins."[19] If blood was not the criterion, then the proper starting place was the political community constituted by recognized borders. This was a nationhood obviously well suited to the American challenge of finding common ground in a nation of immigrants as well as former slaves.

Brownson's conception of the American nation dovetailed with Lincoln's. This was a nation constituted in part by an idea: it was "conceived in liberty"; and yet with an emphasis not found in Lincoln's writing, this liberty had to be understood as liberty under law. The Americans were a nation under God, but then, Brownson was quick to add, so were all peoples: "Every nation is, in some sense, a chosen people of God."[20] What made the Americans special was neither their nationhood nor their relationship to the divine. The mission of the United States was to propagate the reciprocal connection between liberty and law. "Its idea is liberty, indeed, but liberty with law, and law with liberty."[21]

Brownson's respect for the law brought him to understand the special place of loyalty in political theory, and on this point I read him sympathetically.[22] The concept of loyalty has its roots in the law and following the law. The pair "loyalty and law" stands in contrast to another conceptual pair: patriotism and the nation. Loyalty and law are, as it were, the rational anchors of politics; they induce stability, perseverance, and self-control. Patriotism and faith in the "mystical" nation are their romantic opposites. They stand for the passion and the possibility of radical politics. These passions, unrestrained by respect for principle, can have dangerous consequences—as we know from the history of the twentieth century.

In Brownson's thinking, the idea of law links up the emergence of an enduring nation. He sees the United States as having matured from its romantic faith in revolution to a recognition that only law and loyalty could provide the nation with a stable constitution. The tendency in antebellum America, he argues, was to revere "the sacred right of rebellion" and to sympathize "with insurrectionists, rebels, and revolutionists, wherever they made their appearance."[23] "Traitors were honored, feted, and eulogized as patriots."[24] The Civil War transposed our ranking of these values. Loyalty and faith in the established order empowered the British to govern their dutiful colonies; patriotism undermines the law for the sake of the nation's independence. Thus, patriotism was revered by the founders, but it became an evil when invoked by Dixie to shake the foundations of the Union and the legal order ratified in 1788.

The great appeal of Brownson's thinking is that he simultaneously invoked and rejected the romantic tradition. He relied upon the concept of nationhood to ground our aspirations of unity and he cast the Confederacy in the role of irresponsible revolutionaries, the heirs of patriotic fervor that leads to the breaking of bonds and the undoing of the legal order.

Brownson's conservative emphasis on loyalty captured the political sentiments then coursing though the minds of the victorious leaders of the North. Loyalty to the Union became the premise for reconstructing the South. Yet, this form of loyalty, as I shall explain in greater detail, enjoyed the twist of being linked with the crystallization of national consciousness.

Lincoln himself, we should add, might have favored the values of patriotism over those of loyalty. His devotion to the American nation, as evidenced both by his speeches at Gettysburg and the second inaugural address, stresses a passion for unity and reconciliation, regardless of legal forms. The question in Gettysburg was whether the nation—not the Constitution, not the legal order—"would long survive." Lincoln's own policies toward the law made it clear that the law was to serve the nation and its projects, including the war. This is why he refused to obey Justice Taney's order overruling his suspension of the writ of habeas corpus in Baltimore. That is why in his rhetoric he thrust to the fore the Declaration of Independence and downplayed both the Constitution and federal law. When Lincoln did contrast the Declaration with the Constitution in an incomplete text dated early January 1861, he invoked an image from Proverbs 25:11: "a word fitly spoken is like apples of gold in a setting of silver."[25] The Declaration is represented as the apples of gold and the Constitution as the "picture of silver subsequently framed around it." The important point is this: "The picture was made not to conceal, or destroy the apple but to adorn and preserve it. The picture was made for the apple—not the apple for the picture." He averred that neither document "shall ever be blurred, or bruised, or broken," but it is clear that he regarded the apples of gold as more important than the frame subsequently added. The legal frame—the Constitution—was dispensable so long as we remained faithful to the eternal verities of the Declaration of Independence.

It is fair to attribute to Lincoln, then, a sense that the Union required a constitution that would express the basic values he articulated at Gettysburg. This is, in effect, a constitution for a new republic based on nationhood, equality, and democracy. Brownson and other political theorists at the time also had a sense for a new constitution aborning. Brownson writes as though the constitution of the United States were not yet in place:

> The real mission of the U.S. is to introduce and establish a political constitution, which, while it retains all the advantages of the constitutions of states thus far known, is unlike any of them, and secures advantages which none of them did or could possess.[26]

The war had forever recast the American nation and that meant a new constitution must be forthcoming. It is hard to know whether

Lincoln's ambivalent attitude toward the 1787 Constitution went as far as Brownson's conception of a nation, unified after its travail, finally prepared to bring forth its constitution and to realize its mission in history. I would prefer to think of Brownson's view as an outer benchmark that makes it plausible to think of Lincoln as preparing the nation for a new constitution.

The great triumph of Brownson's philosophy was to work out the distinction between the nation as a living, spiritual entity and the organization of the American government. The unity of the nation was one thing, the centralization of the government another. There was no reason, in his view, why unity implied what he called "consolidation" of the government in Washington. "The great problem of our statesmen has been from the first, How to assert union without consolidation, and state rights without disintegration?[*sic*]"[27] In postbellum politics, as we will see, these distinctions carried regrettably little weight. The problem of nationhood was reduced to the question: How much power was centralized in Washington and how much was retained by the states? Brownson, however, understood that these were separate issues. The nation was a spiritual issue that went beyond politics. The organization of government was a matter of practical power sharing.

Brownson, then, is a sympathetic voice supporting my reading of the Gettysburg Address. Whether all aspects of his philosophy would appeal to us today or not,[28] his conception of the nation, if read into the mood of 1863, supports our understanding of Lincoln's speech. The shift in terminology—from peoplehood to nationhood—brought Lincoln into line with the romantic ideas of those who yearned for unity and solidarity in postbellum America. This was yearning for an identity, a consciousness of what it meant to be American. It did not necessarily imply the consolidation of government in Washington or the curtailing of states' rights.

If the United States is understood as a nation forged in the Civil War, the question remains whether it is a nation in the same sense as European nations thought of themselves in the mid-nineteenth century. No one claimed of the American nation that it derived from the bloodlines of a limited number of tribes. The question is whether the myth of tribal descent—critical, for example, in the biblical self-understanding of the Jews—need play a role in the modern conception of the nation.

On this point, the passionate writings of the German immigrant Francis Lieber illuminate the tie between European and American thinking. His personal quest conveys a particular charm. Born in 1800, trained in Kantian philosophy and nurtured as a youth in German romanticism, he tried in his early twenties to join the Greek fight for independence. Following the example of Lord Byron, who fought and died in Greece, young romantics in the early nineteenth century yearned to identify themselves with the struggle for national liberation. Yet, Lieber did not quite make it to Greece. His papers were not entirely in order and, therefore, he got stuck in Rome for a number of years and worked tutoring the children of a German theologian. When he came to the United States in his twenties, he opened a swimming school in Boston and by the sheer force of his personality he managed to cultivate the acquaintance of the leading intellectuals of the time. He found his way into teaching in a minor college in South Carolina and he began writing about prisons, criminal law, and government.

Lieber retained his love for the nation of his birth, as evidenced by the disarming story of his reaction to the outbreak of the German Revolution of 1848. Hearing the news in the midst of a lecture, he broke into tears and left immediately for Germany. By the time he arrived, he had found that liberal sentiments had run their course and that his former countrymen were hardly prepared to carry out the democratic dreams of his youth.

Returning to the United States, he eventually became a professor of political science at Columbia College and held a post teaching in the law school as well. His most notable achievement came in the Civil War. His personal associations brought him to the attention of General Henry Halleck, the Army Chief of Staff, who asked him to draft rules of engagement for the Union troops in the field. Lieber brought to bear his Kantian sensibility in drafting 157 articles of *Instructions*. This proved to be a turning point in the history of the law of war. His draft code was used by the Union forces and it became the foundation, at the end of the century, for the first Hague treaty on the rules of warfare.[29]

Lieber's thoughts on the American nation found their expression in his essay "Nationalism and Internationalism," published in 1868.[30] His views on the relationship between the national identity and the form of government concur with Brownson's. "Centralism remains an inferior form of government," he claimed.[31] As an example of a strong nation with decentralized government, he invoked England, which, in his view, had for centuries cultivated a sense of nationhood under a decentralized government. For philosophers such as Brownson and Lieber, the issue of nationhood had little to do with the debate then brewing about the future of federalism and states' rights in the United States.

Lieber brought a special sensitivity to language to the discussion of nationhood in the United States. The English language had spontaneously swept across North America, displacing German, French, and Spanish. This remarkable phenomenon proved to be essential to the emerging sense of nationhood. Sharing a common language may not be sufficient for a sense of nationhood, but it is certainly necessary. Wherever languages divide, as in Canada, the former Czechoslovakia, or the former Yugoslavia, the ever-present threat of secession haunts political life.

Lieber was acutely aware of the unifying effect of the English language in the United States for several reasons. First, his native language was German, which made him more aware than native English-speakers of the significance of their language to their sense of identity. And, second, the Germanic romantic movement, particularly the writings of Johann Gottfried Herder, emphasized the role of language in the crystallization of national self-consciousness. Lieber argued that great writers preceded statesmen in pointing the way toward the nation as a political entity:

> Dante, singing in the Tuscan dialect, raised it thus to the dignity
> of the language for all Italy, as later Luther by his own transla-
> tion of the Bible, made his dialect the German language.[32]

For the people of a given territory to become a nation, Lieber argued, it was critical that "the inhabitants [speak] their own language [and have] their own literature and common institutions, which distinguish them clearly from other and similar groups of people."[33] It is possible, though historically rare, for a nation to consolidate without a common language. The Swiss provide the enduring exception—a cross-linguistic nation with a long history of national confederation. Language was to prove a critical foundation for the coming together of a common nationality in the United States. Although the Americans were politically divided, they affirmed their common identity every time they called upon the English language to debate their differences.

As Lieber suggested, a common literature captured the spirit of American distinctiveness in the mid-nineteenth century. Harriet Beecher Stowe's *Uncle Tom's Cabin*, published in 1852, had become an instant bestseller and contributed to the sense that Americans were a nation with a special problem that set them off from other peoples.

The American language was taking hold and expressing itself not only in literature but in the newspapers that carried news of the war's battles to the entire nation. The journalists were on the scene and they telegraphed home reports and stories. The reading of printed reports about events ranging from the crushing Union defeat at Fredericksburg to the subsequent turnabout at Gettysburg fed, in Benedict Anderson's apt phrase, the imagination of nationhood.[54] The newly invented telegraph spread the news and made the Civil War the first war with a contemporaneous audience. Americans reading the news in Maine or Tennessee could imagine that others whom they had never met were reading the same paper, engaged in the shared ritual of following the advance and retreat of their boys in blue or gray. They were all encountering the same national drama conveyed in the same language.

The soldiers, too, brought home a sense that might have seemed remarkable had they given it any thought: All these young men from different parts of the country, fighting under the banner of Maine or of Virginia, were speaking the same language. Even if some of them spoke German or Dutch at home, they spoke English in the field. The nation was at war, but the war was strengthening the sense of reciprocal recognition and the understanding that all the combatants shared a common culture.

The final achievement of the war was the inclusion of former slaves in the effort to consolidate the nation. At the outset of the war, none of the four million American blacks bore arms. Congress authorized service for emancipated slaves in 1862, and a year later Union regiments of trained black soldiers began to see action. These soldiers first showed their heroism in June 1863 at Milliken's Bend, Louisiana, and then right after Gettysburg at Fort Wagner, South Carolina, where the Massachusetts 54th performed so well that the names of the battalion and of the battle have entered the annals of black American pride. The units were segregated and until the summer of 1864 black soldiers received less pay. But the courage and sacrifice of black fighting men did more to generate a sense of unity in the nation than all of the abolitionist rhetoric about brotherhood.[35]

Lieber did not have it quite right when he suggested that one of the ingredients of nationhood was a "numerous and homogeneous population."[36] This might have typically been the case in the development of European nationhood but the generalization did not hold for the Americans. Sometimes countries are held together precisely by their differences. They become proud that they have mastered certain difficulties that have torn others asunder. Germans point to the stable and unproblematic relationship between Catholics and Lutherans negotiated in the Treaty of Westphalia in 1648. The Swiss revel in their union of distinct cultural pockets, a medley of different languages and dialects. Americans, too, have evolved from resignation about the racial division of the country to a recognition in many quarters of the beauties of a diversified culture, bound together by a common language and a shared drama of national unification.

Otherwise, Lieber was an astute theorist of nationhood, with a particular sensibility for the difference between the notions of "nation" and "people." He claimed that in all European languages, except English, the "nation" had an aura of "grandeur" while "the people" had become identified with commonness, as it were, with the rabble. He pointed to a then-current French dictionary for support.[37] The linguistic problem is probably more complicated. Today the French term *peuple* hardly carries the negative connotation noted by Lieber.[38]

Nothing in this argument turns on the precise choice of word, "nation" or "people." The relevant question is whether one thinks of Americans as a collection of autonomous individuals bound together by their project to "make a more perfect Union." If so, they would be "simply the inhabitants of a territory," as Lieber put it.[39] Or are they a group destined by the accidents of birth and location to share a common historical fate? The common way of posing the same question in the mid-nineteenth century was to ask whether the group had a "national character."[40] Lieber insisted that Americans had this quality and that, moreover, "Without a national character, states cannot obtain that longevity and continuity of political society which is necessary for our progress."[41]

These, then, are some of the philosophical reflections on the nation that emerged from the Civil War. Brownson and Lieber, two of the leading thinkers of the time, understood the links forged in the American experience. Politicians understood them too. The sense of nationhood comes to the fore in the rhetoric of right and wrong that dominated the postbellum period. Here we need to listen to the complaints of those who felt betrayed by the secession and by the war.

CHAPTER 4

LOYALTY
AND BETRAYAL

"For all my devotion to the Union, and the feeling of loyalty
and duty of an American citizen, I have not been able to
make up my mind to raise my hand against my relatives, my
children, my home."

—Robert E. Lee

Gunfire breeds fear. When brothers start firing muskets and cannons at each other, danger fills the air. For human beings the sense of impending death has a positive or negative valence. The violence comes in shades and hues. Mass killing typically has a purpose, sometimes good, sometimes bad. We learn to see differences. Killing in self-defense differs fundamentally from killing for profit. Executing a murderer is not the same as an act of cold-blooded murder (though it may look that way to some). All of us think, in effect, like lawyers: we seek to confer meaning on violence, to distinguish good from bad, civilized from uncivilized, the battles of armies from the self-interested actions of criminals.

The problem of understanding the violence inflicted between blue and gray became one of the enduring legal and philosophical problems of the Civil War. The range of possibilities is wide. The simplest response would have been to see the assault of each against the other as simple criminal homicide. Union boys killing two thousand of their Southern brothers in the first battle of Bull Run could be understood simply as two thousand individual acts of criminal homicide. The same would be true of the three thousand Union deaths wrought at the hands

75

of General Beauregard's troops. Yet, this description fails to capture the momentum of war. It treats the Confederate military action as equivalent to a terrorist attack. When another enemy of the government in Washington blew up the federal building in Oklahoma City, we treated the assault as simply homicide. When terrorists plant bombs in marketplaces in Israel, the government treats them as criminals. Yet, the killings in the Civil War were dignified as killings in battle.

War has it privileges. The ordinary domestic law of homicide does not apply. Two groups of armed and uniformed "belligerents" meet on the field of battle. At least as to combatants seeking to kill each other, there is no crime of engaging in battle, there is no punishable homicide in killing the enemy. The international law of war takes over. Significantly, Francis Lieber, whose career we discussed in chapter 3, was commissioned to write the first rules of engagement for military troops in the field. His draft of military conduct became *General Field Order 100* and, subsequently, the basis for the Hague treaties and the robust body of international law that governs acts of violence in the fields of war.

It is typically better for those who kill and maim to be treated as prisoners of war. They are never punished for actions committed within the conventional bounds of warfare, and they are held in detention, separated from the "criminals" punished to expiate their crimes. Prisoners of war are released when hostilities are over.

JOHN BROWN'S RAID: CRIME, WAR, OR TREASON?

But drawing the line between crime and war is not so easy. Consider John Brown's raid against Harper's Ferry, Virginia, which we now regard, in retrospect, as the opening salvo of the war. It will be recalled that Brown and eighteen of his followers from Kansas assaulted an armory in order to seize weapons and initiate a campaign to stimulate an uprising of slaves throughout the South. The local people held their own in the skirmish and drove Brown's band to refuge in a firehouse. A young lieutenant colonel named Robert E. Lee arrived on the scene, and with his regulars he handily retook the firehouse. Brown and his men were responsible for causing several deaths in Harper's Ferry. But what kind of crime did they commit? Was it an act of war? Could they claim the special treatment of prisoners of war?

There was not much chance of treating the raid as an act of war, but nor did the state of Virginia wish to try Brown as a simple criminal. They charged him, paradoxically, with treason against Virginia. I say "paradoxically," because treason differs fundamentally from other crimes. As treason was understood in English common law and as it came to be adopted in the United States, treason is committed only by those who, by virtue of citizenship or residence, owe a duty of loyalty to the government. Homicide, theft, rape, robbery—these can be committed against any victim regardless of the previous relationship between the perpetrator and the victim. The bond between them is irrelevant. There is nothing personal in committing the crime. That is one way to understand the famous line in *The Godfather*: "Even the shooting of your father was business, not personal."

In contrast, treason is nothing but personal. The origins of criminal betrayal lie in the bond of fealty that the serfs owed to their lord and above all to the king under the feudal order. In United States, with no king to whom we could attach the required sentiments, the entire country became the object of our loyalty. The purpose of the constitutional clause of treason, however, was to limit the expansive English definition of treason to two cases. The first was "levying war" against the United States, and the second was "adhering to their Enemies, giving them Aid and Comfort."[1]

These two lapidary clauses carry rich overtones. They say nothing about the required allegiance of the traitor to the United States, but the implication is obvious. In order to commit treason by "adhering" to an enemy, the recipient of "aid and comfort" must be an enemy nation. Those who engage in warfare do not commit treason against us. There is nothing wrong in adhering to the enemy if one belongs to the enemy. The problem arises when one of our own goes over to other side. Treason is possible only if the perpetrator stands in a bond of loyalty with the nation that claims betrayal.[2]

The crime closest in nature to treason is adultery. Only those who are married can commit adultery. Only those in monogamous relationships can betray each other. Only those bound to the nation can commit treason. The required "marriage" with the nation is often, but not always expressed as the requirement of citizenship. When William Joyce (Lord Haw Haw), born and raised in England, employed his impeccable accent to broadcast wartime propaganda on behalf of the Third Reich, his actions violated his duty of loyalty to England—at least it was so decided in the Old Bailey. Presumably, Joyce felt no loyalty toward England. In his heart, he had disengaged himself from the country that nurtured him to adulthood and, therefore, it was perfectly natural for him to render "aid and comfort" to the side of the war that he believed in. Resolving their initial doubts, the English courts concluded that even though he was not a citizen and regardless of the state of his emotional disposition toward England, Joyce was guilty of treason. The English sensed that he was one of them and that he owed a corresponding duty of loyalty, regardless of the way he felt.

Though lawyers now speak of citizenship or permanent residence as a requirement for treason, the required bond is in fact more mystical, more elusive than a legal definition of membership in the polity. The required fealty runs not to the state, which grants citizenship, but to the nation, which demands everything and grants nothing. The nation and the duty not to betray are two sides of the reality—a reality that exists more in the minds of people than in the forms of the law.

And, thus, the state of Virginia charged John Brown with treason. The raid on Harper's Ferry could have been considered a simple felony or, at the opposite extreme, an act of military belligerence. Yet, neither of these options captured the particular injury and fear that Virginia felt as a result of Brown's futile effort to raise a slave revolt. Charging treason converts the acts of violence into a calculated act of betrayal. Also, the charge of treason underscored an important political point. Virginia was a sovereign and autonomous entity. It had the kind of relationship with its nationals that one could expect of any nation. The charge of treason expresses as well a sense of solidarity in the group, a self-understanding of nationhood as opposed to the voluntary association of a people. Traitors deserve to die, or so it is popularly believed. The Virginia Court convicted John Brown and had him hanged within three months. Adhering to a different nation and a different set of basic values, Brown went to his death without guilt and without remorse. The North celebrated him as a hero, as the vanguard of men who would die for the cause: "His soul goes marching on."

As levied against John Brown, however, the charge of treason is rife with paradox. Virginia may have felt threatened and injured in its dignity, but as "foreigners" to the state, John Brown and his men had no duty of loyalty to Virginia. This was the first of many contradictions that would run through the use of nationalist rhetoric in the effort to conceptualize the conflict between the North and the South.

A striking feature of mid-nineteenth-century America was, in fact, the preoccupation with issues of nationhood and loyalty. Ordinary crime was of lesser interest. The breach of the "bonds of affection," as Lincoln described them in his first inaugural address, cut more deeply than wounds to the flesh. The preeminence of relationships over consequences is not likely to resonate well with modern readers. Today we gravitate toward the idiom of crime. The frontier of international criminal justice is defined by war *crimes* and *crimes* against humanity. The great evil of Germany's sending its own people to Auschwitz constituted a breach of faith with the German Jews who placed their trust in the nation of their birth. But the tribunal in Nuremberg interpreted the crime as one that violated the duty of all people to humanity in the abstract. In order to understand the ideas that shaped the mind of the Brothers' War, we have to think our way back into the mentality of the times. We must grasp the powerful reality that consists in the bonds that tie us to the history and the nation into which we are born.

Even before Fort Sumter was fired on, the idiom of loyalty guided the ways people expressed both their sense of duty and the wrongs that they suffered. Robert E. Lee, who assumed command of the Confederate forces, was in fact loyal to the Union, and he opposed slavery. Nonetheless, he chose to put his loyalty to Virginia, to his kith and kin, ahead of his loyalty to a distant government. This was not a decision that could be understood as morally right or wrong. The issue of loyalty transcends conventional questions of morality. This is where Lee made his personal stand, and he won respect for his integrity.

Northern leaders made similar use of the rhetoric of loyalty and betrayal. In a major speech on July 4, 1861, defending his policies in the war, Lincoln repeatedly referred to the Confederate soldiers as traitors. And in a very important opinion issued by the Supreme Court at the end of 1862, an opinion we now take up in detail, we find this sentence: "They [the Southern states] have cast off their allegiance and made war on their Government, and are none the less enemies because they are traitors."[3] This language came easily to the lips of those who sought to describe the behavior of their brothers on the other side.

THE PRIZE CASES: WAR AND NO WAR

The issues of loyalty and betrayal preoccupied the Supreme Court in the *Prize Cases* of December 1862, as the litigation about the validity of the Northern blockade of Southern ports came to be called. In late April 1861, immediately after the firing on Fort Sumter, Lincoln declared a blockade of Southern ports. Federal vessels apprehended several ships running the blockade that were flying the Mexican and English flags. They seized the vessels and confiscated the goods. The shippers sued to get the goods back. The question was whether the president was entitled, without a congressional declaration of war, to blockade the ports of the rebellious states and to treat vessels violating the blockade as acting illegally under the law of nations, so that their cargo could be seized as contraband.

The problems were many-layered. Did Lincoln have the authority, without congressional authorization, to order the blockades? Let us leave aside for the moment the question whether Lincoln violated his duties under the 1787 Constitution. As I have argued earlier, in light of the exigencies of war and the necessity of a new constitutional order, Lincoln did not take these obligations particularly seriously. The more pressing questions were the international relations between the United States and foreign powers who were poised, for reasons of the cotton trade, to intervene on the side of the Confederacy. Lincoln needed a judgment from the Supreme Court that would explain to the English and the French why the United States was entitled, under international law, to impose a blockade and to seize ships that sought to ply Southern ports.

The basic rule of international law is that in a state of war between "belligerents," governments are entitled to impose blockades as a way of isolating the conflict.[4] Lincoln wanted the Court to uphold his actions as legitimate, but he did not want the price of his vindication to be the recognition of the Confederate forces as an independent foreign army under international law. He always referred to the military action of the Confederacy as a rebellion or an insurrection, not as a war. The problem was how the blockades could be declared legal under international law if the South was not treated as a belligerent engaged in war in the international sense. Five justices on the Court mediated between these contradictory extremes. They held, in their bare majority, that as of late April 1861 a state of "Civil War" existed as a matter of fact and that the president, acting alone, could take military measures to put down the insurrection.[5] It followed, under international law, that neutral powers were obligated to recognize the de facto blockades. If their ships ran the blockades, they were subject to arrest and seizure. Somehow the Court managed to reach this conclusion without conceding that the Confederacy represented an independent belligerent power waging full-scale war.

Lincoln's victory was complete—domestically and internationally. His authority was upheld, his gunboats could seize ships and cargo in violation of the blockades, and the South could not secure the recognition it desired. Not only were the seizures legitimate under the laws of war, but the secessionists could, in good faith, still be branded as traitors. It was international war and domestic war at once. Somehow they were foreign enemies whose goods were subject to seizure and domestic traitors at the same time. Justice Grier's opinion for the majority reasons that the leaders of the Confederacy were traitors and "none the less enemies because they are traitors."[6] This is the kind of logic that should be expected when brothers go to war.

"LUSTRATION" BEFORE INVENTION OF THE WORD

As the battles were being fought, we faced inevitable contradictions in perceiving and labeling the opponent on the other side of the battlefield. But after Appomattox, we encountered a whole new set of problems. How would we bring the formerly disloyal back into the government of the nation and of their local communities? At least three different veins of policy ran through this problem. There was Lincoln's policy of reconciliation toward those who were distracted by the passions of heart. They were good Americans before their indulgence in the romantic war of secession and they would be good Americans now that the affair was over. When Lincoln mobilized the country for war, he allowed himself to use derogatory language toward the traitors on the other side but, as the climax approached, he adopted the neutrality we hear at Gettysburg. In his second inaugural address of March 1865, he articulated the famous words of reconciliation already implicit in the Gettysburg Address:

> With malice toward none; with charity for all; with firmness in the right, as God gives us to see the right, let us strive on to finish the work we are in; to bind up the nation's wounds; to care for him who shall have borne the battle, and for his widow, and his orphan—to do all which may achieve and cherish a just and lasting peace, among ourselves, and with all nations.

Opposed to the desire for reconciliation we encounter the natural tendency, among politicians and among the people, both to punish the vanquished and to insure that secessionist tendencies were forever rooted out of state government. The conflict between these two tendencies has recurred in contemporary struggles to make the transition from dictatorial regimes to democracy. The general problem is: How does a nation, in the shadow of mass indulgence in violence and betrayal, redeem itself and start anew? How does it absorb, after apocalypse, all those who might be regarded as former enemies? This is the problem the Germans faced after World War II, and it has become the common theme in Eastern Europe and Latin America as numerous nations seek, if not a "new birth of freedom," at least a first embrace of the values that motivated Lincoln at Gettysburg.

Since 1989 and the fall of Communism, the recurrent problem for the West has been: How do we make peace with the past? Do we prosecute the former communists for crimes against their own societies? Do we disqualify them from public office? Or do we simply suspend memory in the hope that time will pass, that the formerly disloyal will die off, and that a new generation will take their place.

In the politics of transition in Eastern Europe, two patterns of reconciliation and punishment have taken hold. According to one group of countries, typified by Hungary, the proper way to come to grips with the past is to honor the martyrs who fell to communism but not to disqualify the former Communist Party officials from the current political scene. Thus, the Hungarians have engaged in elaborate rituals of reburying dead heroes such as reformist political leader Imre Nagy, whom the communists summarily executed after the abortive 1956 revolt. (The Hungarians have a self-mocking aphorism to capture their propensity for symbolic funerals: "Hungarians know how to bury their dead.") Honoring the dead has left the living, some with blemished records, to flourish. Party leaders from the period of reform communism in the 1970s and 1980s have retained their influence and some, such as Gyula Horn, even rose to power under the system of democratic elections.

The alternative pattern is illustrated by Czechoslovakia and, even more radically, by the Federal Republic of Germany after its unification with the former German Democratic Republic. In the immediate aftermath of their "velvet revolution," the Czechs enacted "lustration" laws to prevent former communists from participating in public life. The Germans took the more radical step of suspending the employment of all judges and law professors in the East, thus requiring them to undergo individual examinations to determine their suitability for life in a democratic legal system. Since that time, West German "carpetbaggers" have come to occupy virtually all the available professorships of law in the Eastern universities.

The theme of "lustration" was well known in the period of American Reconstruction—although the usage of the word in a political context lay more than a century in the future. The problem interests us because of the way the issues of loyalty and betrayal reveal the underlying sense of American nationhood. Those who sided with Lincoln's policies of reconciliation had a deep sense of nationhood that could survive the plague that had descended on the land from 1861 to 1865. Those favoring "lustration" urged the propagation of these differences between "them" and "us."

The "others," those who had sympathized with the Confederacy, were regarded as ipso facto disloyal and unsuitable for participation in the postbellum legal order. Yet, the nation came to be torn by wrenching conflict among different segments of American government. The Supreme Court did as much as it could to hold back policies of disqualification based on presumptive disloyalty. The major case of the time was

Cummings v Missouri, which brought to the attention of the Court the tensions that prevailed throughout the war in the slave state of Missouri.[7] This state on the border between North and South was a microcosm of the entire war. Over one hundred thousand of its young men fought for the Union, but another thirty thousand fought on the side of the Confederacy. Missouri never seceded, but its governor, Claiborne Jackson, tried to engineer an alliance with the states to the South. He refused Lincoln's call for troops in May 1861 and set up his own garrison of state troops in the outskirts of St. Louis. When these troops were suspected of pro-Confederacy sympathies, a fiery young Union general, Nathaniel Lyon, victoriously led a charge against them. Yet, Jackson regrouped and later defeated the Union troops at Wilson's Creek. For much of the war, it was not clear who was in charge of the state. Jackson called a meeting of the legislature in the fall of 1861, but less than a quorum showed up.

As the war was winding down, Missouri began the process of drafting a new constitution. Finally adopted by a vote of the people in June 1865, the new charter sought to exclude from practicing their professions all lawyers and men of the cloth who would not take an oath testifying to complete loyalty to the Union during the war. A Catholic priest named Cummings refused to take the oath, he was fined $500, and the state imprisoned him to coerce payment of the fine. On his appeal to the Supreme Court in late 1866, Cummings claimed that the state was not constitutionally entitled to deprive him of his calling on the basis either of his past conduct or his refusal to take an oath.[8] A parallel case reached the Court when a lawyer was denied the right to practice because, although he had been fully pardoned by President Johnson, he had once held state office in the Confederacy.[9] Both cases raised the question whether the legislature, either state or national, could infer present political unfitness either on the basis of the failure to take the oath or past loyalty to the Confederacy.

These were "lustration" laws, pure and simple. The idea was to rebuild society without the participation of those who had been the enemy. The way to do this was to infer present unreliability from past disloyalty. But the inference reeked of overkill. Everyone who had opposed the Union was thrown into the same basket of presumed unfitness for office. This was both unfair to the individuals affected and detrimental to the process of Reconstruction. The legal problem was how the Supreme Court could intervene, particularly in the Missouri case, to overturn the state's overly broad policy of disqualifying the supposedly disloyal from the ministry and the bar.

This was 1866. The ratification of the Thirteenth Amendment in 1865 had sealed the demise of slavery. But the new constitutional order had not yet entered into force. The "due process" and "equal protection" clauses of the Fourteenth Amendment, still two years in the future, would have provided a suitable framework for analyzing the issues. But all the Court had at its disposal were several provisions in the 1787 Constitution that, despite the movement to reconstruct the nation under a new legal order, still controlled the legal argument.

The Court had to decide the issue of loyalty oaths for participation in the postbellum Reconstruction, and therefore it invoked an obscure clause from 1787 that prohibited any state from passing "any bill of attainder."[10] As imposed by parliament, bills of attainder typically named enemies of the regime and imposed punishment on the specific individual. These laws differed because they did not name specific individuals, and indeed the Missouri law required the guilty to identify themselves by refusing to take the oath. The essential feature of both bills of attainder and ex post facto laws (also forbidden in the same 1787 provision) is that they, in the Court's view, imposed "punishment" either without trial (attainder) or retroactively (ex post facto). The punishments imposed on Cummings were multiple: fine, imprisonment and prohibition from acting as a priest.[11] The latter was sufficient, in the Court's view, to convert the Missouri constitutional provision into a bill of attainder. In addition, the provision was an ex post facto law, for it imposed an additional punishment of professional disqualification on the act of "treason" against the state.[12]

The Court's intervention in these cases, by bare majorities of five votes to four, testified to the Court's willingness to uphold a policy both of national reconciliation and the protection of individual rights in the face of those seeking to hunt out and punish the disloyal. The Court's decision suggested that the old Constitution might be sufficient to cope with the problems produced by the effort to reintegrate the formerly disloyal into postbellum political and social life. The policy of "lustration" had not tainted the old Constitution, and perhaps we could negotiate the postbellum era without vengeance toward the disloyal.

But Congress was of a different mind. When the radical republicans secured passage of the Fourteenth Amendment, under circumstances of dubious legality,[13] the amendment contained several provisions aimed explicitly at punishing the South and those who supported the cause of the Confederacy. Section 3 of the amendment was aimed at turncoats: People who had once sworn an oath of office to the Union, as had Jefferson Davis, and then supported the Confederacy, were presumptively banned from office in the reconstituted Union government; their only recourse was to petition Congress for a personal exemption.[14] Section 4 of the amendment canceled the debts of the Confederacy and outlawed compensation for emancipated slaves.[15]

Section 2 of the amendment had a different thrust. Its purpose was to provide a sanction against the states that refused to grant blacks the right to vote. Indirectly, this provision carried forth the policy of chastising and branding the formerly disloyal, for it provided that a state could, without sanction, disqualify someone from voting "for participation in rebellion."[16] This is quite a remarkable change from 1866 to 1868, from the attitudes of *Cummings* to the Fourteenth Amendment. The Supreme Court had taken a strong position in favor of reconciliation and the protection of individual rights. Congress and the ratifying states preferred to write into the Constitution their intolerance of those who had been disloyal to the Union.

The political uses of disloyalty take many forms. President Johnson apparently desired to use the lustration laws for the sake of destroying the influence of the large plantation owners. By his proclamation of May 29, 1865, he pardoned all participants in the rebellion and reinstituted their property rights (except of course for their former property in slaves), but there were various exceptions, notably for major Confederate officials who possessed more than $20,000 in taxable property. This group, namely those who were both rich and presumptively disloyal, had to apply to the president for a special pardon. The plan ascribed to Johnson was to delegitimate the economic élite and to prevent them from participating in the constitutional conventions that designed the new postbellum governments. At the same time, he hoped to withhold political participation from African Americans (before passage of the Fifteenth Amendment in 1870). Without the influence of the élite and the blacks, the way would be supposedly open for the smaller farmers, the Southern yeomanry, to gain power.[17]

The emancipated slaves were, by contrast, a paradigmatically loyal force. Republicans praised their patriotism.[18] If devotion to the country were the issue, the blacks had unquestionably earned the right to vote. But there was no such simple theory motivating the distribution of the franchise. On the part of some, the motive was to punish and disenfranchise the disloyal. On the part of others, the game was political: Promote those and only those who will vote for their own party. The great issue of loyalty and disloyalty dissolved into the pursuit of partisan advantage.

JEFFERSON DAVIS AS SYMBOL OF THE CONFEDERACY

All of these issues—reconciliation, punishment for disloyalty, lustration, political advantage—peaked in the popular fixation on resolving the fate of the president of the defeated Confederacy, Jefferson Davis. His was the story of a patriotic American whose loyalties went the wrong way at the wrong time. A war hero in the Mexican-American War, a former congressman and senator from Mississippi, Davis personified the spirit of men who loved America but were loyal first to their region and to their way of life. He was so devoted to the cause that even after Lee's surrender on April 9, 1865, Davis remained defiant. He took his rump government into hiding in the Deep South and was not captured until May 11. One of the leading topics of conversation in the period after his arrest was whether Davis, languishing in a cell in Fort Monroe, Virginia, would be prosecuted for treason or possibly even for murder. One participant in many of these conversations was a French observer, the Marquis Adolphe de Chambrun, who was visiting the United States during this period and received considerable attention from key personalities of the time, including Charles Sumner and Lincoln himself. Chambrun's sympathy for Davis comes to expression in his diary, published many years later.[19]

The problem of shifting loyalties had troubled France earlier in the nineteenth century, when Napoleon's future was uncertain. Chambrun recalled the fate of Marshall Michael Ney. Originally one of Napoleon's lieutenants, Ney offered his service to Louis XVIII after Napoleon had abdicated and been banished to the island of Elbe. But after Napoleon left Elbe and began his hundred-day campaign, Ney joined him. After

Napoleon's definitive defeat at Waterloo, Ney was in the embarrassing position of having joined the losing side twice. Intolerant of his displays of disloyalty, the House of Peers condemned Ney and had him shot the following morning.

Chambrun saw an analogy between the actions of those who supported Napoleon and those who fought for the Confederacy. He was troubled by the contingencies of victors' justice, of punishing someone like Ney or Davis, both of whom were loyal heroes to the defeated. Whether you sympathized with John Brown or Jefferson Davis had little to do with abstract morality and justice. It was a function of the side you were on.

As John Brown was charged and convicted of treason against a southern state, Davis was indicted for treason against the United States. But the trial never took place. Many leading Northern figures, including Horace Greely, intervened on Davis's behalf and in 1867 he was finally released and allowed to continue his life as a civilian. Chambrun reports the conflicting sentiments of the leading figures of the time. He rode with Lincoln in a carriage after the fall of Richmond, the Confederate capital. It was "impossible to discover in Lincoln any thought of revenge or bitterness toward the vanquished."[20] When someone suggested that they hang Jefferson Davis, Lincoln repeated the line from the second inaugural, "Let us not judge lest we be judged." Apparently, "Lincoln was for mercy at any cost."[21]

Lincoln's vice president and successor Andrew Johnson was, according to Chambrun, a horse of another color. "Johnson is a partisan of those who favor banishment or even the death penalty for the guiltiest among the rebels."[22] Chambrun quotes Johnson as saying, "I'll teach them that treason is a crime, perhaps the greatest of all crimes."[23]

The analysis of Jefferson Davis's treason is hampered by the absence at the time of an established law of war detailing war crimes and crimes against humanity—the kind of offenses applied in the Nuremberg trials. Francis Lieber was then drafting Rules of Engagement for Union troops, and these rules would eventually form the nucleus of the Hague conventions. But this did not solve the problem of whether the conduct of war could in itself be considered criminal behavior. The law of war, as it has taken form in the twentieth century, carries the significant negative implication that ordinary warfare is exempt from criminal responsibility. Only the excesses described as war crimes, aggression, and crimes against humanity can generate the basis for a criminal conviction.

All of these concepts were in flux in the mid-nineteenth century. The relatively clear lines established in international law and in the domestic law of homicide and treason still eluded the sensibilities of the time. The various sides to the debate—those favoring reconciliation, those favoring punishment of the "rebels"—were groping for the concepts to express their moral insights. From the Supreme Court to the man in the street, they did not know how to label the sense of wrong that they had experienced. Virginia called it treason when John Brown led his raid on Harper's Ferry, but in 1867 people were hopelessly divided about how to classify the conduct of Jefferson Davis.

At the time, the United States needed a healthy tolerance for contradiction and self-deception. The Confederacy consisted of traitors, but they were people the North had to live with. The South had been at war, but in Lincoln's view they had never left the Union. In 1868, their senators could sit in the halls of power, but only if they accepted the Fourteenth Amendment.[24] Their endorsement was "voluntary," but they had a debt to pay. These are fissures in American thought that hardly withstand scrutiny.

The country needed a framework for understanding and mediating its contradictions. The appeal of the Gettysburg Address would grow in time because, despite the complexities that set in immediately after the war, the message of November 19, 1863 was still clear and simple. The United States was committed to being a single *nation.* Its people were "conceived in liberty and dedicated to the proposition that all men are created equal." The nation would not perish. We would experience "a new birth of freedom," and we were on the way to becoming a democracy—"government of the people, by the people, for the people."

These great maxims of nationhood, equality, and democracy entered American consciousness precisely because they were so simple and direct. Yet, they would be put to the test. The claims of nationhood would face resurgent claims of states' rights. But none of the three ideals for the new postbellum United States would encounter the moral complexity of the central premise that motivated both the Declaration of Independence and the Gettysburg Address: the proposition that "all men are created equal." The simplest and clearest ideals can sometimes be the most troubling.

CHAPTER 5

EQUALITY

"Democracy arises out of the notion that those who are
equal in any respect are equal in all respects."

—*Aristotle*

The genius of the Gettysburg Address is that it took the words
of the Declaration of Independence and found in them a
crystallization of a meaning suitable for the refounding of
American democracy. In 1776, the idea that "all men are created
equal—for all purposes" had no precedent in the declarations of political leaders. Even the great French Declaration of the Rights of Man, issued thirteen years after the French Revolution, preached a more
limited version of equality—"All men are born and remain equal under the law."[1] In its original context, the famous five words "all men are
created equal" had a limited function. They undermined the pretension
of King George III to rule under the divine right of kings. If all men
were of equal stature under God, then no one could claim to have been
anointed as ruler by supernatural authority. At the same time, however,
the famous maxim could also be understood as referring to "men" as collective entities: "all peoples have equal status." It was not particularly
novel to argue that all nations, all states, had an equal claim to govern
themselves. The principle of national self-determination, urged so
adamantly in the twentieth century, derives from the same source: Every
nation is entitled to preserve its own culture, cultivate its language, and

express itself as a subject of the international community. International law is based on the idea that nations, anchored in the form of states, enter into legal relationships. The states in which nations are embodied enjoy legal personalities. They incur debts and, significantly, these debts are not extinguished by revolutionary changes of government. The forms of the state come and go, and the nation endures through it all. It is no wonder, therefore, that the Declaration of Independence would assert that the American people were equally entitled, with all other nations, to determine their form of government.

These two senses of the famous "all men are created equal" capture the ambiguous quality of the American revolt against the British. It was both a revolutionary and an anticolonial war of independence. The revolutionary spirit was captured in the categorical rejection of monarchy. The anticolonial thrust appears in the assertion of the Americans' equal claim to rule by "consent of the governed."

More far-reaching than both of these original meanings, however, is the individualist interpretation: All human beings are of equal dignity. They are created equal and remain equal in the eyes of their Creator. There can be no foundation, therefore, for the claim that whites are superior to blacks or that men should count more than women. Of course, many framers of the Declaration were slave owners and most, if not all of them, were patriarchal heads of households. Yet, they bequeathed to the world a rhetorical phrase that was pregnant with meaning deeper than many of them may have intended. This deeper meaning lay, embedded in the text, ready to come alive for the first time as their Declaration became the sacred text of the American abolitionist movement.

Legal texts often bear one meaning on their surface and a higher meaning that requires faith and personal investment beyond the surface meaning. A good example is the commandment in the Decalogue prohibiting homicide. Allow me a short digression on the commandment against killing to illustrate the phenomenon of a text that carries one meaning on its surface and a more radical meaning beneath.

The Hebrew expression in the Sixth Commandment, *lo tirtsach*, is generally read: Thou shall not commit murder. The term "murder" implies a prohibition only against unjustified killing, implying the permissibility of killing in self-defense. Yet, a survey of the sources in Jewish law reveal that the term also bears the interpretation found in many

Christian translations: Thou shall not kill. "Thou shalt not murder" is a rule that we can expect people to follow, but "Thou shalt not kill" hardly lends itself to the same strict enforcement. The morality of not killing becomes an aspiration, a challenge for people to realize in their struggle with imperfection. Whether they can renounce self-defense, as the Mennonites appear to have done, is a matter of personal moral realization. Whether they can extend the prohibition against killing to all living creatures, as some exemplary spiritual leaders have done, depends on their moral evolution. Those who eat meat are not wrongdoers or sinners. They simply have not yet reached the highest point of aspiration. One should respect the Buddha, for respecting all forms of life by not killing, but those who fall short of the Buddha are not subject to blame.

The same contrast can be drawn between the equality of all nations and the equality of all human beings. The equality of nations has become a postulate of the international legal order. There may be debate about which groups of people constitute nations entitled to self-determination and representation in the international community, but the principle seems to be accepted by all. For the community of nations, so recognized, equality—let us, say, with regard to voting rights in the General Assembly of the United Nations—becomes a norm readily enforced.

Not so for the equality of all human beings. First, it is not at all clear what we mean by equality, why we should recognize it in all human beings, and what we should do to realize equality in practice. Even Lincoln did not favor the equality of blacks for all purposes, including social and marital relationships. And even if we think that all children are equal in the sight of God, we might understandably bequeath our property to our own kin. How much equality and the form that it should take remain a matter of constant debate.

As in the case of "not killing," in the field of granting equality, there is always more that one can do. The minimum is recognizing an equal "right to life, liberty and the pursuit of happiness." This requires, to be sure, the abolition of slavery. But there arises then the question of equality in the exercise of basic legal rights, like owning property, serving on a jury, and testifying as a witness in court. Some of these basic legal rights of equality did not accrue to women until well into this century. At a further frontier is political equality, namely the right to express opinions, to vote, and to hold office. Further up the scale of equality, we encounter equality of opportunity in economic competition: Every individual should have the right to compete on an equal footing, with equal education and the basic resources required for the market.

At this point in the spectrum, we begin to make the transition from equality of opportunity to equality of outcomes. Everyone should arguably have an equal claim to the world's resources. The manna of life, in Bruce Ackerman's apt metaphor, should be distributed equally.[2] The accidents of birth prevent us all from having equal talents, but perhaps those born with lesser talents should receive some form of compensation for their deprivation. All other outcomes, as John Rawls argues, would be "arbitrary from a moral point of view."[3] A similar form of compensation might be urged for those who fall short in the unfolding of their lives. Some have bad luck in romance, fail at their creative efforts, suffer the accidental loss of a child. An extreme egalitarian might see an injustice, requiring compensation, in these differential life paths.

We might refer to this layered set of possibilities as the spectrum of equality. As in abstaining from killing, one can cross the initial stage of this spectrum and remain unsure about how far to ascend on the scale. To whatever height one ascends on the spectrum of equality, there should be a strong connection between that perch and the *reason* for recognizing human equality in the first place. Once again, the analogy with the commandment against killing (or murder) proves instructive. However much one becomes convinced that killing is wrong, one needs a reason for that degree of conviction. In order to renounce self-defense you need a reason, something to the effect that violence only breeds more violence. Or, if you wish to emulate the model of Albert Schweitzer, you must say something like: All living things are the creatures of God, they all deserve to live. This is not to say that your reason must be demonstrably correct, but you need a reason for your commitment for it to make any sense at all.

The abolitionists, too, must have had reasons for believing in equality in a way that both Northern and Southern fellow citizens rejected. Abraham Lincoln, too, followed an inner logic in cultivating the deeper meaning of the Declaration of Independence. And today we must also have grounds for taking human equality seriously as a basic ideal of social and political justice.

Providing these reasons turns out not to be so easy. As a descriptive claim, the thesis "all men are created equal" is obviously false. People differ in every conceivable respect—size, strength, intelligence, musical talent, beauty. But being equal is not equivalent to being the same, identical, or similar. Equality is a curious relationship, and its model is arithmetic relations. Two sides of an equation are stipulated as equal, but this may not be apparent to the untrained eye. For example: 17 x 17 = 289. The two sides of the equation are not identical in notational form but equivalent in numeric value. The suggestion is that all our differences are like notational form. My DNA, my biography, my talents, are certainly not the same as yours, but these differences become superficial in light of the deeper equivalence of moral value. What gives us this deep equality of value?

Some philosophers have tried to analyze human equality by searching for some single factor by virtue of which we are equal. We might all be equal because we can use language and say things like, "I am as good as you are."[4] Utilitarians claim that we are equal because we feel pleasure and pain.[5] John Locke argued that we are all equal because we are all the property of God.[6] Or as contemporary secular thinkers claim, we are all equal because, in principle, we can act both rationally and reasonably.[7] All these arguments suffer from the same objection. Suppose someone could not speak, would he not be equal to other human beings? Suppose she could not feel pleasure or pain, would that put her outside the human community? If he were not rational, would he not be one of us? None of these criteria alone could be an adequate test of equality unless it was accompanied by a theory that explained why that factor, and that factor alone, was sufficient to generate the strong sense of human equality. Of little value, as well, is Locke's influential argument that we are the property of God. Animals also belong to the same Creator but that does make them equal to humans.

Modern philosophical approaches toward equality all suffer from the same flaw. They are strongly committed, vaguely, to some position on the spectrum, but they offer no reason why they are so intensely committed to this value that has become so powerful in the English-speaking West. Human equality seems to be an unquestioned postulate—one of those truths that we hold to be "self-evident." And those things that are obvious apparently require no grounding in reasons. In the contemporary

liberal culture, equality is one of those values that has become so deeply
held that it is neither questioned nor justified.

Given the long history of popular belief in the intrinsic superiority of
certain classes of people—men, whites, Christians, Americans—the
philosophical belief in equality stands as a critique of commonly held
beliefs. It is clear that the popular culture still harbors many biases about
some people being intrinsically better, entitled to greater privileges, than
others. Yet, the long-range popular trend favors overcoming our biases in
favor of a belief in the equality of all humanity. The American Revolution took the first step by abolishing the privileges of the nobly born.
The 1787 Constitution prohibits both the states and the federal government from granting "titles of nobility."[8] There was this much equality
in the founding, but anchoring the "peculiar institution" of slavery in
the Constitution was the great "offence" against equality that could be
expiated only on the killing fields of Gettysburg and Antietam.

The postbellum history of the United States has carried the egalitarian message of Gettysburg into the liberation of ever more marginal
groups. After the emancipation of blacks, the movement for women's
suffrage gained strength and finally triumphed in 1920, and then in un-
clear succession came the contemporary efforts toward the equal treatment of homosexuals, "illegitimate" children, the handicapped, and
even undocumented aliens.[9] The thrust toward inclusion of more and
more groups within the inner circle of the equally privileged has been
one of the central themes of American life. Yet, even the victory of the
Civil War is not yet complete. The badges and vestiges of slavery still
haunt the land. The quest for redemption from the original sin of slavery continues in our own time.

Our sensibilities are conditioned by our history. But, however difficult the struggle, we have a history of which we can be proud. We
Americans were the first to conceptualize the great maxim of equality
and to label it a self-evident truth. No other legal system, so far as I can
tell, relies explicitly on the principle that all human beings are created
in the image of God. Yet, all modern legal systems and international
documents of human rights today subscribe to the principle of equality
before the law. Typical of the American influence is the 1789 French
Declaration of the Rights of Man, which provides in the second part of
Article 6: "The law must be the same for everyone, regardless whether it
serves to protect or to punish."[10]

Equality before the law is the most limited claim of human equality. This form of equality applies only to fellow nationals and residents subject to the same legal order. More ambitious are the arguments of the philosophers such as Ackerman and Rawls who claim that equality is the first principle of social justice. At the outer reaches of principle, we find the great maxim invoked in the Gettysburg Address: All human beings are equal in the sight of God.

Let us limit our thinking, for the time being, to the most modest claim—that all individuals, black and white, men and women, gay and straight, born in wedlock and out of wedlock, should be treated equally under the law. We did not recognize this principle in the 1787 Constitution. It came into our positive law—the law actually applied by the courts—in 1868 with the Fourteenth Amendment. But what is the grounding for this transformation in our attitudes toward equality under law? Did we need the more radical faith in equality in the sight of God to discover the imperative of treating everyone equally under the law? Is equality under law limited to Americans? If so, why does the Fourteenth Amendment literally protect all "persons" against the American states that deprive them of equal protection of the laws? These are the difficult issues to which we now turn.

THE NATION AS THE CRUCIBLE OF EQUALITY

Gettysburg forged a link between the nation and egalitarian thinking that we sometimes forget. The connection between the limited nation and unbounded equality has paradoxical overtones. The *nation* is dedicated to the proposition that all men are created equal. The thrust toward equality has universalist implications. Neither Lincoln in 1863 nor the founders in 1776 argued that only "Americans" were created equal. The claim was that all people—in principle, all human beings on the planet—are born with equal dignity. Yet, this universalistic thinking thins our commitment to equality to a point of fragility.

Equality flourishes in an environment of mutual sympathy and reciprocal identification. The love for each and the needs of each come to the fore in the affective bonds of family, friendship, tribe, and, by extension, in the reciprocal attachments of nationhood. The limited political sphere of the nation facilitates the recognition of others as human beings sharing a common history. If blacks and whites, Northerners and Southerners, eventually men and women, could respect each other as Americans participating in the same national drama, they would lay a foundation for affirming their mutual equality. They need not be brothers and not exactly friends, but they could at last recognize each other as compatriots with a common language, a single history, and a shared future.

The source for this association between bonds of affection and equality lies outside the Judeo-Christian tradition, notably in the philosophy of the ancient Greeks. The fullest development comes in Aristotle's *Politics* and in the *Nicomachean Ethics*. The idea of universal human equality was foreign to Aristotle, but he did believe in the mutual recognition of equality within the bonds of friendship and other close associations. Indeed, wishing well for the other as an end in himself is an essential component of *philia* or friendship understood broadly, and this sentiment, Aristotle believed, provides the necessary foundation for all virtuous behavior.[11]

Equality appears as a central theme in the virtue of justice as well as friendship. The just person is one who pays due regard to his own interests as well as to those of others. He is able to maintain the proper balance between his own interests and those of others. This is an aspect of distributive justice that generally requires each person to receive a due or proportionate share of the good to be distributed. Aristotle describes this proportion as an expression of geometric equality. Similarly, when one person wrongs another, some correction is necessary. This species of justice is also based on equality, understood arithmetically. The wrongdoer and the victim should both be restored to the state they were in prior to the wrong. This might be done by compelling the wrongdoer to pay compensation from the gains that he has received in order to make up the loss to the victim.

These virtues of friendship and justice require cultivation, for they contribute to the flourishing of the virtuous individual. Adapted to the nationalist argument for equality among all Americans, Aristotle's argument about friendship would go something like this. We should treat all members of the American polity as equal, with equal concern for their lives, precisely as we would treat friends. By so doing, we as a nation will flourish and we as individuals will flourish from our taking the ends of our compatriots as seriously as we would those of friends.

Each nation must seek equality for the sake of its own flourishing. The sense of common destiny is nowhere better expressed than in the Jewish expression: *Kol Jehudim eruvim ze bze* [All Jews are responsible for each other]. In the rhetoric of American nationalism, the metaphor of the chosen people, of the substitution of Americans for Jews, recurs as a familiar trope. The sense of organic closeness is implied. The responsibility of the American nation should run to all members of the nation, defined in the Fourteenth Amendment as all those naturalized or born on the soil of the United States and subject to its legal jurisdiction.

Nationalism becomes a virtue if it avoids hatred of outsiders as it encourages mutual respect among insiders. This, indeed, was Lincoln's ambition in seeking reconciliation in the Gettysburg Address and in his second inaugural address. Accepting his idea of a "new nation dedicated to the proposition that all men are created equal" would have enabled Americans to negotiate the postbellum period without self-seeking and rancor. But this was not, as we saw, the way it happened, particularly after the tragic turn at Ford's Theatre.

Andrew Johnson's plan for Reconstruction was plagued by controversies about whether the previously disloyal were still full members of the nation and whether blacks, once emancipated, should ascend a step higher and receive the franchise on equal terms with whites. Lincoln imagined grounding the equality between black and white, Northern and Southern, in a shared sense of nationhood. With the rancorous infighting that dominated Congress in the period 1865 to 1870, the relevance of nationhood began to recede. More important were the ideological issues of loyalty, personal desert, and political self-interest. The question of the black franchise became associated with the fears of Democrats that a coalition of freedmen and Republicans would dominate the postbellum South.

But this should not surprise us. Politics merely occupies the surface of our lives. The give-and-take of daily conflict can lead us easily to forget both our shared purposes and our enduring principles. The Civil War had ushered in a commitment to the equality of all members of the nation. Whatever the struggle for adoption may have been, the language of egalitarian principle came into force. By 1868, we had in place a clause in the Fourteenth Amendment that was unique in American constitutional history: no state could "deprive any person of the equal protection of the laws." What this clause would imply in practice, no one quite knew. We did know, however, that the legal idea of equality carried no historical gloss. The Constitution had already spoken of "privileges and immunities"[12] and the Bill of Rights, of securing "life, liberty, and property" against deprivation "without due process of law."[13] But the Constitution had never before contained the notion of equality of persons before the law.

The remarkable feature of this ideal-bearing language is that it protects all persons within the power of the state — all those whom the state can touch with its legal power. This was hardly a self-evident way for the provision to be drafted. Given the nationalist background of our sentiments of equality, one could readily have formulated the clause: "No state shall deny to any *American citizen* within its jurisdiction the equal protection of the laws." That is, because we were bound together foremost as fellow Americans, one would expect a commitment first to the equal treatment of all Americans. The Weimar Constitution in Germany found this to be a perfectly natural way of formulating the commitment to equality: All Germans are equal before the Law.[14] It was not until the postwar Basic Law came to be in 1949 that West Germany recognized that a commitment to equality had to be universal. The provision now reads: All human beings are equal before the Law.[15] The striking fact is that Americans came to this principle of universalization as early as 1868.

As the distinguished German constitutional law scholar and philosopher of the Weimar period Gerhard Leibholz pointed out, the Western theory of equality has united two distinct strains of thought.[16] The first is the Aristotelian principle, which grounds the virtue of equal treatment in the affective bonds of friendship or, by extrapolation, in the ties of nationhood. The Civil War enabled Americans of different cultural strains, some with power, others without, to see themselves as compatriots of a single nation. Their mutual recognition as partners in a common struggle generated a sense that at least they — the Americans — were created equal.

The second great principle in Leibholz's egalitarian synthesis stressed the universality of all humans in the love of God. This universalization derives from the biblical faith that all persons are created in the image of God.[17] The first is limited and circumscribed by the bonds of affective identification. The second breaks the bonds of the nation and extends to persons unknown and unimagined. We will allow ourselves a slight detour to explore these religious ideas and to understand their impact on the theory of equality as it developed under the Fourteenth Amendment.

THE RELIGIOUS BASIS OF EQUALITY

The abolitionist movement began on the heels of the Second Great Awakening of the first three decades of the century. The country overflowed with the religious pursuit of self-perfection, talk of the millennium—the thousand years of peace before the Second Coming of the Lord—and of the hand of God in human affairs. The American revivalists adopted the Jewish idea that our purpose on earth is to complete and perfect God's creation. As historian William G. McLoughlin sums up the fervor of the times: "The new consensus also included the belief that Americans are a peculiar race, chosen by God to perfect the world."[18]

Many of the preachers of the Awakening supported the abolitionist cause but many others did not. Faith in God and the higher law of revelation enables some people to confront the injustice they see around them; it enables others to retreat and to find solace in their personal quest for salvation. Religious beliefs also supported the cause of those who believed in slavery. Lincoln summed up the ambivalent role of religious faith in the Brothers' War: "Both [sides] read the same Bible, and pray to the same God; and each invokes His aid against the other."[19]

Religious faith hardly lays out a straight path leading to the affirmation of human equality. Yet, it is hardly an accident that many of the great abolitionists such as William Lloyd Garrison and Theodore Parker were ministers whose faith fired their dedicated opposition to the great sin of one man's owning another. These men carried with them an intimate knowledge of the Bible, yet they did not require a consensus of biblical interpretation to support their political commitments. Frederick Douglass argued that slavery was a sin because by "subjecting one man to the arbitrary control of another, it contravenes the first command of the Decalogue. . . ."[20] He was appealing to the basic principles of monotheism. But sophisticated biblical exegesis was unnecessary for those who shared the root intuition that slavery was an abomination.

Lincoln thought it obviously wrong for men "to ask a just God's assistance in wringing their bread from the sweat of other men's faces."[21] These were strong intuitions of evil, tutored by religious faith but obviously not determined by the Bible.

The religious abolitionists had every reason to be drawn to the Declaration of Independence; there they found the religious inspiration for which they could search in vain in the secular monument called the Constitution. "We hold these truths to be self-evident, all men are *created* equal." Behind those *created* equal stands a Creator—the source as well of our basic human rights, for the text continues by listing the truths we hold to be self-evident: "that they are endowed by their Creator with certain inalienable rights, that among these are life, liberty and the pursuit of happiness." This noncommittal Deist theme runs through the rhetoric of 1776. God is mentioned only as "nature's God," by virtue of which every people is entitled to "a separate and equal station" in the community of nations. This is the basis for the American people's claiming that no government may rule them without their consent. The end of the Philadelphia Declaration resonates with another invocation of a higher power: "with a firm reliance on the protection of Divine Providence, we mutually pledge to each other our lives, our fortunes and our sacred honor."

The religious refrain in the charter of our independence differs radically from the flat, secular tone of the 1787 Constitution, which makes no reference to any of the words, "God," "Creator," "Providence," "divine," or any of their synonyms. The Constitution recognizes no power higher than the will of "We the People." Yet, the close bond of religious zeal and American politics returns in the Awakening in the early decades of the nineteenth century, a period leading not only to the abolitionist movement but also to the expression of religious passion in foreign policy, particularly in westward expansion under the ideology of manifest destiny.

The invocation of God in the Gettysburg Address is both accidental and entirely predictable. It is accidental in the sense that Lincoln spontaneously added the divine invocation as he neared the end of the address.[22] The innovation was predictable. Lincoln's association of the nation and God derived from his deepest convictions. He thought of Americans as God's "almost chosen people," successors to the Jews in a relationship with the Divine that could be described as "almost a covenant."[23] In the mid-nineteenth century, it was relatively easy to believe that we were in the grip of a great historical force, possibly emanating from a higher power. "IN GOD WE TRUST" became a popular motto, appearing for the first time on the nation's coinage in 1864. Trust in God can generate diverse conclusions, but this does not subtract from the obvious way in which, at the time, faith in God and the Bible nourished the radical claims of human equality.

For modern readers, those who do not think instinctively in the idiom of Genesis and the Psalms, it is worth reviewing the kind of argument for equality found in biblical sources. The central idea that generates the concept of universal humanity or universal brotherhood is that we are made in the image of God. As the story has come down to us from Genesis 1, 26, and 27:

> And God said, Let us make man [Adam] in our own image after our likeness, and let them have dominion over the fish of the sea, over the birds of the air, over all the cattle, and over every creeping thing that creeps on the earth. So God created man in his own image, in his own image He created him, male and female He created them.[24]

There is much to be said about the proper reading of this passage, particularly in relation to the contrary story of creation in Genesis 2, a story that supposedly justifies the subordination of women. The proper reading of the text, as I have argued elsewhere,[25] has God creating a single being, both male and female. God gives this being, called Adam, dominion over all the animals but not over the first woman, yet to be created. Only in the later story of the Garden of Eden do we encounter the curse and subordination of Eve. For those who look to the Bible for guidance, therefore, it makes a tremendous difference whether one relies primarily on the egalitarian message in chapter 1, of ultimate human dignity for all, or on chapter 2, with its story leading to the curse of women that they be "ruled by their husbands."

That creation in the image of God resonated in the culture of the abolitionists is undeniable; the advocates of emancipation readily read into the line "all men are created equal" the vision of creation set forth in Genesis 1. If you believe that an individual is created in the image of God, it is difficult to deny his or her ultimate worth. There is no higher value than God, and therefore partaking of that value confers upon all human beings ultimate human dignity. This point is brought home in the grounding of the prohibition against homicide in Genesis 9:6:

> Whoever sheds man's blood by man shall his blood be shed;
> for in the image of God he made Adam. . . .

The infinite dignity of the potential victim generates an absolute ban on killing. The dignity of the victim is as great as any person who might wish to kill him and, therefore, the homicide of an innocent is never justified. This is a remarkable passage for an era in which the killing of the stranger, the "other," was a routine occurrence.

The basic ideas of Genesis receive their best secular rendition in the moral philosophy of Immanuel Kant, who takes the idea of creation in the image of God and bequeaths to us the idea of universal humanity. We are all essentially alike as members of the human family. We all partake of infinite human dignity:

> In the kingdom of ends everything has either *value* or *dignity*.
> Whatever has a value can be replaced by something else which
> is equivalent; whatever, on the other hand, is above all value,
> and therefore admits of no equivalent, has a dignity.[26]

The idea of human dignity, which we now take to be a shared premise of Western civilization, became the backdrop for our current faith in human rights and crimes against humanity.

The Fourteenth Amendment is our placeholder in the evolution of egalitarian thinking. We know very little about how much equality the framers of the amendment intended to secure, and frankly it does not matter. Each generation must struggle to assay how far they are willing to go in the name of egalitarian justice or, by contrast, how far they wish to surrender to the surviving counter-values of hierarchy. In the aftermath of the Civil War it was clear, ironically, that black men were far ahead of white women in ascending the scale of egalitarian possibilities.

Black men acquired, at least nominally, both the right to vote and the right to serve on juries. White women and black women alike would acquire neither until well into the twentieth century.

Some might argue that because the United States lagged in recognizing equal legal rights for women, the mood of 1863 would have been hostile to recognizing that women as well as men were equal in the sight of God.[27] When Lincoln said, "All men are created equal," therefore, he meant *men*—only males were equal in the sight of the Creator. This objection is easily countered. Lincoln explicitly invoked the figures of women in his discourse on human dignity. In 1857, in his speech attacking the *Dred Scott* decision, Lincoln explicitly refers to the dignity and inherent equality of black women:

> In some respects she certainly is not my equal; but in her natural right to eat the bread she earns with her own hands without asking leave of any one else, she is my equal, and the equal of others.[28]

Even if the textual evidence were silent, however, we would have to interpret "all men are created equal" as inclusive of all human beings—all variations of women, men, and children. This inclusiveness follows from anchoring the great maxim in the idea that human beings were created in the image of God: "So God created man in God's own image, in the image of God created God it, the first being, male and female God created them."[29] (I recognize that one reading of the biblical text, widely accepted in various religious traditions, holds that God did create a male Adam in his own image and later removed a rib to create Eve.)

Recognizing the inherent moral equality of women in 1863 did not mean, however, that they would receive full legal and political equality as did black men. The notion of "appropriate roles in life" still governed relations among equals and it would take decades for Americans to grasp that the politics of equality can not brook the coercion of women into domestic, apolitical roles, nor could some misguided theory of social organization tolerate the relegation of blacks to a limited number of lower-status professions.

HUMAN DIGNITY AS A
PLACEHOLDER FOR EQUALITY

One basic value remains curiously absent from those enthroned in the postbellum legal order. The movement to redeem ourselves from the evil of slavery should have prompted a commitment to a value even more basic than equality: the infinite human value of all human beings. In the wake of the Holocaust, the Germans recognized that this was the proper way to initiate the catalogue of basic rights in the 1949 Basic Law (Constitution): "Human dignity is inviolable. All state power is obligated both to protect this value and to respect it."[30] This provision clearly bears the imprint of Kantian moral philosophy, which treats respect for human dignity as an absolute duty of all individuals, including officers of the state.[31]

The structure of Article I of the German Basic Law bears a striking resemblance to the Thirteenth Amendment, which in its core provides: "Neither slavery nor involuntary servitude shall exist within the United States." If we think of the prohibition against slavery and involuntary servitude as an affirmation of autonomy, then the passive sentence of the Thirteenth Amendment could be rewritten, without change of content, in the form of the German Basic Law:

> Human dignity and autonomy are inviolable. All state power is obligated both to protect and respect autonomy, by eliminating slavery and involuntary servitude.

This would, admittedly, be an unconventional way of formulating the demands of the Thirteenth Amendment. The usual commentary on the amendment stresses simply that it omits the requirement of action by state officials that we find in the Bill of Rights and in the Fourteenth and Fifteenth Amendments. Yet, it is clear that the postbellum order sought to declare a fundamental value as the symbol of the new United States. The motive was similar to the impulse of the German drafters seeking to ground their postwar constitution in the humanistic values of human dignity. There may be intriguing and important differences between human dignity and autonomy, and we shall return to these later. For now, it is important to note merely that the postbellum legal order begins with a commitment of all state power to eliminate the evil that had cursed the United States since its founding.

Significantly, both human dignity and autonomy, both due process and equality, transcend the limits of the nation. It is not only our nationals who are entitled to these basic human rights. All human beings, all persons, should enjoy the same rights—at least so far as they are within the jurisdiction of the state securing those rights. Our commitment to nationhood generates the reciprocal sympathy that enables us to make the move from particular to universal. We may come to understand the meaning of basic rights in the context of the nation but then we are driven to see that all persons, whether members of the nation or not, are entitled to the same treatment.

ALTERNATIVE READINGS

Not everyone agrees that the equality of all persons represents the moral breakthrough of the Fourteenth Amendment. In an alternative version of the postbellum legal order, also based on the value of nationhood, Charles Black stresses the reliance on national citizenship in the first sentence of the Fourteenth Amendment: "All persons born or naturalized in the United States, and subject to the jurisdiction thereof, are citizens of the United States and of the State wherein they reside." Membership in the nation is now defined by birth on the land, and the fact of nationality, legally recognized as citizenship, generates the most basic right of the new legal order. Black reasons that the amendment places citizenship at the center of the new constitutional order. "No State shall make or enforce any law which shall abridge the privileges or immunities of citizens of the United States." The centerpiece of the new order, therefore, should have been citizenship and the elaboration of the "privileges and immunities" of citizenship.

The appeal of Black's reading of the postbellum legal order is that it, too, draws on the Declaration of Independence and the Gettysburg Address. The key phrase in his reading of the Declaration is not the commitment to equality but the clause immediately following: "that they are endowed by their Creator with certain inalienable rights, that among these are life, liberty and the pursuit of happiness." Black imagines these words coupled with the language of the Ninth Amendment, which implies an unspecified catalogue of rights "retained by the people." These "inalienable rights" should express themselves in a catalogue of human rights, including the right to sexual privacy, to reproductive freedom, and to governmental services necessary for the "pursuit of happiness."[32] The latter might plausibly encompass education, medical care, a minimal standard of welfare, and perhaps even guaranteed employment.

There is much to be said for Black's interpretation of the constitutional text. He brings together strands of our legal culture that until his writing seemed to lack internal coherence. He grounds his argument in the familiar rhetoric of rights. He builds his interpretation on critical planks of the postbellum legal order, namely the ideas of nationhood and national citizenship. Yet, the content of his argument reverts back to the language of rights, inalienable rights, rights retained by the people. He invokes the rhetoric we associate with our eighteenth century Constitution enthroning freedom over equality. True, as the title of Black's book reminds us, Lincoln's address does rely on one phrase to establish a link with the old legal order: *A New Birth of Freedom*. Yet, Black ignores the cardinal values of equality and democracy, which, along with nationhood, represent the cornerstones of the postbellum legal order.

Taking the "privileges and immunities" of citizens as the pivotal value of the new order, as Black does, creates its own problems of equality under law. Why should only citizens and not resident aliens enjoy the inalienable rights of "life, liberty and the pursuit of happiness?" Do not immigrants and even undocumented illegals have rights as human beings? The universalist language of the Declaration of Independence hardly dovetails with the parochial category of citizenship in a particular governmental polity. If all men are created equal, if we are endowed by our Creator with certain inalienable rights, it cannot be the case that these rights are limited to those who are classified as the subjects of a particular sovereign.

To be sure, the Reconstruction Amendments had to define citizenship in the United States, at least to heal the divisive scars left by the *Dred Scott* decision. That infamous act of judicial will, which served only to fuel the passions for war, held that a former slave could never become the citizen of any state. That is why the amendment adds that citizens of the United States are citizens also "of the State wherein they reside." They could avail themselves, therefore, of a body of law already developed to secure the mutual recognition of the states of "all Privileges and Immunities" of citizens in sister states.[33] As history would have it, however, the "privileges and immunities" clause of the Fourteenth Amendment has not had—at least until recently—any impact on constitutional debates.[34] The language has lain latent in the text of the Fourteenth Amendment. Whether it will find a suitable purpose in a constitutional scheme built on equality and due process remains to be seen.

Black pursues the theme of freedom and ignores the phrase that in fact requires emphasis in reading Lincoln: a *new* birth of freedom. The redemption and renaissance of our country would become possible only by confronting our "offences," and that meant recognizing and compensating for the evil of slavery. The issue that could stimulate a new birth of the nation, therefore, was not freedom itself but freedom tempered by equality before the law.

Yet, there is reason to applaud Black's reading of our history, as there is to honor the divergent views found in Bruce Ackerman's and in Akhil Amar's writings. Ackerman focuses on the de facto transformation of government wrought by the Fourteenth Amendment, enacted by a rump Congress in violation of the express language of the Constitution.[35] Amar, too, reads the history in his own way. The postbellum legal order, in his view, shifts our focus from rights that enable us to participate in government to rights that celebrate individual freedom.[36] May all these readings flourish. They testify to the innate multiplicity of meanings inherent in the second founding of the United States in the postbellum legal order. Our only problem, then as now, is that we are not sure which way the revolutionary refounding of the nation should go.

THE CUSP OF REVOLUTION

By 1868 and the enactment of the Fourteenth Amendment, we were perched on the threshold of a constitutional revolution. An entirely new legal order was yearning to work its way clear from the turmoil of the 1860s. The foundation of this new order was painted bold in the phrases that resounded at Gettysburg: nationhood, equality, and democracy. The mechanism for implementing these exhortations would be the new grant of congressional authority in the final clause of the new amendments: "The Congress shall have power to enforce, by appropriate legislation, the provisions of [these articles]." A more powerful central government was a critical part of the new constitutional order. This would be a government that would raise income taxes, as it started to do during the war. This government would enact welfare legislation to care for the widows and orphans of the war. And, most important, it would be a government that would have the capacity to supervise private relationships. The Constitution was no longer focused just on the individual struggling to secure his freedom against the government. The government would have an active role in protecting and securing the autonomy of its citizens. As my rewriting of the Thirteenth Amendment would have it: Securing and protecting the autonomy of labor would become the duty of all state power. Government would have to keep a vigilant watch on all labor transactions to insure that there never again would arise relationships bordering on slavery or involuntary servitude.

In 1866, Congress began to act on its responsibility to guard against the aftershocks of slavery by prohibiting discrimination in all facilities open to the public. African Americans were part of the public, and they should be entitled, as a matter of equality with others, to have access to public transport, theaters, and hotel accommodations. The first Civil Rights Act, therefore, would seek, in the later words of Justice Harlan, to eliminate "the badges of slavery."[37]

The commitment, first and foremost, of the new constitutional order was to the equality of all persons affected by the laws of the United States. No one knew how far our collective promise to realize equality in American life would take us. The Fourteenth Amendment could conceivably have been sufficient to insure equal voting rights for all, doing away with the need for the Fifteenth, the Nineteenth, and later amendments to secure the franchise.

With these ideals in place, we have to recognize that the guns of war had stilled very few of our fundamental social conflicts. The rough and tumble of postbellum politics pitted one segment of the nation against the other. The freedmen could aspire to power in the region where they previously had been slaves. Northern carpetbaggers could join forces with Southern scalawags to remake the agricultural South in the image of the industrial North. At stake was the class structure of the South with its landed gentry commanding a servile class of laborers. Behind the political conflicts, however, was a remaking of the American conception of government. And the states would fight by any legal means necessary to realize the position they could not secure with their sacrifices on the battlefields of recent memory.

If war, in the famous saying of Clausewitz, represents a continuation of politics by other means,[38] then postbellum legal disputes stood for a continuation of war by other means. All the disputes that eventually led to armed conflict between the states would begin, in the period after 1865, to plague the courts and throw into question the values that the war should have secured. States' rights, the holding of blacks in a form of servitude called segregation, withholding the franchise from women—all of these would remain central issues for at least another hundred years.

CHAPTER 6

THE REVOLUTION
THAT NEVER WAS

"Only when Lee handed Grant his sword was the Confederacy born."[1]

—*Robert Penn Warren*

Revolutions are never easy. The people who inhabit the new regime are the same as those who dominated the old detested order. They cannot be expected to change quickly. The judges who interpret the new law are basically the same as those who interpreted the old law. Even if the law changes, even if there is a nominally new constitution, the process of reading the new document will gravitate toward the old. The regime changes, but the people are, after all, the same.

The ancient Israelites would spend forty years wandering in the desert before the passing of time would generate a new people, unaffected by the mentality of the "fleshpots of Egypt." Modern political conditions rarely offer this luxury. The Soviets dreamed of creating a "new man" who would regard the communist system as the natural backdrop for cooperation. History never gave them the chance. But Germans could engineer a radical transformation after the fall of the Berlin Wall and the unification of the country. The West Germans absorbed the former German Democratic Republic and then restaffed the courts and the law faculties with new personnel, drawn overwhelmingly from Western ranks.

For Americans in the postbellum period, the obstacles to revolutionary change were daunting. Emancipating the slaves was one thing, changing attitudes toward blacks was quite another. Americans of the 1860s were essentially the same people who had tolerated the institution of slavery; their judges were of the same background and schooling as those who had declared in the *Dred Scott* decision that persons of African descent, whether born free or born in bondage, could never become citizens of the United States.

As part of its reconstructing the former Confederacy, the victorious North tried to cleanse the formerly rebellious governments of their "treasonous" followers. The Fourteenth Amendment, which the rebellious states were expected to ratify as the price for reinstating their right to representation in Congress, included a clause disqualifying from public office, in either the states or the federal government, anyone who had taken an oath to uphold the Constitution and thereafter "engaged in insurrection or rebellion against the same."[2] This provision could conceivably have rid the South of those who supported the war for Southern independence, but it could not liberate the North from its judges and politicians who were ambivalent about the equality of all citizens. The membership of the Supreme Court changed entirely between the time of the *Dred Scott* decision in 1857 and the first major constitutional decision of the postbellum period in 1872. Yet, the judges who came onto the court still carried with them the values and confusions of their antebellum youth. They could not easily imbibe an entirely new spirit of nationhood and a strong commitment to equality. Their justice did not express the vision of the victor but rather the reluctant judgment from within that the vanquished, too, had arguments on their side.

Securing a nominal legal change in the form of the black-letter rules of constitutional revisions was not so difficult. The Thirteenth Amendment was ratified as soon as the war was over, and the Fourteenth and Fifteenth followed within five years. By 1870, the language of revolutionary change was in place. The only question was whether the words on paper would bring about a fundamental change in American self-government.

The three promises of Gettysburg—nationhood, equality, and democracy—should have become the guiding values for interpreting the amendments that would govern postbellum America. These amendments had the form of a new constitution. They set forth the basic principles of government and each of them granted authority to Congress to realize the amendment with appropriate legislation. The amendments needed only the backdrop of the three branches of government then in operation. It would not have overtaxed the legal imagination simply to incorporate the existing structure of the federal government into the new constitutional order.

Had the United States been able to begin anew, with judges educated in the values and vision of Gettysburg, with a new generation unaffected by old habits of thought, Lincoln's prophecy at Gettysburg might have prevailed. The commitment to "a single nation" of black and white would have provided the foundation for a jurisprudence of equality in the courts. The federal government would have become the watchdog of private relationships that approached too close to the forbidden line, defined in the Thirteenth Amendment as "slavery" or "previous condition of servitude." The "self-evident truths" of the Declaration of Independence—the inalienable rights to life, liberty, and the pursuit of happiness—could have generated the foundation of a new constitutional order. Yet, this was not to be the fate of postbellum America.

Part of the problem is the way we came to think of the great sacrifice that occurred on the battlefields of Gettysburg, Antietam, Vicksburg—all the places where Americans rushed to give their lives for the sake of vague principles. If we did not have the great articulation of the war's aim that Lincoln gave us at Gettysburg, the entire enterprise would have reeked of the absurd. "I am fighting for my rights," a Confederate soldier might have said—not too sure what those "rights" were. On the other side, in blue rather than gray, he might have said, "I am fighting for the Union" with the nagging sense that dying for a governmental structure was slightly ridiculous.

The Gettysburg Address was pregnant with the sentiment that the war expressed the fraternity of Americans. The bond was expressed not only toward the slaves who were liberated but also toward the two hundred thousand black men who fought side by side, though in separate battalions, with white men to liberate those still under domination.[3] The national tie—the "bonds of affection"[4]—is expressed as well toward the Confederate men in arms who, in Lincoln's view, never ceased to be part of the American nation. This was a war between brothers. It was necessary to settle the inevitable family quarrel about the kind of nation the United States would become.

As American history took its course in the decades that followed the "war for the nation," we managed to betray the inner meaning of the great sacrifice that Lincoln sought to consecrate at Gettysburg. We absorbed the war into the preexisting political and legal vocabulary. We could have celebrated a new vocabulary of politics—a vocabulary we shared with Europeans who were then moving toward nation-states of internal solidarity. And, yet, we ignored the appeal of the new for the sake of the old. We drove the solidarity of Gettysburg underground. We converted the ideas that should have become our new activist national charter into our passive Secret Constitution.

The issues that concerned postbellum America were not the ideas of solidarity and reconciliation that Lincoln managed to articulate both at Gettysburg and in his second inaugural address. With the assassination in April 1865 of the man who had preached a new order of ideas, the United States became a country obsessed with power. The great issues of the postbellum period breathed the tensions of institutional conflict.

The party of Lincoln became the radicals in Congress, and Lincoln's successor, Andrew Johnson, himself from Tennessee with roots in the yeomanry of the former Confederacy, was less eager than Congress to effectuate a cleansing of the governments that had supported the rebellion. He was opposed to the Fourteenth Amendment, which would have subjected the states to continuing federal scrutiny, and he was at odds with Lincoln's secretary of war, Edwin Stanton, who concurred in the effort to seek radical reconstruction of the South. Fearing that Johnson would fire Stanton, Congress passed a statute requiring congressional approval to remove a member of the presidential cabinet. Johnson resisted; he fired his secretary of war. In retaliation, the House began impeachment proceedings. After a fierce trial that Johnson himself did not attend, the president survived, by one senatorial vote short of the required two-thirds majority. Johnson was humbled and offered less resistance thereafter to congressional policies, including the enactment of the Fourteenth Amendment.

Behind the *Sturm und Drang* of the nation's first impeachment trial was a struggle for power between the Congress and the presidency.

Would the constitutional structure that emerged from the war more closely resemble the European style of parliamentary democracy, with the executive cabined by congressional directives? Or would the presidency remain an independent third force of government? Wars have a way of throwing open basic questions of this sort, and by unleashing aggression within a society, a Civil War inevitably invites a redefinition of governmental power. Thus, a whole new set of issues came onto the agenda of constitutional discussion.

Among the most important of these was the proper relationship between the federal government and the states. This is the question of "federalism" that still preoccupies American constitutional lawyers. There is no doubt that the federal government came out of the war more powerful than ever. It had experimented with an income tax and, therefore, could look forward to more effective funding. It had coordinated the armies of the states and now it would undertake to guide the redevelopment and integration of the South in a society governed by a new set of values. The question now was whether under a new governmental structure with Washington at its head, the individual states could nourish the principle that they were the residual source of governmental power as set forth in the Tenth Amendment, "The powers not delegated to the United States by the Constitution, nor prohibited by it to the States, are reserved to the States respectively, or to the people."

In 1791, when the Bill of Rights was ratified, it made sense for the Tenth Amendment to affirm that all federal power derived from the states and from the people. The Constitution represented a pact among preexisting states. But the states that entered the Union between the founding of the nation and the end of the Civil War, all twenty-three of them, could hardly be thought of as enjoying the same history of a prior state of independence as the original thirteen.[5] The new states, with the exception perhaps of Texas, came into being by federal fiat. They were born, in almost all cases, of territories already possessed by the United States. They were created as administrative units and then recognized as states. To think of them as being the residual source of powers delegated to the governments that created them is the kind of self-deception that only lawyers can devise.

The new states admitted by 1865 should have enjoyed only the autonomy that the federal government allowed them to have. Yet, the great myth of American constitutional theory—that the new states were just like the original thirteen—prevailed. Perhaps this sleight-of-hand was necessary to maintain equality among the states. It would not do to regard the original thirteen as constituting one country superior to a second country constituted by states thereafter recognized. Yet, it would have made sense, after the Civil War, to recognize that the Tenth Amendment had lost its relevance to a United States that embodied a nation of equal Americans.

This is not to say that for the purpose of administrative efficiency, it would not make sense to divide functions between the federal and state governments. This kind of efficient allocation of functions would make sense against a conception of the nation as the foundation of governmental power. Perhaps this concern for efficiency is all that lawyers mean when they talk about the problems of states' rights and a limited federal government. Yet, the discussion remains haunted by the myth that the states admitted after the founding retroactively granted authority to the federal government that created them.

An institution emerged to articulate and preserve this myth of autonomous states enjoying residual powers under the Tenth Amendment, and that institution was the Supreme Court. The Court had assumed the power to declare federal and state laws unconstitutional ever since Chief Justice John Marshall so interpreted our basic charter in 1803.[6] In the fifty-five years leading up to the Civil War, the Court used this power sparingly.[7] In the postbellum institutional shakeup, however, the Court would become more aggressive in exercising its power to overrule decisions by other agencies of government. It would articulate the ideas—it would, as we now say, give the "spin" to our basic concepts—that would define the fate of nationhood, equality, and democracy in postslavery America.

How the Court accomplished these acts of reinterpretation constitutes a major chapter in the intellectual history of the United States. It is the history of the way in which we took the words of the postbellum legal order, betrayed their inner sense, and assimilated the new legal order into the original Constitution of 1787. Blending the new language into our old habits nullified the vision of a new legal order. The principles that should have inspired postbellum America became our Secret Constitution, remaining latent for decades before they would reappear to shape the contours of American law. The story may be disheartening but it must be told. To explore the process of reinterpretation, I will focus on two leading Supreme Court decisions of the time, the first *Slaughterhouse* decision, and the *Civil Rights Cases*.

THE PLIGHT OF THE NEW ORLEANS BUTCHERS

In 1869, four years after the war was over, the Louisiana legislature passed a statute that brought home the persistence of a dispute about economic freedom that reached back to the earliest stages of modern European and English legal history. The great virtue of the case was to remind the legal community that many issues of freedom had nothing at all to do with the war of solidarity to preserve the nation and emancipate the slaves.

At the time, about one thousand people in New Orleans were engaged in the business of receiving shipments of livestock from boats coming down the Mississippi, slaughtering the animals and packing the meat for distribution. The 1869 Act claimed to concentrate the management of the livestock and meat packing trade into selected areas. It provided that animals could be unloaded and slaughtered exclusively on the properties owned by two of the many enterprises engaged in the trade. All the butchers in the area had the right to use these facilities, but they had to pay a prescribed fee to the patented monopoly. The ostensible reason for consolidating these activities was "to protect the health of the city of New Orleans."[8] The Act was entitled: "An act to protect the health of the city of New Orleans, to locate the stock-landings and slaughter-houses, and to incorporate the Crescent City Live-Stock Landing and Slaughter-House Company." The Act named seventeen people who were entitled to exercise the privileges of the incorporated company, and, further, it imposed fines for every violation of the patent. The excluded local butchers were enraged. They thought as landowners they were entitled to use their land to house and slaughter animals as the market required. They wanted nothing more complicated than to pursue their trade as they saw fit on their own land.

On the assumption that the legislature had acted in good faith, that there was no graft involved in vesting this authority in the Crescent

City Slaughter-House Company, the controversy seemed to be an easy one—at least by contemporary standards of public regulation. This was a reasonable exercise of the state's "police power," its general authority to promote the common good. The single slaughterhouse was in the nature of a public utility—much like a telephone or electric company that has received a franchise from the government to provide service to a particular area. In describing the case, Charles Black dismissed the controversy as trivial.[9] The complaint by the butchers should not even have generated a serious constitutional question.

At the time, however, the dispute claimed attention as posing fundamental issues. The dispute reached the Supreme Court within seven years of Appomattox. The passage of the Reconstruction Amendments was still fresh in the minds of everyone. The age overflowed with vision—but not in the Supreme Court.

The argument was close, but in the end the advocates of state power won in the Supreme Court the battle they could not win on the killing fields. Five justices voted to uphold the 1869 Act granting a monopoly to the Crescent City Company. All three of the articulated dissents empathized with the independent butchers' economic freedom to carry on their trade without paying tolls to those favored by the Louisiana legislature. Justice Stephen Field honestly expressed the intuition that motivated the search for legal arguments for the dissent: "No one will deny the abstract justice which lies in the position of the [independent butchers]."

The reader will forgive me, I hope, for dwelling on these 1872 opinions of justices whose names we barely remember. The confrontation was so deep and so wrenching for the history of the Constitution that these conflicts have taken on epic proportions. Speaking for the majority favoring the autonomy of state power there was Justice Samuel Miller, appointed to the Court by Lincoln in 1862, and on the other side, we encounter three passionate opinions expressing sympathy for the plight of the independent butchers. I shall focus here on the conflict between Justices Miller and Field.

The "abstract justice" mentioned by the dissenting Justice Field derives from the weight of history. In the early stages of capitalism, independent entrepreneurs found themselves embedded in a feudal system of overlords and toll collectors. The lawyers for the butchers eloquently expressed the historical associations in prerevolutionary France:

> The peasant could not cross a river without paying to some no-
> bleman a toll, nor take the produce which he raised to market
> until he had bought leave to do so; nor consume what remained
> of his grain till he had sent it to the lord's mill to be ground, nor
> full his cloths on his own works, nor sharpen his tools at his own
> grindstone, nor make wine, oil, or cider at his own press.[10]

The plight of the craftsman is expressed equally poignantly: "the pry-
ing eye of the government followed the butcher to the shambles and the
baker to the oven."[11]

Reading this passionate language today, we can grasp the way so
many people felt about the principles of "abstract justice" favoring the
butchers. The struggle for the right to work and to retain the fruits of
one's labor was one of the passions of the nineteenth century. The same
sense of justice that inspired Marx worked its way, in the same middle
decades of the century, into the disputes of the butchers against the City
of New Orleans.

The problem was to capture in concrete legal terms the abstract
wrong committed against the butchers. The lexicon of American jurisprudence was freshly stocked with high-sounding language in the
Thirteenth and Fourteenth Amendments. Were these restrictions on the
butchering trade an "involuntary servitude" as prohibited by the Thirteenth Amendment, or were they a violation of the "privileges and immunities" of citizenship, either state or federal, or an infringement
against the state's duty to accord all persons subject to its power both
due process of law and the equal protection of the laws?

Before they reached this rich stock of possible constitutional arguments, the lawyers for the butchers tried a simple tack: The Louisiana
statute infringed the common law of England, the basic principles of
which had become the bedrock of American law. One of these principles was that monopolies were per se invalid. The leading jurist of the
seventeenth century, Sir Edward Coke, articulated this principle in a
case in which the Crown had granted an exclusive franchise to a London merchant to buy and sell playing cards of a certain type. When a
competitor was sued, he claimed that he was free to engage in his chosen trade; celebrating the principles of free enterprise, the court declared the monopoly invalid.[12]

This case would have been persuasive precedent for the butchers but for two hurdles that counsel had to negotiate. The first was to brand the New Orleans slaughtering franchise a "monopoly." That proved to be problematic. The dissenting judges had no trouble concluding that requiring the butchers to use, for a fee, a single slaughterhouse was as "much a monopoly as though the act had granted to the company the exclusive privilege of buying and selling the animals themselves."[13] But the majority, led by Justice Miller, balked. The Court was willing to accept the label of "monopoly" but denied "the assertion that the butchers are [thereby] deprived of the right to labor in their occupation."[14]

If the analogy with common law monopolies had held, the second problem would then have consisted of transplanting the English practice of invalidating statutes simply because they violated, as Edward Coke said in another leading case, "common right or reason."[15] There was no evidence that courts in the United States would or could invalidate statutes simply because they violated the "common law." The Supreme Court never took this attack on the Louisiana statute seriously. It interpreted Coke's decision in the *Case of Monopolies* to be about whether the king could grant a monopoly. Coke supposedly took the side of the Commons against the king, but left open the question whether parliament could grant monopolies. The impermissibility of the statute is dismissed with the rhetorical question: "Whoever doubted the authority of Parliament to change or modify the common law?"[16] The notion of legislative power to regulate the economy prevailed. The elected representatives of the people enjoyed wide-ranging discretion in the legislature to enact measures that had at least the nominal purpose of promoting the public good.

To find a way of striking down the Louisiana statute, the New Orleans butchers would have to invoke a constitutional prohibition that would override the presumed competence of the legislature. The specific clause would have to capture the sense of "abstract justice" favoring the butchers, the sentiment of right and wrong that, in the opinion of Justice Field, no one could deny.

In exploring the lawyers' and the Court's arguments, our primary concern should be the fate of the ideas proposed at Gettysburg as the foundation of the postbellum legal order. Our task is to ponder the fate of the ideals of nationhood, equality, and democracy, to understand how the second founding of the United States imploded and merged, at least nominally, with the first Constitution and the Bill of Rights.

NATIONHOOD AND CITIZENSHIP

As much as Lincoln sought to evoke a consciousness of American nationhood, this idea did not readily resonate in the minds of lawyers. The word "nation" was not used in the postbellum amendments. I doubt if it even occurred to counsel for the butchers to come into court and argue that independent tradesmen had a right, granted to them by the American nation, to practice their trade without the duty to pay tolls and use specific facilities. Their rights derived, if from anyplace, from universal principles governing the free market and dignity of working people. Yet, this very argument—that the nation was the source of rights acquired under the Thirteenth and Fourteenth Amendments—would show itself, remarkably, in a majestic dissenting opinion in 1883.[17]

The idea of the American nation may have been in the air in the 1870s, but it was not part of the stock of concepts that the Court would draw on directly to domesticate its abstract sense of justice. The concept of an American nation was part of the American creed, but it had yet to become a fixed feature of American law. It enjoyed a fate comparable to the inalienable right to the "pursuit of happiness" as articulated in the Declaration of Independence. The latter is sometimes mentioned in legal opinions,[18] but it never became the rationale for decision making in the courts. It remains an article of faith, as does the commitment to think of the American people as a single nation.

The faith in the American nation, along with the inalienable right to happiness, constitute affirmations of the American civic religion. They belong side by side with the frequent invocations, on the currency of the affirmation of faith: "IN GOD WE TRUST." These are the background assumptions by which we live. The same is true of the sense of nationhood. In 1892, the secular prayer to the flag and the nation—the Pledge of Allegiance—would spontaneously sweep the country.[19] It stood for the idea that the United States was "one nation indivisible"—a residue of "the war between brothers" that occurred thirty years before. However important these ideas may be in American civic religion, however much they dominate the thinking of Americans in the civil society that exists side by side with government, they might not be suitable as legal doctrines for deciding court cases.

Nationhood rings of romance. It appeals not to the analytic mind but to the sentimental heart. As between thought and emotion, lawyers have a bias for the linear creations of mind. The appeals of nationhood are left to poets. Lawyers opt for its analytic counterpart: citizenship. As used in the Fourteenth Amendment, citizenship is a purely formal idea, dependent solely on one's place of birth. In the debates about the rights of New Orleans butchers before the Supreme Court, the notion of citizenship and its privileges became the stakeholder for any residual yearnings to express the rights of the nation.

Perhaps, as Charles Black and other scholars have argued, the privileges and immunities of *national* citizens capture whatever relevance the nation has to constitutional law. The position is defensible, though in my view, there remain important differences between the romantic extralegal idea of nationhood and the formal legal concept of citizenship. But let us leave these differences aside and imagine that if nationhood is to play a role in constitutional law, it must become domesticated under the rubric of citizenship.

The original Constitution recognized both state and U.S. citizenship. Only citizens—not merely residents—of different states could bring their cases to the federal courts.[20] More important, the 1787 pact sought to equalize the legal status of citizens across the country by guaranteeing that "the Citizens of each State shall be entitled to all Privileges and Immunities of Citizens in the several States."[21] National citizenship, either for a specified period of time or by birth, was necessary to run for national office.[22] Yet, the charter of 1787 said nothing about how one becomes a citizen either of a state or of the national polity. The matter was left entirely to state law, as it is today in the European Union. In antebellum America as in the European Union today, citizenship in the larger entity requires that you first pass the local hurdles set for local citizenship. Leaving the matter of citizenship to the states meant that slave states could deny citizenship to blacks or to anyone they chose. This proved to be disastrous in the *Dred Scott* decision, where first Missouri and then the Supreme Court held that the bloodline of Africans forever excluded them from citizenship.[23]

The first item of business in the Fourteenth Amendment was to establish who, as a formal matter, belonged to the American polity. To find a simple definition, the Constitution adapted the traditional English rule that it is not blood but place of birth that matters: "All persons born or naturalized in the United States, and subject to the jurisdiction thereof, are citizens of the United States and of the State wherein they reside." Applying the traditional rule of *jus soli* to everyone born on American soil—except for the children of diplomats and other people "not subject to the jurisdiction" of the country—had the radical effect of eliminating family and racial history from the definition of the bond between citizen and government in the United States.

This part is simple and direct. Complications begin to arise as soon as we note the difference between U.S. and state citizenship. It would have been much simpler to have a single conception of national citizenship, the same idea that one finds in virtually every other country in the world. If the Reconstruction Amendments had really been an entirely new constitution, the courts could have ignored the concept of state citizenship altogether. Alas, the Fourteenth Amendment itself mentions it: Every national citizen becomes a citizen of the state in which he resides. And to make things more complicated, each form of citizenship carries its own privileges and immunities. The original body of the Constitution prescribes that every state must respect the privileges and immunities of citizens of other states;[24] the Fourteenth Amendment extends the same duty of recognition to the privileges and immunities of national citizenship.

The problem that confronted the Supreme Court in the *Slaughterhouse* case, therefore, was twofold: first, how to interpret the relationship between two kinds of citizenship and second, how to fit the "abstract justice" favoring the butchers' claim into the confines of the privileges and immunities of either form of citizenship.

Dissenting Justice Field constructed an ingenious interpretation of the Fourteenth Amendment that had the effect of promoting the butchers' cause. The first step in the argument was to find a principle of equality embedded in the 1787 clause prohibiting discrimination against citizens of sister states. Although the original Constitution does not mention the word "equality," the "privileges and immunities" clause can be read as a mandate of equal treatment regardless of the state of origin— at least as to citizens. Now, let us suppose that Louisiana enacted a statute prohibiting out-of-state butchers from using the Crescent City Slaughter-House Company. This kind of preference for one set of butchers over another would have been clearly unconstitutional, as the case law in this area readily reveals.[25] It follows that if Louisiana cannot arbitrarily disfavor citizens of other states, it would seem odd that they could do the same thing to a group of their own butchers. Prior to the postbellum constitutional amendments, there were a limited number of clauses that made the states accountable for wrongs committed against their own citizens. The most notable were the prohibitions against ex post facto laws, bills of attainder, and laws impairing the obligation of contracts.[26] But these provisions hardly provided a foothold for attacking the special privileges accorded to the butchers of the Crescent City Company.

At this point in the reasoning process, Justice Field made his striking claim: the very purpose of U.S. citizenship was to fill this gap left by the other clauses in the Constitution. It made no sense for the federal courts to guarantee better protection for butchers out of state than for those within the state. To bring about parity between these two classes—the protected citizens of other states and the unprotected citizens of one's own state—the concept of U.S. citizenship should protect people against the actions of their own states.

The intellectual problem was similar to the situation that occurred in international law after World War II. The legal order among the nations protected citizens of foreign states against atrocities committed by the Germans, but it did not protect Jews living in Germany against their own government. This was a remarkable omission in the structure of international law. To correct it, the architects of the Nuremberg tribunal generated the idea of crimes against humanity. Today, in disputes from Rwanda to Kosovo, we take it for granted that states have duties, under international law, toward their own citizens. The *Slaughterhouse Cases* struggled to achieve the same breakthrough in the relationship between individual states and their own citizens.

The conceptual hurdle in 1872 was the same as in 1945. In order for a state to have duties toward its own citizens, the citizens must be considered as members of some entity higher than the state to be held accountable. In other words, the citizen and the state must both be considered as subjects of a higher legal order. Nuremberg located German Jews within the higher legal order called humanity. The victims of

German terror were to be protected simply because they were human beings. Justice Field thought, correctly in my view, that the notion of United States citizenship was akin to being the member of a legal order higher than the states, a legal order to which the states themselves owed a duty to treat citizens of their own state no worse than the citizens of other states in the United States.

There is little doubt that Justice Field's analysis, though rejected in the *Slaughterhouse* decision, eventually became the guiding principle for interpreting the Fourteenth Amendment. The proper home for this analysis turned out not to be the dual concepts of the citizenship clauses but rather the due process and equal protection provisions in the neighboring clauses of the same amendment. Both of these latter provisions, it will be remembered, are directed to the protection of "any persons" (due process) or "any persons within the jurisdiction" (equal protection). The drafting of the Fourteenth Amendment thus anticipated the theory underlying the Nuremberg principle of a crime against humanity. Under the Nuremberg standard, the international order imposed a duty on nation-states to treat their own citizens decently. In the postbellum legal order, the same result derived from federal constitutional principles.

But this gets us slightly ahead of the story. The question remains why and how the majority of the court rejected Justice Field's ingenious construction of harmony between the two levels of citizenship. Keep in mind what the stakes were. There was no question that the states were subject to a higher legal order. The only question was whether that higher order would be the order established by the federal government or the order implicit in the idea of humanity. Would the controlling feature of the butchers living in Louisiana be their membership in the polity called the United States or their status as "persons" entitled to due process and the equal protection of the laws?

Field's argument carried four votes. The other five members of the court recoiled at the thought that the states owed duties to a higher legal order called the United States. U.S. citizenship did not have the effect of leveling the distinction between local citizenship and being the citizen of another state. To read the Reconstruction Amendments in this way would "fetter and degrade the State governments by subjecting them to the control of Congress."[27] The primary issue, as understood by the majority, was whether the states would retain their own special authority over their own citizens, an authority that was expressed in the "police power" to legislate for the common good. The implication was that states could readjust private rights and obligations among their own citizens if doing so served the overall advantage of the state's residents. Granting a special franchise to the Crescent City Slaughter-House Company was simply an illustration of a general authority to help some citizens and hurt others—all within the state. What no state could do, however, was to seek to promote the interests of its citizens over the citizens of other states.

This, we should note, carried forth the struggle of the Civil War by other means. The special solicitude shown to "the relations of the State and Federal governments to each other and of both these governments to the people" harks back to the rhetoric of the 1830s about the asserted autonomy of the new states to decide whether they would go one way or the other on the issue of slavery. It is almost as though the Civil War had accomplished only one objective, namely settling the issue of secession, while doing nothing to define the nation of the United States or to establish a principle of equality among all its citizens.

Nonetheless, writing for the majority, Justice Miller constructed a plausible theory of what it should mean to be a citizen of the United States. The picture presented is something like the posture of a supplicant toward a distant protector. The citizen should be able to address representatives of the U.S. government in person, make claims against the higher power, and receive its protection as a citizen abroad or on the high seas. None of this is particularly radical, and it fails, to be sure, to incorporate the commitments to nationhood and equality bequeathed by the Civil War.

On these larger issues, the opinion of the Court proves to be a great historical disappointment. The Miller opinion's perception of our unity as a nation comes across in this remarkable sentence:

> And quoting from the language of Chief Justice Taney in another case, it is said "that for all the great purposes for which the Federal government was established, we are one people, with one common country, we are all citizens of the United States. . . ."[28]

The date of this "other opinion" is not mentioned, but Chief Justice Taney, it will be recalled, was the author of the *Dred Scott* opinion, which did indeed affirm that we were one [white] people and that persons descended from slaves could never become a part of it. To cite Taney on the issue of American nationhood is a bit like invoking Al Capone on the rule of law.

EQUALITY

And equality—that glaring omission from our original Constitution? How did the Fourteenth Amendment's attempt to rectify the sins of 1787 fare in the grip of the antebellum intuitions that drove the Miller court? The five majority justices could have applied the "equal protection" clause and achieved the same result that Justice Field had engineered under his construction of the dual tracks of citizenship: the butchers rendered dependent on the Crescent City Company were subject, they could easily have concluded, to impermissible discrimination. That would not have been a particularly radical result, and it would have established an enduring commitment to equality under the postbellum constitution. But no, the Court turned away from the larger issue of principle for the sake of overcoming a narrow historical injustice. The "evil to be remedied by this [equal protection] clause," the Court writes, was "the existence of laws in the States where the newly emancipated Negroes resided, which discriminated with gross injustice and hardship against them as a class."[29] In other words, the only point of the new commitment to equality should be simply to eliminate the institution of slavery and its concomitant legal institutions. But if that was the only purpose of the Reconstruction Amendments, the Thirteenth had already done the job. There was no need for the Fourteenth Amendment and its commitment to the larger principle of equality among all "persons in the jurisdiction."

Susan B. Anthony had already begun her campaign for women's suffrage, but as of the date of the *Slaughterhouse* opinion there was little sympathy for moving the spectrum of equality up one notch to include women as a class worthy of protection. Immediately after resolving the

Slaughterhouse dispute, the Court turned to the petition of Myra Bradwell to be admitted to practice law in Illinois.[30] There was no dispute about whether she was qualified. She was a citizen of the United States and of Illinois, and she had the training and character to make a fine lawyer, but there was one problem: She was a woman. This was sufficient for the state to bar her admission, and the Supreme Court, with only one justice dissenting, thought this was an acceptable exercise of state power. After the *Slaughterhouse* decision, it was a minor stretch for Justice Miller to conclude that practicing law did not fall within the ambit of "privileges and immunities" of citizens. The amazing feature of the Court's decision in this case is that it did not even occur to the judges to justify the discrimination against women as compatible with "equal protection of the laws." The opinion is totally silent on the issue of equality. This was the temper of the times. In 1874, another woman, Virginia Minor, argued to the Supreme Court that Missouri's denying her the right to vote violated the Fourteenth Amendment. The Court resolved the matter by unanimous vote.[31] It did not even mention the possibility that the discrimination violated equal protection of the laws.

Apparently, it lay beyond the imagination of the justices in the 1870s that someday equal protection would be extended to protect all those created in God's image. It would protect not only racial minorities but also women, children born out of wedlock, aliens, and all groups that suffered the stigma of arbitrary social and legal exclusion. They ignored the "abstract justice" that screamed at them from the bold language of the new constitutional structure. Rather, they read the language to narrow it, to confine it to historical circumstances, in effect, to defeat the vision of a new, more just society. Supreme Court justices are an inherently conservative lot, but they are rarely as reactionary as these justices of the postbellum era. The Reconstruction Court did as much as possible to convert the vision of a new order into our Secret Constitution.

Yet, the values of nationhood and equality would not remain forever hidden, camouflaged in the deep structure of constitutional thought. They would begin to reassert themselves both in the political arena and in the courts. The debate in the *Slaughterhouse* case had failed to take seriously the issues either of nationhood or of equality. The dissent never got to the question of equality because they were satisfied that the Louisiana statute violated the "privileges and immunities" of United

States citizenship. The majority never reached that point because, as far as they were concerned, the Fourteenth Amendment had the limited function of eliminating statutory discrimination against African Americans. The Court's view that the purpose of "equal protection of the laws" was solely to protect blacks from apartheid-like legislation was so clearly narrow-minded that it could not hold for long. Fourteen years later, the Court would extend the principle of equal protection to Chinese launderers in San Francisco subject to discriminatory enforcement of zoning regulations.[32] This was the first step toward a sensible jurisprudence of equality.

The historical associations of the *Slaughterhouse* dispute lend themselves to multiple perspectives. For the advocates of the butchers' economic rights, the critical perspective was the long history of emancipating craftsmen and laborers from the feudal bondage that subjected them to a network of service and financial obligations. For the dissenting judges, the challenge posed by the case was the creation of a single national polity in which the states were obligated to treat insiders as well as they treated outsiders. And for the majority, the issue was the one that should have been resolved by the Civil War: the struggle for power between the states and the federal government. Unfortunately, that struggle would continue to haunt the court for decades of contentious litigation.

APARTHEID IN THE THEATER

It is tempting to read the *Slaughterhouse* case as a decision by the Court to turn its back on the struggle for racial equality in the United States. In fact, as we should keep in mind, the case had nothing to do directly with discrimination against former slaves. The decision does, however, signal a great concern for the autonomy of the states, for the revival of states' rights against the federal government. This could have generated a jurisprudence of deference to the states in their exercise of police power, even if executive and legislative decisions had the effect of discriminating against former slaves. In subsequent decisions, however, the Court established the basic principle that in the field of criminal justice at least, the states could not treat blacks as an inferior class. In one 1880 decision, the Court upheld a federal penalty against a Virginia state officer who disqualified blacks from jury service.[33] And another decision in the same year reversed a state court conviction of an African American tried by a West Virginia jury on which blacks were not permitted to serve.[34] With respect to African Americans' exercising the basic rights of citizenship, particularly in the field of criminal justice, the Court would be vigilant.

The more contentious issues arose in defining the way the emancipated slaves could move and function as supposedly free citizens in American society. The most fundamental rights of former slaves could not be taken for granted. The first Civil Rights Act, enacted in 1866 on the basis of the Thirteenth Amendment's commitment to suppress slavery and involuntary servitude, established elementary civil rights for former slaves: the right to sue in the courts, to be witnesses, to have the same legal remedies, and to be subject to the same penal and tax obligations as other citizens. The act provided criminal penalties against any official who subjected any person to one of these basic legal inequalities on grounds of race, color, or status as an alien.[35]

The difficult question was whether Congress could properly legislate under the Thirteenth Amendment to protect former slaves against informal but rigid forms of customary discrimination, for example, the denial of service in restaurants, the refusal to rent rooms in hotels, and the segregation of theaters. The Civil Rights Act of 1875, Section 1, provided that all persons should enjoy equal access to "inns, public conveyances on land or water, theaters, and other places of public amusement" regardless of race, color, or previous condition of servitude.[36] Section 2 attached a fine and a prison term of up to thirty days for committing the misdemeanor of denying someone access to these facilities for the prohibited reasons. On the basis of these provisions, the federal government indicted various suspected violators around the country—New York, San Francisco, Tennessee—for having denied access to theaters and other public facilities. Significantly, all of these prosecutions were brought in areas that had been loyal to the Union in the war. The defendants appealed their jury convictions on the ground that the Civil Rights Act exceeded the authority of Congress. Their appeals were consolidated on appeal to the Supreme Court.[37]

Eight justices decided that the Congress's effort to prevent segregation and apartheid in public life overstepped their authority under both the Thirteenth and Fourteenth Amendments. Accordingly, the Court reversed the convictions and set free the defendants who enforced the color line in public accommodations. The Court reasoned about the Reconstruction Amendments in the same sterile and truncated way we have already witnessed in the *Slaughterhouse Case*. This discrimination in access to public transportation, inns, and theaters did not constitute an "involuntary servitude," for, as the Court had the temerity to suggest, these interactions in public were in the realm of "social rights of men and races in the community."[58] The purpose of the Thirteenth Amendment was merely "to declare and vindicate those fundamental rights which appertain to the essence of citizenship."[59] Of course, this was obvious discrimination on the basis of race. Why should it not qualify as the denial of "equal protection of the laws" under the Fourteenth Amendment? The Court focused on the wording of the amendment: No *state* shall deny to any person within its jurisdiction the equal protection of the laws. Only the states could violate the amendment. And the particular persons who enforced the color bar at trains, inns, and theaters were not agents of the state. Their actions did not constitute legislation by any government or executive action by any official wearing a badge of state authority. And, therefore, the state was not responsible for these private persons denying "social rights" to black citizens. The conclusion: If the wrongdoing was purely social or private, then the federal government could not punish it under legislation designed to enforce the Fourteenth Amendment.

This cramped and faithless reading of the Constitution has become obvious to us over time, but it was apparent in 1883 as well. The lone dissent by Justice John Marshall Harlan records, with allusion and insight, the betrayal of what should have been the postbellum constitutional order. Harlan pinpoints the intellectual moves that led the court astray. On the issue of state action, Harlan recognizes the spectrum of possible positions ranging from purely private actions to the actions taken as the policy of the state. To grasp the subtleties of the problem, think of the following points on a spectrum of actions ranging from purely private action at home to the purely public functions of state officials:

1. Actions taken at home, in the family, with friends.

2. Actions taken in public by employees of private companies that serve the public, for example, a store clerk refuses to sell goods to a black person.

3. Actions taken in public by employees of an organization entrusted with a public function, for example, ushers at the opera or conductors in railroad cars refuse to seat blacks.

4. Actions by a privately owned utility that has a state franchise to provide service in a particular area, for example, Bell Telephone refuses to sell service to former slaves.

5. Actions taken by local officials on their own, in defiance of governmental policy, for example, a local judge refuses to include blacks on the jury list.

6. Official policies of the government, discriminatory legislation, executive decisions not to hire blacks.

Except for purely private actions at home and official policies at the other extreme, the other points on this spectrum represent a mix of private decision making and government policies. In fitting the Fourteenth Amendment to the reality of these diverse combinations, the Court could have insisted on stage six as the threshold of behavior included within the scope of the amendment, thus limiting the supervisory power of the federal courts to the official action of state officials. But it was clear from the outset that this would make little sense. Discriminatory application of sound laws could not escape federal scrutiny simply because state officials acted beyond the scope of their authority. Limiting "state action" and official policies of the state would encourage officials to act beyond their legal competence. Thus, stage five came to be included within the ambit of state responsibility.

The fatal mistake in 1883 was concluding that everything below stage five could properly be classified as private or "social." Justice Harlan's dissent stresses that stages two, three, and four are also actions in the public domain that implicate the state in various ways—as enforcer, as beneficiary of the surrogate private enterprise, or by direct or indirect funding (e.g., tax incentives). Reading the Fourteenth Amendment with a view to what it was intended to accomplish would have yielded a more generous understanding of "state action." The range of constitutionally relevant action would have included at least actions fulfilling the public functions of providing transportation, accommodations for travelers, education, and culture. And if the Court had so interpreted the notion of state action, it would have had no difficulty sustaining both the Civil Rights Act of 1875 and the convictions brought against the violators of the provision requiring equal access to theaters and other facilities open to the public.

Furthermore, as Justice Harlan pointed out, the Court had read the new rights established by the Reconstruction Amendments as though they were just like other restrictions imposed on state governments, for example, the prohibitions against the states enacting bills of attainder, impairing the obligations of contract, or granting titles of nobility.[40] Therefore, the Court could engage in close analysis of the specific prohibition against state authority and assess whether it was really the "state" that was responsible for the wrong committed against those who were shut out of facilities supposedly open to the public.

The Court ignored, in Harlan's clearheaded view of the case, the critical feature of the Reconstruction Amendments, namely that each of them grants Congress authority to effectuate the amendment with "appropriate legislation." This was the first time in our history that constitutional amendments carried with them an expansion of Congressional authority.[41] Accordingly, it was up to Congress to decide how best to implement the general commitments explicit in the Thirteenth and Fourteenth Amendments. Congress had acquired a general police power in this area comparable to the state legislative power upheld in the *Slaughterhouse Case*.

Harlan's most devastating argument was that the courts had long assumed that Congress enjoyed a general legislative power to regulate the conditions of slavery. The constitutional text of 1787 had stipulated a right of slave owners to recover slaves who had escaped into free territory.[42] On that basis, Congress enacted the Fugitive Slave Law of 1793, which in a manner similar to the Civil Rights Act under attack had imposed a federal penalty on those who refused to cooperate in the return of runaway slaves.[43] If Congress could elaborate on a constitutional clause securing slavery, surely they enjoyed an analogous power, reasoned Justice Harlan, under an express grant of legislative authority in the Reconstruction Amendments to eliminate slavery and secure equal protection of the laws.

Justice Harlan's position eventually triumphed—but not until our own time. After a long process of litigation, addressed primarily to the constitutionality of New Deal welfare legislation, the courts expanded the authority of Congress to legislate on all matters affecting "interstate commerce."[44] This became the basis for the Civil Rights Act of 1964, which finally enacted the broad-gauged protection against discrimination that the Court had declared beyond the competence of Congress in 1883. Grounding congressional competence to counteract discrimination in its power to regulate interstate commerce smacked of legal convolution. The better ground would have been precisely the original claim of authority asserted by Congress in the Civil Rights Act of 1875.

Justice Harlan's fidelity to Lincoln's vision of the postbellum constitutional order becomes clear in his appeal to the concept of nationhood. Of all the opinions surveyed in leading cases decided in the aftermath of the Civil War, Harlan's is the only one that comes close to conceptualizing the United States as a nation acting as a single unit. When the term appears in the other opinions, it is always as the adjective "national." Yet, Harlan's opinion is studded with references that replicate the usage that we heard in the Gettysburg Address and then found in selected poetry and philosophy written at the time. The nation is not just a government. It is an organic entity, a source of authority. As Harlan repeats nearly thirty times in the course of his opinion, the "*nation* has liberated"[45] the slaves, "the *nation* has established universal freedom in this country,"[46] and blacks, denied citizenship in the *Dred Scott* decision, acquired their equal citizenship "in virtue of an affirmative grant from the *nation*."[47]

Reasoning like Orestes Brownson or Frances Lieber, Justice Harlan distinguished clearly between the nation and the federal or national government. The nation is not a constituted government. It is rather the source of authority that legitimates government. This conception of nationhood, synonymous with the spirit of Gettysburg, is evident in expressions stressing the logical priority of the nation's will. For example, Harland writes that to insure that "the purposes of the nation might not be doubted or defeated . . . the Fourteenth Amendment was proposed for adoption."[48] Equally poignant are passages that treat the rights and privileges of the Constitution as "derived from the nation"[49] or that stress "what the nation through Congress has sought to accomplish."[50]

John Marshall Harlan's entire philosophy, expressing the heart of the Secret Constitution in dissent, is summed up in this sentence:

> Exemption from race discrimination in respect of the civil
> rights which are fundamental in citizenship in a republican
> government, is, as we have seen, a new right, *created by the na-
> tion*, with express power in Congress, by legislation, to enforce
> the constitutional provision from which it is derived.[51]

It is clear in this passage that the nation, as distinct from government, creates rights, grants citizenship; it has objectives that it seeks to
accomplish, but it must act through the prescribed processes of the law.
The nation acts initially in the process of constitutional amendment,
and then, by means of delegated authority, through the Congress. The
nation has expressed its will by precisely these means in the Reconstruction Amendments, which delegated Congress authority to engage in the
kind of legislation under attack in the *Civil Rights Cases*. The logic of
the argument traces the genesis of the nation-state. First the nation
comes into being as a prelegal organic unity, and then the nation expresses itself in a governmental structure.

One might properly inquire how the idea of the nation's expressing its
will differs from "We the People" acting in concert for the sake of a better government. The differences are admittedly subtle. Perhaps the accent in Justice Harlan's mind was on the historical bond implied in the
war that held the nation together. Yet, it is no accident that the expression "We the People" is absent in the rhetoric of his dissenting opinion.
The problem he addressed was not one that the people could decide for
themselves. The question "Who constitutes the nation?" does not lend itself to democratic resolution. The question of nationhood logically precedes both government and the popular will. For the nation to express
itself as "government of the people," it must first come into being.

The nation does not constitute itself by popular vote or by a decision
of government. The nation comes alive, as Lincoln viewed our history,
as a bond forged in an historical struggle. The bond was first cast in
1774 with the first stirring of independence or, at the latest, in July
1776. The inclusion of emancipated slaves within the nation came as
the only consequence of the Brothers' War that could make sense of the
national search for redemption.

Remarkably, the eight justices who signed the Court's opinion invalidating the Civil Rights Act of 1875 used the vocabulary neither of peoplehood nor of nationhood. They had no conception of the American

nation—or at least not one relevant to their legal analysis. Of course, they refer to the national government, a phrase in which "national" is synonymous with "federal" or "central." Yet, they use the term "nation" in reference to France![52] I suppose that in the minds of the majority of justices, the United States constituted not a nation but a people still living under the Constitution they had designed and ratified in the 1780s.

No one chose to create an American nation consisting of North and South, white and black, native and immigrant, and there were undoubtedly many people displeased by the idea. Yet, this was the situation in which we found ourselves in 1863. Lincoln had conceived of rooting our history in the identity generated by the struggle for independence. History had forged a unique nation of people of diverse origins. Justice Harlan understood what the nation had become and what it could do to further its own internal harmony. His magisterial dissent leaves us with a historical record of what constitutional thought in the postbellum period could have been.

Instead of integrating our nationhood and the commitment to equality into constitutional discourse, the *Civil Rights Cases* completed the process of driving Lincoln's vision into the deep structure of our constitutional thought. The Court generated a surface discourse to camouflage the Secret Constitution. It bequeathed to us a narrow conception of state action that we are still struggling to overcome. And, more to the point, by undermining federal authority to remove the incidents and marks of slavery, the Court facilitated segregation in American society. It would be a mere dozen or so years until the Supreme Court upheld the idea that public facilities, including schools, might be "separate but equal"—thus institutionalizing apartheid for generations.[53] At the same time that the courts drove the postbellum legal order underground, concerted action by the children of slave owners organized to frustrate the purposes of the Fifteenth Amendment. Various measures, including poll taxes, literacy tests, and organized violence, were used to prevent African Americans from realizing their right to vote. The Democratic Party gained the loyalty of white Southern voters and remained in power for more than half a century, largely on the basis of segregationist principles.[54]

Yet, there is an important difference between the courts' betraying the Thirteenth and Fourteenth Amendments and the people's frustrating the purposes of the Fifteenth Amendment. With regard to the first two of the Reconstruction Amendments, the courts gutted the great aspirations of the new constitutional order and led many professorial observers to teach that our Constitution really was what the segregationist courts said it was. This tendency to take the Courts at face value derived largely from academic skepticism about the possibility of a higher law prevailing over the uses of judicial power in our understanding of what the Constitution really required.

The Constitution became what the courts do in fact. Legalism prevailed. The legal philosophy of the Confederacy triumphed, both in substance and in style.[55] The ideals of Gettysburg became, for the lawyers in the second half of the nineteenth century, a matter of history. For the nation as a whole, however, the values of Gettysburg—nationhood, equality, and democracy—retained their promise, and these principles would eventually return to the field of litigated law.

At least the commitment to democracy had begun to make inroads in the official documents of the lawyers. The language of the Fifteenth Amendment, the first federal measure directly securing a right to vote, betokened the beginnings of popular democracy. No state could deprive African-American men of the right to vote—at least in theory. Missing was not the constitutional language but the will to enforce it. The campaign to overcome impediments to black voting would take several generations, including additional amendments and legislation abolishing poll taxes and literacy tests. As the Secret Constitution would again reassert itself in American politics, we would also take the promise of the Fifteenth Amendment seriously.

As a sequel to World War II, when black and white had again fought side by side, although still in segregated units, the will would again arise to fight for equality in a single nation. It would take a campaign of restaurant sit-ins and bus boycotts finally to correct the great error of the *Civil Rights Cases.* In 1964, four-score-years-and-one after the initial defeat in the Supreme Court, the country could once again say that equal access to theaters and public accommodations was the law of the land.

If we look at the legacy of the *Slaughterhouse Case* and the *Civil Rights Cases* together, we should note two additional casualties to the vision of a new postbellum legal order. In the first case, counsel raised the issue of economic discrimination, which had never received due attention from the

Supreme Court. We turn in the next chapter to the legacy of that failure in ongoing economic discrimination in education. As race came center stage in the truncated arena of "equal protection," the Supreme Court would ignore the tragedies of the states' toleration of wealth and class discrimination. As we shall see, other countries have confronted the problem of wealth discrimination as an aspect of their commitment to equality. It will eventually be incumbent on the Supreme Court to do the same.

The second major casualty was the concept of "involuntary servitude" as invoked in the Thirteenth Amendment. Counsel tried, but they could not persuade the Supreme Court to think of the burdens imposed on the New Orleans butchers and on African Americans subject to public segregation as variations of the servitudes prohibited by the Thirteenth Amendment. That concept had the potential of inducing a new role for government in the relationships between private parties. If servitudes should be understood as relationships of domination, then an open-ended approach to the concept would have generated a watchdog role for the federal government in inspecting and supervising private relationships of potential exploitation and domination. The Crescent City Company's domination of the independent butchers, who had to pay tribute to practice the slaughtering trade, should have been a paradigm of impermissible domination. And the other paradigm of coerced servitude would have been the domination of blacks by whites in a segregated society.

Had these two decisions gone the other way, a triadic relationship with government would have emerged. The triangle would have consisted in the potentially dominant private party, the potentially subservient private party, and the government as the guarantor of relationships of equality and nondomination. It is not clear which branch of the federal government would have benefited most from a triadic relationship with private parties. Congress would have exercised its authority to legislate under the Thirteenth Amendment. The executive would have established commissions to keep tabs on relationships that came to public attention. Although the judiciary probably would have prospered as well, the Supreme Court of the 1870s and 1880s did not want to see the federal government become the watchdog of economic and semipublic racial relationships. Our history took a different course, one that required us to confront, in ways that we hardly expected, the moral difficulties of understanding equality under law.

CHAPTER 7

EQUALITY WITHOUT VISION

"It is obviously contrary to the law of nature, however it may be defined, for . . . a handful of people to gorge themselves on superfluities while the starving multitude lacks necessities."

—Jean-Jacques Rousseau

A remarkable irony of the Civil War was that the states remained entities even more powerful than before their fight about secession. The destruction of plantation society meant, as Eric Foner insightfully argues, that the states had to assume new functions of social control.[1] The understanding of the times was that the emancipated slaves, no longer under the supervision of their masters, could not simply roam the countryside in search of work. They had to come under a new form of discipline. The only agency available to assume this new function of social control was the state governments.

Defining crimes and imposing punishments became the preferred mechanism of social control. The notion of crime had the advantage of stigmatizing ways of life that the white establishment found threatening. Imprisonment was a way of returning the emancipated slave to a status close to bonded servitude. Some of the laws enforced against the freed African Americans had been on the books for centuries, for example, those outlawing vagrancy and miscegenation. Vagrancy apparently had its origin in the fourteenth-century English legislation designed to control the poor and to prevent uprooted laborers from wandering from town to town.[2] The elastic definition of this offense gave the police wide discretion to stop, investigate, and detain blacks who seemed to be out of place.[3] Sexual relations between whites and slaves had been under the local supervision of the slave owners. With emancipation, the state took charge of the intimate lives of men and women who might tread against ingrained attitudes about racial purity. The crime was nominally limited to marriage between blacks and whites. Thus, the public and the courts had an arena in which to play out their obsessions about who was really white and who was really black.[4]

New statutes, known as the "Black Codes," were enacted as well. These laws conferred some rights on the freedmen but also regulated their lives with crimes specially designed to keep them under the control of their employers and most definitely to keep black men away from white women.[5] The state had assumed a major burden of social control. It had to be supervisor, judge, and custodian of a vast population numbering roughly four million souls. There was an explosion of work for the courts and, in the legally less precise ways of the street, for the police.

This was the beginning of the now-simmering relationship of distrust between African Americans and local police forces in the United States. From the beginning of emancipation, the police and the courts saw it as their task to keep the blacks "in line." In 1881, the great scholar Oliver Wendell Holmes, Jr. wrote approvingly of an antebellum case in which a young male slave was convicted of attempted rape for walking too closely to a white woman on the street.[6] "Dissing" the police was a dangerous move, for there was virtually no legal supervision over harassment by state police officers. Each police department was local and independent, and there were virtually no federal techniques for intervening against cops on the street. The Civil Rights Acts, based on the Thirteenth and Fourteenth Amendments, should have provided a partial remedy, but their impact was limited to the most egregious cases.[7] Local police were, in effect, the heirs to the unrestrained power of the slave owners.

Police and prosecutors functioned on the county level, but the law was defined by the state legislature and interpreted, finally, by the state supreme court. By taking charge of an expanding criminal law, the states gained power in objective and absolute terms, and they celebrated this new power by codifying their criminal law. The first major wave of state criminal law codification occurred in the first decade after the surrender at Appomattox Court House. Also, we should keep in mind that the institution of the prison was relatively new, both in the United States and in the world at large. Although there were some other systems of confinement in use during the first half of the nineteenth century, the first modern penitentiary, based on long-term incarceration and parole for good behavior in prison, opened in Elmira, New York, as late as 1876. Since then, the American prison system has not only become a major industry (the union of prison guards has come to be a powerful political lobby in itself), but the business of confining and supervising people has become a major instrument of state political power. Today, with nearly two million people behind bars, the United States has one of the largest prison populations in the world. Over 90 percent of these inmates live under the supervisory power of the fifty states. The rest spend their days in federal penitentiaries.

Not surprisingly, the brunt of this state power has fallen on the descendants of emancipated slaves. A few years ago, we were appalled to learn that one out of four young black men was under the supervision of the criminal justice system—in jail, on parole, or on probation. Since then the figure has risen, in many places, to one out of three. The primary device for gaining this intense supervisory control over the lives of black people are the drug laws. Punishing the sale and use of crack cocaine, heroin, and other hard drugs has become in our time what the law of vagrancy was when blacks first tasted the freedom of being their own masters. Here are a few figures. In 1995, 22 percent of all adults incarcerated in the United States were sentenced for drug law violations.[8] African Americans constitute a high percentage of those imprisoned: over 42 percent of those convicted under federal drug laws, and almost 60 percent of those convicted under state drug laws.[9] The drug laws alone do not account directly for the fact that nearly 50 percent of all prisoners, state and federal, are African American, but they generate a large percentage of this "new class" of men under supervision.[10]

The states have gained power not only as the heirs to the plantation owners but as the agents responsible for the protection of basic human rights. In the way the Reconstruction Amendments came to be understood in the *Slaughterhouse* and *Civil Rights Cases*, the primary actors are not individuals but state agents. A new body of law came into being—which might be called metaphorically "a federal law of state misbehavior." If the states misbehaved by denying individuals "due process" or "equal protection of the laws," the federal courts would intervene to "punish" the states by nullifying their actions, thereby chastising them for violating the Constitution.

Thus, the states were required to stand trial. They had increased authority but also increased responsibility under the due process and equal protection clauses. They could not act with impunity. The idea of "states' rights" remained vital after the Civil War, but the idea came to be modified by the principle of "states' duties." They could exercise vast powers of criminal jurisdiction, but they could not escape, forever, the requirements of the Fourteenth Amendment. Yet, the states' exposure to responsibility also served their interests. Their rights and duties hung together as a single package. The more responsibility they had under the Fourteenth Amendment, the more autonomy they had. After all, the states had to answer for the blacks within their jurisdiction. And the judicial attention came to be riveted on the states, their officials, and whether they were fulfilling their duties under law. The question that the Fourteenth Amendment led the courts to pose was not "How are people being treated?" but rather "How is the state behaving?"

Thinking of the judicial approach to the equal protection clause as a "federal supervisory law of state behavior" enables us to understand the resolution of some important modern debates about the criteria for judging state misbehavior. It is not enough, as the Supreme Court made clear in 1976, for a state law or program to have a highly unfavorable impact on a group of people generally protected against discrimination. For certain state actions to be impermissibly discriminatory, it must be motivated by a hostile intention, a malicious discriminatory purpose.[11] The state must have a *mens rea*, as criminal lawyers are inclined to say. But a hostile purpose is not enough. For example, when a city closed its swimming pools in order to avoid integration, it acted out of hostility toward blacks but the impact fell equally—at least nominally—on whites and blacks. The Court held the hostile purpose was not enough.[12] There must be a union of harmful action and malicious intent. These are criteria taken straight from the criminal law.

Holding people criminally accountable for bad actions with bad intentions may seem like a humiliating process of supervision. But in fact the very process of indictment and trial affirms individual autonomy and responsibility. As constitutional law became the "federal supervisory law of state misbehavior," the states also gained in their sense of dignity and autonomy. To be sure, the states often violated their duty to protect the rights of the emancipated blacks and of other weaker members of the body politic. But behind every controversy in the Supreme Court, the same principle of state autonomy has asserted itself.

From the very beginning, the Supreme Court found the states wanting on some issues of racial discrimination. Explicit disqualification of ex-slaves from jury service was struck down as early as 1880.[13] And eventually, in our time, the Court has intervened to strike down other residual effects of slavery and apartheid in the United States. Miscegenation,[14] loitering laws,[15] police brutality,[16] the framing of black defendants[17]—particularly in rape cases—the failure of white Southern courts to convict whites who commit crimes against blacks[18]—they all have come under the watchful eye of the Supreme Court. That the states are sometimes "convicted" of unconstitutional behavior, however, hardly subtracts from their dignity and authority. They, the states, are always the ones on trial. They are the bearers of rights and duties, powers and liabilities.

THE PROBLEM OF VOTING RIGHTS

The most remarkable vestige of the antebellum legal order is state control over all voting rights, both registration and providing access to polls, in both state and federal elections. The federal government has no presence anyplace, except in the District of Columbia, in the day-to-day operation of the means by which democracy is realized in the United States. Washington's role is limited to supervising the states and making sure that they do not discriminate against voters for the wrong reasons. The pattern for all future amendments was set by the Fifteenth Amendment:

> The right of citizens of the United States to vote shall not be denied or abridged by the United States or by any State on account of race, color, or previous condition of servitude.

The reference to the possibility that the federal government, here equated with "the United States," might deny or abridge the right to vote seems surprising today, for the power to abridge the right to vote suggests that the federal government might undertake directly to secure voting rights in its citizens. Yet, no one can go to the polls with a copy of a federal statute in hand and declare, "This law secures my right to vote." The most the citizen can argue is that the local registration authorities have discriminated against him in violation of federal law (either the Constitution or a statute enforcing the Constitution), but in order to make out this claim the citizen must demonstrate that the basis for denying the right to vote is in fact an impermissible act of discrimination. The Fifteenth Amendment, the first in a long series of amendments adding other impermissible reasons for denying the franchise, mentions only "race, color, [and] previous condition of servitude." It says nothing, for example, about granting the right to vote to women—either white or black, either previously free or previously slave.

How the victorious Union would regulate the voting rights of emancipated blacks was, in the late 1860s, an open question. The Fifteenth Amendment could have read: "All citizens shall have the right to vote in all state and federal elections." In other words, it could have proceeded positively (the right shall exist) rather than negatively (the rights shall not be denied or abridged for certain reasons). If a constitutional amendment can outlaw all private relationships of "involuntary servitude," the postbellum nation surely could have intervened directly to secure the most basic political right in any democracy, namely the right to vote.

Congress and the states had good reasons for taking a negative strategy toward the first national effort to regulate voting rights. In the mid-nineteenth century, popular democracy was still a relatively new idea. In the aftermath of the Civil War, there were still many who urged the limitation of the franchise to white males.[19] Even if the "democrats" of principle had desired to take an aggressive, positive tack, they would not have known how far they wanted to go. The extension of the franchise has proceeded by tentative steps, with a series of amendments extending voting rights a bit further—to women,[20] to those who could not pay a poll tax,[21] to all those over the age of 18. Federal legislation has taken the additional step of eliminating literacy tests.[22] These steps proceed toward expanding the franchise in the name of equality of all citizens.

The negative strategy of accumulating small steps at the federal level has left the states in charge of regulating the franchise. Placing the states in charge of this issue as well as making them guarantors of due process and equal protection of the laws affirmed the basic principle of American government. Whatever the Civil War might have been about, the states were in charge and the federal government accepted being relegated to the status of supervisor.

One of the more striking consequences of this negative approach to the franchise has been the persistent practice of disenfranchising felons. A long history, yet to be fully told, supports the idea of treating the category of criminals called felons as "civilly dead." The idea stems apparently from the Roman institution of *infamia*. In a time when all felons were subject to the death penalty at English law, perhaps it made sense to treat a surviving felon as equivalent to a decedent, incapable of exercising civil or political rights. The distinction between "felony" and "misdemeanor" was introduced to distinguish between the graver offenses that carried the death penalty and minor offenses subject to lesser penalties. As the distinction evolved, however, it became a purely formal matter resting on the length of the prison sentence: felons could be punished by a year or more in the penitentiary. The connection between felony and "infamy" lost its force.

Yet, the practice of disenfranchising has survived in the United States. According to voting qualification laws and constitutional provisions in the vast majority of the fifty-one jurisdictions, felons serving time are not allowed to vote.[23] The disqualification applies in varying degrees to convicted felons on probation, on parole, and after release from prison. Disenfranchisement is permanent in at least thirteen states. The Sentencing Project reports the mosaic of American law in these terms:

> In 46 states and the District of Columbia, felons are prohibited from voting while in prison. In addition, 32 states prohibit offenders from voting while on parole and 29 bar voting while on probation. Felons are barred for life from voting in 14 states, a prohibition that can be waived only through a gubernatorial pardon or some other form of clemency. Only four states— Maine, Massachusetts, New Hampshire and Vermont—allow prison inmates to vote.[24]

It is not easy to understand how this practice survives in a modern democracy. It is quite common in other countries to recognize the voting rights even of those serving time in prison. They are, after all, still citizens. Germany recognizes no disenfranchisement based simply on conviction of crime.[25] And recently, in the 1999 campaign in Israel, a convicted felon (Aryeh Deri) orchestrated his party's campaign from his jail cell.

The American hostility toward felons bears devastating consequences for the voting rights of African Americans. The statistics are disquieting. Fourteen percent of African-American men are ineligible to vote because of criminal convictions. In seven states, one black man in four is permanently barred from voting because of his criminal record.[26]

Alarmingly, the Supreme Court has allowed this discrimination against black voters to continue. The agency that is supposed to censure the irrational and discriminatory behavior of the states has let this mode of discrimination pass. True, in one case, the Supreme Court, without dissent, struck down an Alabama constitutional provision that disenfranchised everyone who committed a crime of moral turpitude. The Court found a current of racial motivation in the convention that adopted the disenfranchising amendment to the state constitution, and in fact the rule, as applied, had a disproportionate impact on blacks.[27] Yet, in another decision, where the question was simply disenfranchising felons without a showing of discriminatory motivation, the Court let the policy stand.[28] Deliberative discrimination against convicted felons was simply insufficient cause to censure the antidemocratic and antiegalitarian practices of the state.

The surprising fact of constitutional history is that an ignored corner of the Fourteenth Amendment itself provided an argument that permitted Justice Rehnquist to write an opinion upholding disenfranchisement—at least when there is no proof of a racially discriminatory purpose. The Fourteenth Amendment includes three provisions, all of which have a distinctively historical purpose. Section 4 of the amendment was designed to cancel the confederate debt. Section 3 had the aim of disqualifying from public office anyone who had taken an oath to uphold the Constitution and then participated in the rebellion. Section 2 had a similar purpose of correcting the defect in the Constitution that permitted states, for the purpose of representation in Congress, to count all free persons but only three-fifths of the "unfree" population. This section of the amendment could have ended after its first sentence:

> Representatives shall be apportioned among the several states
> which may be included within this Union according to their re-

spective numbers, counting the whole number of persons in each State excluding Indians not taxed.

But the drafters wanted also to add a sanction to cover the case in which the states did not grant the right to vote to emancipated slaves. In anticipation of the Fifteenth Amendment, the rest of Section 2 provided (with two exceptions yet to be made clear):

> But whenever in any State the elective franchise shall be denied to any portion of its male citizens, not less than twenty-one years of age, or in any way abridged . . . the basis of representation in such State shall be reduced in the proportion which the number of such male citizens shall bear to the whole number of male citizens not less than twenty-one years of age.

In other words, if black males over the age of 21 constituted 20 percent of the local population and a state denied them the franchise, the state's representation would be reduced by 20 percent. But then the drafters had second thoughts: perhaps there might be some good reasons for denying some males over the age of 21 the franchise. If Section 3 prohibits former leaders of the Confederacy from holding public office, then perhaps they should also be denied the right to vote. Therefore, the amendment provides an exception in cases in which the state denies the right to vote "for participation in rebellion." Just to be sure that the exception was broad enough, the drafters tacked on the phrase "or other crime."

The phrase "or other crime," added seemingly as an afterthought, gave Justice Rehnquist and his majority all they needed to dismiss an equal-protection challenge to the disenfranchisement of felons. This could not possibly be a violation of the Fourteenth Amendment, their argument went, because the amendment, in Section 2, recognizes the possibility of disenfranchisement for committing a crime.

It is remarkable that American judges could have taken this argument seriously. Seizing on the single phrase "or other crime" ignores both its place in the text of Section 2 and the historical context of this provision as a response to the Civil War. The exception provides merely that if states do restrict voting rights for "participation in rebellion or other crime," their representation in Congress will not be affected. It would

make sense to read "crime" as referring to crimes related to "participation in rebellion;" but even if a broader reading is accepted, the
only point of the provision is to say that a particular remedy—pro-
portional reduction of representation in Congress—will not apply. It
does not follow that disenfranchisement of all "convicted criminals"
is constitutionally desirable. And it certainly did not follow that as the
principle of equality under law became more comprehensive, there
would always remain an entrenched exception for those convicted of
crime.

The Supreme Court's reading of this provision as creating an exception to the principle of equal protection disregards the obvious historical
context of these three middle provisions—Sections 2, 3, and 4—in the
amendment. (Section 1 is the familiar provision on due process and
equal protection, and Section 5 authorizes Congress to enact legislation
to enforce the amendment.) The middle provisions were not meant to
have lasting application. Sections 3 and 4 are about as relevant today as
the biblical instructions on conducting sacrifices in the Temple. One
scholar has argued insightfully that Section 2 implicitly recognizes a
background of state policies skeptical about granting the franchise to
emancipated blacks.[29] In any event, these doubts were resolved in the
enactment of the Fifteenth Amendment, and Section 2, adopted two
years before, became a dead letter, never enforced to restrict the representation of any state in Congress. It lives on only in the sting supposedly carried by the phrase "or other crime."

Section 2 also carries other implied restrictions on voting rights that
have obviously been superseded. It refers exclusively to male voters
above the age of 21. At the time women and eighteen- to twenty-one-
year-olds did not count. They acquired the franchise respectively in the
Nineteenth and Twenty-Sixth Amendments. But let us suppose that
women had not acquired the right to vote by constitutional revision in
1920 and today women challenged the denial of the right to vote under
the equal protection clause of the Fourteenth Amendment.[30] Suppose
someone argued in response to the challenge, "Yes, but Section 2 refers
exclusively to male   voters, and therefore the amendment implicitly approves of restricting the franchise to men." The argument would
be laughed out of court. In the current jurisprudence of the Supreme
Court, women would win the vote, with or without the support of the

1920 amendment.[31] The fact that Section 2 implicitly recognizes a franchise limited to male votes is irrelevant.

Section 2 should be read out of the Constitution, and for the most part it is. The only words of this historical encrustation that are taken seriously are those that dovetail with our contempt for criminals—for those who fall in the class we love to hate. The disdain that we once had for those who had participated in the rebellion remains alive, and it applies to the new "untouchables" captured in the criminal justice system.

Thus, we have the following paradox of disenfranchisement. A constitutional amendment was enacted to support the voting rights of emancipated slaves. The text of this amendment refers to the possibility of disenfranchising people who have committed crimes. Because patterns of law enforcement have changed over the years, because the number of felons convicted has greatly increased, and because a large percentage of those convicted are black, the policy of felon disenfranchisement sharply reduces the voting rights of African Americans. The upshot: A constitutional provision designed in 1868 to improve the political representation of blacks has turned out in the 1990s to have precisely the opposite effect.

Reading the arguments in the case law and in the legal literature on the disenfranchisement of felons is enough to induce both laughter and tears. The typical argument against allowing convicted felons to vote is that we must preserve the "purity of the ballot box."[32] If we assume that these people, required to "pay their debt to society," are the new "untouchables," then of course it makes sense to keep them as far away as possible from the sacred institutions of American society, the ballot box among them. There are many signs that this is the way we think today of felons, particularly those convicted of sex offenses.[33] Some writers improperly invoke the texts of political theory to justify felon disenfranchisement on the ground that those who have chosen the path of crime (as evidenced by one conviction) are not fit to participate in the self-governance of a democratic society.[34] On the other side of the debate, the constitutional arguments[35] against felon disenfranchisement are powerful and convincing. Only an instinctive aversion toward convicted criminals could sustain the willingness of the Supreme Court to discriminate against them. Whatever the reasons for this unforgiving disdain for those who pay their debt to society, it would be difficult to argue that they enjoy equal protection of the laws.

EQUALITY IN EDUCATION

As argued earlier, equality is an open-ended blessing, a scale of advantageous possibilities. Emancipated male slaves and their male descendants
gained the franchise under the Fifteenth Amendment, but they have
not been secure against losing it by force of antiquated attitudes about
the rights of felons who have served their time. Black men received confirmation of their constitutional right to serve on juries as early as
1880,[36] but this right did not become secure in practice until the Court,
in the last two decades, took steps to curtail the use of peremptory challenges systematically to remove blacks from the pool of candidates for
jury service.[37] The expansion of egalitarian thinking to protect the
rights of other traditionally disadvantaged groups did not occur until
the late 1960s and early 1970s. For the first time, we witnessed justices
taking seriously the rights of women,[38] of children born out of wedlock,[39] and of noncitizens. These were times of expanding the range of
those who benefited from the principle that states were obligated to
treat everyone within their jurisdiction with an even hand. The language of our commitment to equality was in place, and the Court had
begun to elicit a vision, an advance on the never-ending scale of egalitarian justice, of what that commitment might mean in contemporary
American life.

One would think that the first requirement of even-handed justice,
an initial step in the march toward an elusive goal, would attach to the
disbursement of state monies. If the state built streets and sewers in
white neighborhoods but failed to do so in black neighborhoods, it
would be difficult to maintain that the state had met the standard of
equal treatment under the law. The same would be true if the terms
"rich and poor" took the place of "white and black." If the equal protection clause meant anything at all, it would imply that the state could
not discriminate by providing better services for the rich than for the
poor. Where the law of the state is expressed in the spending of money,
it seems particularly easy to apply the equal protection clause: The state
must treat all recipients of its services equally.

This, unfortunately, has not happened as equal protection thinking
has evolved in the United States. The raising of state money by taxation
and the spending of state money on services have somehow, miracu-

lously, escaped the sensibilities of the courts. It is almost as though a critical expression of state power—the government's influencing the distribution of wealth among its citizens—has nothing to do with equality under the law. As we shall see, the Supreme Court has suffered from a blind spot in its thinking, a blind spot that reflects a policy of indifference toward inequalities generated by wealth and class in the United States.

The battleground in the courts has been in the field of school financing. Schools in the United States are operated under state boards of education but they are financed on the basis of a mixed system of taxation, which includes a varying component of local property taxes. So far as local taxes matter, the funds available to each school district depend both on the taxable property in the community and the willingness of voters to support high rates of taxation. Given these variables, one should not be surprised that the richer school districts may spend twice as much per pupil as the poorer districts. Within the same community, so far as expenditures improve the quality of education, then, children living in rich districts will receive a better education than those living in poor districts. The children of the rich will acquire a competitive edge in seeking university admission and, therefore, in the long run have a better outlook for financial success. It seems fairly obvious, then, that permitting differential per-pupil school financing within the same state perpetuates the class system. It is a "head-start" program for the rich.

In the early 1970s, stimulated by the research and dedication of a few law professors,[41] the state courts began to assess whether differential school financing was consistent with the equal protection clause. California and a few other states decided that it was not.[42] The movement inevitably reached the Supreme Court in 1973 in an opinion that perhaps more than any other of the postwar era exemplifies the lack of vision in the American approach to equality under law.[43] In the *Rodriguez* case, the Court decided, five votes to four, that equal protection of the law did not require the state to equalize expenditures in financing the education of children. It was all right for the school district to spend nearly 70 percent more per pupil on the children of the rich than it spent on the children of the poor. It is hard to imagine how the judiciary in a democracy supposedly committed to the principle that "all men—all children—are created equal" could come to this result.

When I tell European colleagues that the United States Supreme Court has approved the states' spending significantly more on the education of children of the rich than those of the poor, they are nonplussed. They cannot quite believe it. We would not believe it either if we had not simply become accustomed to the lack of vision in the American approach to equality under law.

The *Rodriguez* case represents the low point in the historical influence of the values of nationhood, equality, and democracy that inspired the Secret Constitution. Five score and ten years after the Gettysburg Address, Lincoln's message had become a liturgy recited in school, but it has been reduced to a body of law that tolerates massive class discrimination in the funding of those same schools. One reason for the Supreme Court's ignoring wealth discrimination is that it has become preoccupied with racial discrimination. Yet, in the *Rodriguez* case there was, not surprisingly, a close correlation between poverty and ethnicity. In the poorer school district, which spent $356 per pupil, the children were 90 percent Mexican American, and 6 percent black. In the richer school district, which bestowed $594 on each pupil, the population was over 80 percent Anglo and 18 percent Mexican American. If the state supported a system of financing that deliberately fed more money into the Anglo schools, the Supreme Court would have intervened with little ceremony. That is their business, as they understand it. But the indirect impact on Mexican-American children was insufficient to trigger the conventional response.[44]

The *Rodriguez* case, therefore, was formulated in much the same way as the dispute about the voting rights of felons came to be understood in the Supreme Court. In fact, it was one year after *Rodriguez* that the Court upheld the disenfranchisement of felons as compatible with an obviously weak commitment to equality under law.[45] Disenfranchisement and school financing were state policies that undoubtedly had a strong impact on particular minorities, but without a clear showing of an antiethnic intent the Court would stay its hand. Yet, there was in fact a "discriminatory intent" in both instances—or at least an intent to disfavor particular classes of people. In one, the states have sought to impose additional burdens on persons convicted of certain crimes, even after they have served their sentences. In the other, the states have tolerated and funded a policy of disadvantaging the children of the relatively poor. The problem is that these acts of showing favor are regarded as constitutionally acceptable. Our task is to understand how, with regard to school financing, a policy of spending more on the rich could withstand the scrutiny of the Supreme Court.

There are two ways to begin an argument about equality under law. One can begin with a commitment to the equality of all persons and inquire about what this intrinsic equality requires of the American legal system. The other way, as I have stressed in this chapter, is to begin with the state as the subject of inquiry and ask whether the state has behaved properly with regard to the principles of equality under law. In brief, the former question is: Are the people getting their fair share? The latter standard is: Are the states behaving within the acceptable range? The former question would have led rather rapidly to the conclusion that grossly unequal spending was a violation of the equal dignity and equal merit of all children living in the state. The second approach, in fact adopted by the dissenting four as well as the majority justices, opened the way to reflections whether—despite the injustice to the children[46]—the state had acquitted itself properly under the broad supervisory standards of the federal courts.

Treating the constitutional standard of equal protection of the laws, therefore, as a "federal supervisory law of state misbehavior" gave the state of Texas room to maneuver. It could argue that despite the injustice to the children[47] the state was not "guilty" of a violation of the federal supervisory standards. The first argument was about the proper standard for holding the state accountable. In the last several decades, the Court has spent considerable time and energy debating the problem of fitting different standards for different kinds of equal protection disputes.

The net result of this debate, as expressed in the conventional jargon, goes like this. If a case raises a problem of racial discrimination or the equivalent, then the state is held to the highest standard of supervision called "strict scrutiny." If the dispute is merely about legislative distinctions that favor some commercial interests over others, then the standard is much lower and it is called the "rational basis" test. The latter standard is typified by the question of whether, for example, the state can distinguish between optometrists and opticians with regard to the commercial privilege of prescribing lenses. This distinction was upheld as "rationally" serving the "purpose" of promoting the health and welfare of the public.[48] The distinction between these two types of case is about the hurdle that the state must surmount in order to justify its behavior. In a "strict scrutiny" case, the state must satisfy a tougher burden. It must show "a compelling state interest" to support the discrimination, and it must also show that the distinction used is the "least restrictive alternative" available to accomplish its compelling objective. In a purely commercial case, the state need merely show that the legislative classification meets the minimal criteria of reasonableness and nonarbitrariness. On the surface of things, then, it looks as if it would be much tougher for a state to acquit itself under the "strict scrutiny" standard than under the "rational basis" test.

The way the judges think these days, the foremost question in every case is whether the controversy should be assayed under the higher or lower or perhaps under an intermediate standard of scrutiny.[49] Taking this to be the first question on the agenda, of course, has the effect of steering the inquiry away from the rights of the affected people—whether as persons created equal they have received equal treatment under the law—and focusing judicial thought instead on the behavior of the state officials. The first victory of the state of Texas in defending its grossly unequal spending in school financing was to get the argument centered not on the injustice suffered by the children but on the reasonableness of its behavior in administering its schools.

At this point in the argument the jargon of lawyers takes over. There are two ways conventionally accepted by the Court to get a case classified as a matter requiring "strict scrutiny." One way is to show that the state action operates to the disadvantage of a "suspect class." Race—black versus white—is the paradigmatic "suspect class." In the last fifty years, other distinctions have come to qualify as inherently "suspect" in the same sense, for example, national origin, illegitimacy, and alienage.[50] The question thus posed is whether wealth—having more or less money—is suspect in the same way as the bright line distinctions typified by the practice of segregation between black and white. This was, in fact, the great issue posed by the case. Did the state have a commitment to foster—or at least not to entrench—class differentiations based on earning power and wealth? Differential school financing is likely to have the effect of enabling the children of the rich to attain greater earning power than available to the children of the poor. The five conservative justices who constituted the majority would not tackle the immense social problem of income disparity and class privilege in the United States. They could readily disguise their unwillingness to think about wealth discrimination by concluding that relative poverty was not a sufficiently bright line to come under the principles applied to racial discrimination. In the words of Justice Powell: the class discriminated against was too "large, diverse, and amorphous."[51] The conservatives would not think about this blurred and fuzzy distinction in the same way they were to willing to apply "strict scrutiny" to classifications equivalent to the boundary between black and white.

The alternative track for subjecting the legislative behavior of a state to the higher standard of "strict scrutiny" is, according to the doctrines of the Court, to classify the issue at stake as a "fundamental right." For example, in the late 1960s, the Court applied the higher standard of review to determine whether a state could constitutionally apply a residence requirement of one year as a qualification for welfare benefits. The category of those residents in the state for less than a year (and thus deprived of welfare benefits) was not in itself a "suspect class" traditionally subject to discriminatory treatment. But the Court decided that the right to travel from state to state without suffering financial detriment lay at the foundation of the federal union.[52] This was probably correct, but that leaves us with the question: Why is not the right to education as basic as the right to travel? There is no clear answer to this question. Five justices concluded, without convincing argument, that education was important but not so "fundamental" as to impose the tougher standard in assessing Texas's scheme for financing education.

We should not take this jargon of "suspect classes" and "fundamental rights" too seriously. The simple fact is that the Court was not of a mind to become the national censor of fifty separate schemes for financing education. This terrain was too complicated to tread—better to find some way to leave the entire matter to the states. If they wanted to foster unequal modes of financing, if they wanted to entrench their local class differences, so be it. The fact is that since the *Rodriguez* decision, many states have decided on the basis of their state constitutions that they would not tolerate gapingly unequal financing among the school districts within the state.[53]

The deeper issue deliberately not addressed in the Court's opinion is discrimination on the basis of wealth—state policies that serve the rich more than the poor. American courts have cut a wide swath in the law in order to avoid that basic problem of social justice. Taxation would be the natural arena to begin inspecting whether the legislature was fair to rich and poor alike. It would not occur to American lawyers or judges to question whether the system of, say, tax deductions was compatible with the equal protection of the laws. In the early days of equal protection, the Court did in fact strike down a tax statute for imposing differential standards of taxation against corporations and against individuals.[54] But this case has proved to be a temporary deviation. The five Justices in the *Rodriguez* majority had this to say about wealth discrimination in the tax system:

> No scheme of taxation, whether the tax is imposed on property, income, or purchases of goods and services, has yet been devised which is free of all discriminatory impact. In such a complex arena in which no perfect alternatives exist, the Court does well not to impose too rigorous a standard of scrutiny lest all local fiscal schemes become subjects of criticism under the Equal Protection Clause.[55]

The surprising fact is that other legal systems are willing to consider discrimination in the tax system as a violation of the constitutional provision on equality under the law. For example, the German Basic Law Article 3 provides no more guidance than does the lapidary formula of the American equal protection clause.[56] Yet, the courts have carried the basic mandate of equality under law into the field of wealth discrimination.

To take just one example, a 1976 decision of the German Constitutional Court assays a change in tax policy with regard to expenses incurred in rearing children. A system of direct payments based on the number of children took the place of a scheme granting deductions per child from the parents' gross income. The net impact of the change was that the benefit to the taxpayer was a function solely of the number of children and not of income level. Some taxpayers (they happened to be law professors) with children objected to the change. They claimed that the change in policy had a differential impact on relatively wealthy taxpayers: They lost in the transition because their deduction, worth more in a higher tax bracket, became a fixed payment. The Constitutional Court took the argument very seriously and analyzed it carefully under its principles of "tax justice" and "equality under the law." In the end, the Court upheld the legislative determination to favor one policy over another.[57] Yet, an American lawyer can only wonder at the willingness of the German Constitutional Court to enter the thicket of details in the tax law to consider whether each and every distinction meets the criteria of equal justice under law.

The simple fact is that German jurisprudence has carried the principle of equality into the field of material inequality among those subject to German law. The commitment of the legal system includes the furthering of equality in income and wealth. The reason, often cited in the opinions in this area, is that the German Constitution or Basic Law explicitly declares the Federal Republic of Germany to be a "social state based on the rule of law [*ein sozialer Rechtsstaat*]."[58] The "social" dimension of the legal system includes the leveling of differences in welfare and opportunity.

Admittedly, American courts have no ideological commitment to social justice—as defined by a tendency toward eliminating income disparities. The United States has the greatest disparity between the incomes of rich and poor among the industrialized nations, and these inequalities are only getting worse. The top 1 percent of Americans, about 2.7 million people, now have as many after-tax dollars to spend as the bottom 100 million people.[59] But the problem of social justice is not of the slightest concern to American courts. Our notion of "equal protection of the laws" simply does not include the critical question of wealth discrimination.

The indifference of American courts to social justice remains a remarkable anomaly—particularly in view of the serious philosophical attention paid to the principles of material equality. A few years before the decision in *Rodriguez*, John Rawls published the book that has become the standard theory of egalitarian social justice in the Western industrialized world. *A Theory of Justice* begins on the assumption that all inequalities—whether in basic liberties, economic opportunities, or material wealth—require justification. His argument is that material inequalities are justifiable only so far as they further the class least well off. As applied in the dispute in *Rodriguez*, this would mean the differential spending on schools would be justified only so far as spending more in the richer district benefited pupils in the poorer districts. It is hard to imagine how the pupils receiving an inferior education could benefit from the fact that their rich neighbors were receiving a greater financial investment in their future. Rawls would conclude, without hesitation, that inequalities in school financing were clearly unjust.

Of course, under the Fourteenth Amendment, injustice does not entail unconstitutionality. Justice Stewart, concurring with the majority in *Rodriguez*, conceded that the system was unjust. German courts would have concluded that differential school financing violated their constitutional commitment to social justice as well as equality under law. But the American courts are content to remain on the sidelines of this dispute.

APOLOGIES FOR INEQUALITY

To be fair to the American perspective on the problem of school financing, we should add the dimension of federalism and the value of decentralized power. A vision of equality leads to a single standard applicable to the entire country. Federalism breeds a certain skepticism about the value of visions applicable to all. It is better, the argument goes, to allow local forces to develop their own conceptions of the good—even if the consequence is a certain inequality from state to state. This indeed may have been the argument that really scored in gaining five votes for the decision in *Rodriguez*. The central question was determining the unit within which equality of school financing would be constitutionally necessary. No one has argued that all states in the Union must guarantee the same amount per pupil. There will always be a difference in the allocations per pupil between states more dedicated to public education and those less dedicated. The advocates of reform could accept this inequality among states and insist merely that within each state the financing should be equal. Those who defended the Texas scheme argued instead that the relevant unit of equality was not the state but the school district. Each of the 120 school districts in Texas would be required to insure local equality; not even the conservatives could have accepted the idea that, let us say, the Edgewood school district could, with a convincing justification, have allocated more money per pupil in one school than to another within the same district. Thus, the debate centered on the relevant unit for insisting on the equal distribution of funds.

The majority in *Rodriguez* bought the idea that local control of schools was desirable and that local control implied local financing, at least in part. Local financing entailed the risk of inequality. The decentralized management of the schools is a distinctively American idea. It may sound odd to Europeans who run their schools on the basis of a national curriculum, with a single university qualifying examination— for example, the *Abitur* or *baccalauréate*—for all graduates of secondary school. Yet, the idea has not had great political appeal in the United States. The majority in *Rodriguez* invoked the argument of pluralism and the value of decentralized power:

> Pluralism also affords some opportunity for experimentation, innovation, and a healthy competition for educational excellence. An analogy to the Nation-State relationship in our federal system seems uniquely appropriate.[60]

One might well dispute, as do some of the dissenting justices, whether decentralized political control justifies material inequality from district to district. But the position of the majority is hardly as heartless and indifferent to wealth discrimination and social justice as it appears at first blush.

In some areas, the Court is indeed concerned about the legal consequences of poverty. Where issues of criminal justice or democratic process are at stake, the Justices have intervened to insure that the poor do not suffer from their inability to pay. In the field of criminal justice, the Court has taken pains to guarantee to indigent criminal defendants the same opportunity to defend themselves as available to those capable of paying for a full defense.[61] And the commitment to democratic voting has led to decisions barring financial impediments to voting and running for office.[62]

Apart from the isolated areas of criminal justice and democratic process, the Supreme Court has hardly developed a consistent vision of equality under law. It tolerates a gross injustice against citizens once

convicted of a serious crime simply because the Fourteenth Amendment, Section 2, happened to design a remedy for voter disenfranchisement that at the time did not obligatorily extend to women, men under
the age of twenty-one, or persons who participated in the rebellion or
who had been "convicted of crime." If the Court had a vision of equal
voting rights for all citizens, it would recognize the time-specific nature
of this outdated remedy for voter discrimination and apply the equal
protection clause to eliminate voter disenfranchisement based on super-
stitions about the tainted character of felons. Similarly, if the Court had
a vision of equal opportunity for children, it would insist on statewide
equalization of educational financing. The failure of the Court in these
areas reminds us that our theories of equal treatment under law are still
in their infancy.

American courts and scholars have cultivated a distinctive theory of
equality under the law that can fairly be described as antivisionary. The
equal protection clause is not designed, according to their view, to realize the philosophical ideal captured in the Declaration of Independence
and the Gettysburg Address. The point of the clause is simply to come
to the aid of disadvantaged groups who cannot rely effectively on the
political process to defend themselves. The clause merely provides a cor-
rective for breakdowns in the democratic process. As disadvantaged
groups cannot defend themselves, the Court must come to their rescue.
This view, originally developed in an influential book by John Ely,[63] has
gained a following among professors of constitutional law. The argument has striking relevance to the most hotly disputed cases on equality
under law, namely those surrounding the permissibility of affirmative
action. Yet, as applied in this context, the argument against an egalitarian ideal—the claim that if democracy were perfect there would be no
problem of equal protection of the law—suffers from a fundamental
contradiction, as we shall see in the next chapter.

One reason for skepticism about the egalitarian ideal is that the equal
protection clause lends itself to constant and easy application. Virtually
every dispute can be framed as a mistaken and discriminatory legislative decision. In the hands of lawyers, the egalitarian ideal becomes a
depreciated, knee-jerk mode of argument. As Justice Holmes wrote in
1927, it is the "usual last resort of constitutional arguments."[64]

But disdain for a vision of equal justice under law leaves one unsatisfied. Our tradition begins with a grand proclamation that all persons are equal in the sight of God, and we come to a point of history where we tolerate great injustice simply because the state cannot be properly blamed for having allowed it to occur. We forget the roots of the idea of equal protection in a religious perception of the ultimate dignity of all human beings. A great moral principle has been reduced to but one of the factors bearing on whether the democratic system works the way it is supposed to work.

We are left with the question: What if the ideal of equality in the Gettysburg Address actually became the law of the land? What would happen if the Court actually started their judicial reasoning with the maxim, "All men are created equal?" These are radical questions, for they require us to think about what would happen if the Secret Constitution began to show its face. Would it be possible to tolerate the injustices we have surveyed in this chapter—the callous discrimination against convicted felons and the use of state monies to further a system of education that favors the rich?

The question, as we shall discover to our great relief, is not just hypothetical. In fact, slowly and diffidently, the faith in the egalitarian ideal has begun to reassert itself, and the Secret Constitution is beginning to unfold before our eyes.

CHAPTER 8

A MAXIM OF JUSTICE:
ITS BIRTH AND REBIRTH

"There is only one religion, though there are a
hundred versions of it."

—*George Bernard Shaw*

The United States is unique in tracing the principle of equality under law to the great religious principle of creation in God's image. German theorists have generated an independent commitment to equality under law by deriving the principle from the rule of law. The idea of law is hostile to arbitrary distinctions. The rule of law implies, therefore, the necessity of recognizing a constitutional requirement like the German provision: "All persons are equal before the Law."[1] This alternative, rule-of-law rationale suffices for most purposes. And it may account for why the other English-speaking countries seem to have ignored the rhetoric of the key moments in the evolution of American thinking—the 1776 Declaration of Independence and the 1863 Gettysburg Address.[2]

Our rhetoric in the years 1776 and 1863 has left us with a deep foundation for our commitment to equality. As Americans, we derive sustenance from our Great Maxim, "All men are created equal." One would expect that these famous words would have had a distinguished career in the rhetoric of the Supreme Court. In fact, these words have been recited much less than one would expect—only twenty-three times in the history of the Court, and usually, as we shall see, in dissenting opinions. The

Great Maxim asserted itself in 1776 and then retreated into relative obscurity until roughly the 1830s, when abolitionists began to cite the claim on behalf of their cause. The Maxim reaches its most prestigious moment in the Gettysburg Address and then once again begins to recede from the American agenda. It is only in our time that the Maxim of 1776, the faith behind the Secret Constitution, has asserted itself once again.

How the Great Maxim of equality shows itself at times and then retreats, covers its face, and then hides from view is an entrancing tale of American intellectual history. This story enables us to trace the retreat and return of the Secret Constitution in American political and legal thinking. We shall discover in the history of the Great Maxim an effort by Americans to make sense of their ideological roots and to live out the vision that inspired the Civil War and the second founding of the United States.

FREIGHTED BEGINNINGS

The words "All men are created equal" had an uninspiring debut in the collected opinions of the Supreme Court. Their first citation in a judicial opinion proves to be embarrassing. In the *Dred Scott* decision, that notorious monument to racism that made the Civil War inevitable, Chief Justice Taney invoked the phrase to underscore the contradiction between the Declaration of Independence and the Constitution. The conflict is there for all to see. One document affirms equality-in-creation. The other recognizes and enforces slavery. Today we would unhesitatingly assume that the Declaration of Independence got it right. But Taney came to the opposite conclusion. After quoting the principle of equality in the Declaration, the Chief Justice stained the pages of United States reports with these words:

> But it is too clear for dispute, that the enslaved African race were not intended to be included, and formed no part of the people who framed and adopted this declaration; for if the language, as understood in that day, would embrace them, the conduct of the distinguished men who framed the Declaration of Indepen-

dence would have been utterly and flagrantly inconsistent with the principles they asserted; and instead of the sympathy of mankind, to which they so confidently appealed, they would have deserved and received universal rebuke and reprobation.[3]

These views hardly put Taney in good standing with the White House. One cannot but have sympathy for Lincoln's decision to treat him with contempt when, sitting as a circuit judge, Taney issued a writ of habeas corpus to release persons that the army had arrested in Baltimore in the early, uncertain days of the war.

There was a saving moment in the dissenting opinion by Justice John McClean. The callous views of Roger Taney drove Justice McClean to invoke the principle that all men are created in God's image. About the slave Dred Scott, he wrote:

> He bears the impress of his Maker, and is amenable to the laws of God and man; and he is destined to an endless existence.[4]

This well-crafted theological account of equality never found another citation in the opinions of the Supreme Court, but it stands as a reminder that even in 1857 some judges understood the implications "all men are created equal" for the end of slavery.

In the aftershocks of the *Dred Scott* case, the Great Maxim made a slow recovery, and surprisingly, despite the luxury of time, its rhetorical appeal has fired the imagination of only a few justices on the Court. In the course of its 120-year history in the opinions of the Supreme Court, three members of the Court have been champions of the rhetorical power of this language from the Declaration of Independence. They account for about one-half of the citations to the Maxim.

The first major proponent of the Maxim's deeper implications for equality under law was Justice Joseph P. Bradley, who invoked the phrase in his dissent on behalf of the butchers who were required in the *Slaughterhouse* case to suffer restrictions on the practice of their trade. The emphasis in this opinion, however, is not on the moral equality of all people, black or white, but rather on the sentence following the Maxim in the 1776 Declaration, namely: Having been created equal, all "are endowed by their Creator with certain inalienable rights; that

among these are life, liberty, and the pursuit of happiness." The implication for Justice Bradley is that for the "enjoyment of these rights the
individual citizen, as a necessity, must be left free to adopt such calling,
profession, or trade as may seem to him most conducive to that end."[5]
The primary impact, therefore, is not in the principle of equality but in
the idea that every person enjoys certain basic human rights. Bradley
was hardly an egalitarian, for he voted on the same day with the eight-
person majority to affirm Illinois' denial of the right to practice law to
Myra Bradwell.[6] There is obviously not much consistency in his claim
that the "individual citizen . . . must be left free to adopt such calling,
profession, or trade" as he chooses.

Yet, Bradley was committed to economic freedom, at least for men.
He invoked the Great Maxim in the sequel to the *Slaughterhouse* dispute, in which the Court decided the Louisiana legislature, by granting
a monopoly, could not contract away its capacity to legislate in the future as the public interest required. Bradley concurred, again writing a
major tract against restrictions on economic freedom. Any legislative
monopoly violated the principle of equality:

> To deny [equality] to all but a few favored individuals, by in-
> vesting the latter with a monopoly, is to invade one of the fun-
> damental privileges of the citizen, contrary not only to common
> right, but, as I think, to the express words of the Constitution. It
> is what no legislature has a right to do; and no contract to that
> end can be binding on subsequent legislatures.[7]

It is worth noting, however, that this notion of equality comes closer to
the view, as articulated in the German literature, that the principle of
equal treatment is implicit in the rule of law. This is what Bradley
means by arguing that legislative arbitrariness violates "common
right."[8] The claim of equal treatment was beginning to find a foothold
in American legal doctrine.

TWO PRONGS OF EQUALITY

At the turn of the century, the rhetoric of equality in creation found a
new advocate, Justice David J. Brewer, who invoked the proposition "All

men are created equal" in three opinions for the Court. In these three cases the Court revealed its activist side, demonstrating a resolute will to nullify both state and federal legislation. These cases are worth reviewing, for they illustrate themes that have since become prominent constitutional concerns.

In the first case, the question was whether Congress could enact a statute that would, as applied, prevent a church from paying a minister to immigrate to the United States.[9] The purpose of the statute was to discourage the subsidy of immigrants, presumably for the purpose of working in sweat shops. But the statute literally prevented the Church of the Holy Trinity from hiring the minister of its choice. Writing for the Court, Justice Brewer expressed outrage that the Congress would have unwittingly interfered with the flourishing of the United States as a "Christian country." The contemporary idea of separation of Church and State was obviously far from the thought either of Brewer or the other eight justices who joined the unanimous opinion. The United States was a religious country and Christianity, broadly understood,[10] was that religion.

The justices are drawn to the Declaration of Independence, as the opinion declares, to establish the religious sensitivity of the founders:

> The Declaration of Independence recognizes the presence of the Divine in human affairs in these words: "We hold these truths to be self-evident, that all men are created equal. . . ."[11]

In the mind of the Court in the 1890s, it followed that the country was founded on religious principles and that Congress should and could not interfere with the efforts of a church to secure a minister from abroad. Intriguingly, this opinion replicated the tension stressed in the *Dred Scott* decision, but this time to the opposite effect: the religious-minded Declaration prevailed over the secular Constitution. This was but the first of many cases in which the theme of equality in creation influenced the outcome of disputes on the scope of religious liberty. The other invocations, as we shall see, took a different turn.

In two subsequent cases, Justice Brewer, writing for the Court, relied on the Great Maxim to bolster his conclusion that a state legislature had engaged in unconstitutional discrimination, in violation of its duty to accord "equal protection of the laws" to all those subject to its jurisdiction. In one case, the Texas legislature had imposed a duty on railroads to pay the attorney fees of litigants who sued them and won.[12] The railroad complained that this was unfair discrimination, for only railroads had to pay these fees in the event of a lost lawsuit. The Supreme Court upheld the claim and struck down the Texas statute. Justice Brewer's opinion relied heavily on the image of irrational classification in cases of racial discrimination, particularly in the discrimination against Chinese laundries in the *Yick Wo* case.[13] In this context, on behalf of the railroad, it seemed to be irrelevant to cite the "all men . . ." language from 1776.

In a similarly reasoned case a few years later, the Court confronted another conflict between a state legislature and business interests connecting to the slaughtering of livestock. This time the state of Kansas simply sought to regulate the fees and practices of the larger stockyards in the state, size defined by the number of animals slaughtered. If a stockyard was of the requisite size, then it was declared a public yard and its fees could not exceed a certain level. As the statute operated in fact, it applied only to the large yards in Kansas City and left unregulated smaller yards in Wichita and Jamestown. The shareholders of one of the Kansas City yards sued to have the statute declared void on the ground that it discriminated against them and deprived them of their property. The Court decided unanimously that the legislature had exceeded its authority.[14]

Again, Justice Brewer cited the *Yick Wo* case, prohibiting discrimination against Chinese laundries, and invoked the principle of divinely instituted equality from the Declaration of Independence. These citations, in the context of this dispute about whether the state can regulate the fees of large stockyards, reeked with misplaced sentiment. There was no great issue of principle here as there was in the disputes about the rights of persons to pursue their chosen calling in the earlier *Slaughterhouse Cases.* As well as the case on lawyers' fees imposed against railroads, this suit was a simple problem about whether the state could impose special restrictions on large economic entities. In one case, the railroads, in the other, the Kansas City stockyards, fought for a principle of equality in economic affairs. The large should be treated the same as the small. And the Supreme Court agreed, but it seems morally askew to associate these disputes about free market policies with a religious principle of creation in God's image.

This was a period when the Court was much more concerned about the rights of economic competitors than about the dignity of individuals. Just four years after the Kansas City stockyard case, the Court reached the high watermark of its protection of unrestrained market activity. In the famous Lochner decision, the Court held that the state of New York could not regulate the working hours of workers in the baking industry.[15] And in the same period, the Court clearly retreated from its earnest efforts in the immediate aftermath of the Civil War to protect the interests of emancipated slaves suffering discrimination. Now with at least two generations of blacks born in freedom, as citizens of the United States, the Court declared it was acceptable for the states to segregate their schools according to race. After all, the Court reasoned, schools that were separate could still be equal:[16] A state endorsing apartheid and the degradation of black citizens could still acquit itself under the Fourteenth Amendment.

By the 1890s, the Secret Constitution had gone into full occlusion. Our minds were not on the great issues of nationhood, equality, and democracy. The business of the times was business. Our values were off the mark and on the money.

The postbellum period had begun with a decision in the *Slaughterhouse Cases* upholding the legislative vesting of a monopoly in selected New Orleans butchers. Now, as the emblem of our thinking a mere quarter of a century later, the Court was engaged in a resolute defense of free enterprise. The converse switch occurred with respect to the protection of blacks against the racist impulses of their new masters, the states. For several decades, the Court intervened against the states to protect the emancipated slaves from efforts to institutionalize second class citizenship. In the 1890s, the Court accepted segregation and insisted, in Justice Brewer's opinions, that being created equal was really about the supposed parity of all, rich and poor, in the marketplace. In other words, the states lost power in the field of economic regulation and gained additional authority in the way they would choose to manage racial issues in line with local prejudices.

Testifying to our distorted values at the turn of the century, we find the proposition "all men are created equal" cited in all the wrong places. Instead of coming into play in the debate about whether keeping the races apart was compatible with equality in the sight of the Creator, the Maxim made its debut in the opinions of the Court in cases about whether the United States is really a Christian country and whether it is committed to a free market system. The commitment to human dignity and equality no longer were at the head of our agenda. The moral aspirations of the Gettysburg Address had hidden their countenance. The postbellum vision had become the Secret Constitution. More important than nationhood, equality, and democracy was the burgeoning economy, the protection of railroads and of private entrepreneurs. Equal protection of the laws became a standard not for protecting the weak against discrimination but for indulging in the myth that large and small in the marketplace were of equal value.

Justice Brewer's opinions achieved a melding of two totally different kinds of problems and the courts assume today that the merging is warranted. *Yick Wo*, the case Brewer loved to cite, addressed a genuine problem of human equality. Were the Chinese residents of San Francisco of equal dignity with Americans of European descent? In response to this question, it would have made sense to cite the Great Maxim and to reason that if all persons are equal in the sight of God they may not suffer discrimination under the law. The Chinese in San Francisco were entitled, therefore, to an even-handed and nondiscriminatory application of the local ordinances. This was not the explicit reasoning of the Court that decided that case, but Justice Brewer insightfully read the principle of equality-in-creation into the precedents of the Court.

There is no genuine issue of equality in creation, however, in the problems of railroads having to pay attorneys' fees or slaughterhouses of a particular size coming under the regulatory power of the state. There is, to be sure, an issue of consistency and fair treatment in these cases— of the rule of law—but there is no question that requires us to ponder the nature of creation in God's image. There would be good reason, even for atheists who cared not a wit about the image of God, to strike down legislation that arbitrarily benefited or harmed a single group like railroads or stockyards. Discriminating against emancipated slaves, against Chinese immigrants, against women—this drawing of lines on the basis of color or biology communicates a judgment about the essential inferiority of the group in question. But making the railroads pay attorneys' fees says nothing about their essential worth. And subjecting large stockyards to a special regulatory scheme hardly degrades large companies and brands them as inferior. Yet, for Justice Brewer and the

Supreme Court of the period, these issues represented but different layers in the same sphere of constitutional wax.

Today the Court expresses this structural unity by ranking some forms of discrimination as worse than others, thus requiring "a higher level of scrutiny" in the process of constitutional evaluation. Discrimination based on an inherently suspect classification such as race requires "strict scrutiny," whereas other forms of discrimination under law, such as against the railroads or the large stockyards, merely require ordinary scrutiny.[17] Stated in different language, racial distinctions require a compelling state interest to meet the constitutional standard of equal protection of the laws; ordinary cases of legislative discrimination require merely that the classification be rational and nonarbitrary. Thus, there is a difference in degree between racial discrimination and legislation aimed at certain economic interests, but, according to this accepted view, there is hardly a philosophical difference of kind.

Both forms of discrimination are "arbitrary" but at different levels of judgment. Racial discrimination may be arbitrary in the judgment of the legal élite, but there would hardly be a demand for this form of classification unless it resonated in popular sentiment. One cannot explain the evil of discrimination against blacks and Chinese by saying, "It is irrational, just like a law excluding purple people from public services." Purple people are science fiction, but a long painful reality of prejudice supports the desire to exclude nonwhites and women from the privileges enjoyed by white males. There is a clear social target, therefore, for judicial policies outlawing legislation discriminating against emancipated slaves, against immigrants, or against any of the many groups that have suffered the pains of the inbred desire to exclude. The target is not the legislation but the prejudice that supports the legislation. The use of the Maxim "All men are created equal" is designed to counteract not arbitrary and random attitudes but rather to overcome stable and entrenched sentiments that ignore the creation of all men and women in God's image.

Legislation singling out railroads and large stockyards impresses us as potentially arbitrary in a totally different way. Disfavoring these enterprises reinforces no popular attitudes. There is no tradition of contempt for railroads or large entrepreneurs. The legislative classification is rather accidental. Legislatures invariably intervene for or against certain groups in the economy. This they must do if they are to act for the common good. When a legislature so acts, it exercises an authority that we have come to call the "police power." The federal government requires a specific constitutional mandate for every act of legislation, but the states do not suffer the same restriction on their police powers. So far as they do not violate a federally protected right (including rights under the Constitution) or conflict with regulations properly adopted in federal legislation, they are free to act, to exercise their innate police power, for the common good.

Legislatures cannot award benefits or impose burdens on everyone, and therefore they must design categories for deciding the reach of their programs. This kind of line-drawing, which has nothing to do with ingrained cultural stereotypes, can give rise to claims of discrimination. From time to time, these claims prevail. The danger in legislative schemes allocating economic and social benefits is that they frequently have political sinecures built into them. The equal protection clause provides a good way for testing whether these legislative schemes for distributing benefits and burdens unfairly advantage or tax a particular group. The benefits and burdens are thought to be fair if they stand in an appropriate relationship, typically called a "reasonable" or "rational" relationship, to the legislative goal.

The current mood of the Supreme Court favors deference toward legislative decisions. For example, in a controversial decision, the justices ruled that it was acceptable for the city of New Orleans to award a monopoly to a few push cart venders who had worked in the French Quarter for more than eight years.[18] At the turn of the century, however, the courts were more concerned about fairness in the marketplace.

Justice Brewer's decisions striking down two pieces of economic legislation generated the linguistic and doctrinal foundations for current thinking about judicial application of the equal protection clause. Looking at the language of these two opinions, one cannot but be impressed by the justices' reliance on the language of reasonableness to express the limits of the legislative authority to draw lines favoring some and harming others. In the 1901 decision on legislation singling out large stockyards for regulation, Justice Brewer's opinion invokes the term at least five dozen times. This is important, for the concept of reasonableness conveys an attitude that runs precisely counter to the strict rule suggested by the Maxim "all men are created equal." The latter conveys a principle not subject to qualification and exception, but the ideas of reasonable regulation and reasonable classification convey a sense of discretion and degree. Reasonable is always a little more or a little less. And this is just the opposite of the stringent moral principle of creation in the image of God.

Equality does not lend itself to the values of proportion and degree. When the pigs in George Orwell's *Animal Farm* declare "Some animals are more equal than others," the reader gets the joke immediately. Either you are equal or you are not. It is not a matter of degree, not a question of reasonably relating means to ends. Yet, Justice Brewer's opinions managed to join the slippery slope of reasonable degrees with the high moral plateau of the Declaration of Independence. American law has functioned ever since in the shadow of this convergence.

One consequence of this amalgamation is that we think it possible to justify even racial discrimination—whether or not all men are created equal. If the relation between means and ends is sufficiently "reasonable," if the state has a sufficiently compelling reason, then it may impose burdens on the basis of criteria that one should think irrelevant in an egalitarian society. Thus, in modern times, we find the Supreme Court upholding the wartime confinement of American citizens of Japanese descent.[19] All third-generation Japanese citizens on the West Coast were presumed to be disloyal and dangerous. This decision, justified on grounds of military necessity,[20] strikes many as a source of shame comparable to the *Dred Scott* decision. And we encounter several decisions upholding legislation that privileges women, for example, not requiring women to register for the draft[21] or not subjecting females to the crime of statutory rape for seducing men under the age of consent.[22] Other exceptions can be found in other fields where one would expect an egalitarian commitment to dictate a consistent rule of principle— without exception for seemingly "reasonable" policies of the state.[23]

So informed by the jurisprudence of reasonableness, the Supreme Court has merged two radically different kinds of cases. In one kind, the principle "All men are created equal" has a point. Its invocation refutes ingrained attitudes of superiority toward groups that for one historical reason or another are treated with contempt or, as in the case of women, placed on a pedestal. The argument for equality for all those created in God's image bespeaks the inspiration behind the Declaration of Independence and its adaptation in the Gettysburg Address.

In the second kind, celebrated in Brewer's opinions, the legislature engages in line-drawing that imposes burdens on some more than others and those disadvantaged argued that the legislation is unfairly discriminatory. In this context, the invocation of the claim "All men are created equal" is inappropriate for two reasons: first, the issues, and second, the actors. The issues are typically matters of structuring the system of free enterprise and therefore have nothing to do with moral equality in the sight of God. Second, the actors, the players in these cases, are hardly created by God. They are created by charter under the laws of the state. They are railroads, large stockyards, financial companies, licensed opticians, and the like.[24] Invoking a great moral principle on behalf of their financial interests is something like preaching brotherly love to persuade motorists to put a quarter in the parking meter. The Great Maxim loses its force and its meaning when it is deployed too cheaply.

At the turn of the century, as evidenced by Justice Brewer's opinions, it is fairly clear that the Supreme Court had lost Lincoln's vision of a society inspired by the ideal of equality. The rhetoric of the Gettysburg Address fell to the purposes of the "dismal science" of economics. Lost was the dream of a society in which blacks and whites would stand side by side as equal citizens of the American nation. Segregation—separate but supposedly equal—became the policy of the states that gained control over the descendants of emancipated slaves.

THE REVIVAL OF EQUALITY-IN-CREATION

It would take two more great wars to rekindle America's passion for egalitarian justice. In the immediate aftermath of World War I, the states finally ratified the Nineteenth Amendment granting women the right to vote. In World War II (as in World War I), blacks and whites served in segregated units, but after military victory, when the country again realized that all Americans of all races and ethnicities had laid down their lives for their nation, Hubert Humphrey would stand up at the 1948 Democratic Convention and intone the rebirth of Lincoln at Gettysburg:

> To those who say that we are rushing this issue of civil rights, I
> say to them we are 172 years late. To those who say that this

civil rights program is an infringement on state's rights, I say
this, the time has arrived in America for the Democratic Party
to get out of the shadows of states' rights to walk forthrightly
into the bright sunshine of human rights.[25]

Humphrey's speech elevated Harry Truman's campaign into a crusade
for human rights, with the South bolting and forming the Dixiecrat
Party under Strom Thurmond. The old wounds of the Civil War played
themselves out again. But the country was now ready for decisive action
in the name of egalitarian justice. Within a few years, the Supreme
Court would outlaw all segregation in public schools and facilities, all
pretense of equality in separateness.[26] The long period of indifference
toward human equality was over.

In the 1960s, the Court finally began to cite the Maxim of equality-
in-creation in its proper context.[27] The country stood on the verge of a
revolution in thinking about equality and civil liberties in general. In
the following generation, the rhetoric of 1776 and 1863 finally found its
great advocate. Justice John Paul Stevens began to cite the Great Maxim
but almost always in dissent, as a constant challenge to the Court to do
more to realize the truth that the revolutionaries of the late eighteenth
century had regarded as self-evident.

These dissenting challenges by Justice Stevens stand as the conscience of the times, a constant reminder of what the United States
would be like if it could realize Lincoln's vision, if the Secret Constitution had in fact become the law of the land. Yet, the remarkable feature
of Stevens's romance with the rhetoric of equality is his effort to find a
nuanced understanding of what equality means in the context of the
great issues that disquieted fair-minded people in the closing decades of
the twentieth century.

Stevens began cultivating the language of equality in a subtle case of
disadvantage imposed on children born out of wedlock. The Social Security scheme contains various presumptions about when relatives may in-
herit benefits as financially dependent claimants. Many of these reflect
traditional assumptions about the social organization of American society. The general picture is that, by and large, men support women and
that children born out of wedlock tend to live apart from their biological
fathers. Eventually the Court would have to assess the presumption that
men tended to support women more than vice versa.[28] But the first

question to be addressed was whether the statutory scheme should incorporate the assumption that children born out of wedlock were not likely to be financially dependent on their fathers. So-called illegitimate children had to prove dependency, while "legitimate" children did not. A majority of six justices opined that the classification of children was based on "reasonable empirical judgments" and that building these statistical judgments into the legislative program spared the federal government administrative expenses.[29] Justice Stevens led a minority of three in dissent. The other two, Justices Marshall and Brennan, were well known for taking up the cause of minorities. Administrative considerations could not justify the perpetuation of a cultural distinction based on the irrational stigma of birth out of wedlock:

> The reason why the United States Government should not add to the burdens that illegitimate children inevitably acquire at birth is radiantly clear: We are committed to the proposition that all persons are created equal.[30]

This is the nucleus of an absolutist position. People "inevitably" incur burdens at birth only if they bear some demographic marking that is the object of ingrained social prejudice. They occupy a disfavored position in society simply by virtue of who they are. All forms of prejudice that are directed to characteristics acquired at birth are incompatible with the principle that at birth at least, all persons are of equal dignity. The list of these birth-markings obviously includes race, national origin, gender, legitimacy, physical handicaps, and possibly sexual orientation. Having been born a noncitizen also counts as a demographic burden—but only relative to the United States. It might be advantageous relative to some other legal system. The intriguing question for this purpose is whether birth under modest economic circumstances constitutes the kind of burden that would trigger Justice Stevens's principle.

Imagine the implications of Justice Stevens's rhetoric in the *Rodriguez* case. Because he received his appointment in 1975, he was not on the Court at the time.[31] But if he had dissented in place of his predecessor in the same seat, William O. Douglas, Stevens could have formulated his view like this:

The reason why the Texas government should not add to the burdens that poor children inevitably acquire at birth is radiantly clear: We are committed to the proposition that all persons are created equal.

The same argument would apply on behalf of homosexuals, and indeed ten years later Justice Stevens would dissent from the conservative majority upholding a state decision to define sodomy as a crime and to prosecute two homosexuals found committing the act in their bedroom.[32] Again he would cite the Great Maxim, but to a slightly different effect:

> Although the meaning of the principle that "all men are created equal" is not always clear, it surely must mean that every free citizen has the same interest in "liberty" that the members of the majority share. From the standpoint of the individual, the homosexual and the heterosexual have the same interest in deciding how he will live his own life, and, more narrowly, how he will conduct himself in his personal and voluntary associations with his companions. State intrusion into the private conduct of either is equally burdensome.[33]

The expression of doubt at the beginning of this quote signals a retreat from the absolutist tone expressed in striking down legislation discriminating against "illegitimate" children. In fact, Justice Stevens was at this time engaged in a deep process of reevaluating the implications of the Great Maxim for the most nagging and pressing issue that this generation of justices has encountered: the problem of affirmative action.

The Fourteenth Amendment was drafted before anybody took seriously the possibility of making exceptions to the rule of equal treatment on behalf of those who needed it. Newer constitutions—enacted after World War II—recognize the possibility of deviation from the rule of even-handed legislation. For example, the 1982 Canadian Charter of Rights and Freedoms expressly exempts from its commitment to equality before the law: "any law, program, or activity that has as its object the amelioration of conditions of disadvantaged individuals or groups" and in particular those disadvantaged "because of race, national or ethnic origin, color, religion, sex, age or mental or physical disability."[54] The German Basic Law prohibits discrimination for or against individuals on the basis of the usually suspect criteria (sex, descent, race, etc.) and then the text implicitly authorizes affirmative action on behalf of the physically handicapped by prohibiting only legislation designed to disadvantage the handicapped.[55] A 1994 amendment goes further in the case of affirmative action for women by mandating the state to "further the realization of equality between men and women and [to] seek to neutralize the vestiges of inequality."[56]

Yet, American justices must reason their way through what is now called "benign discrimination" by starting with basic principles, including the principle that "all men are created equal." The cases focus on various techniques of benign discrimination, the two most common being a quota system in university admissions and set-aside requirements for minority contractors in granting federal contracts. The debate about these cases and the proper principles for resolving them goes to the heart of contemporary jurisprudence. Let me review some of the basic lines of argument and assess the way they shape the debate.

Against Affirmative Action 1: The Constitution is and should remain blind to distinctions of race, color, sex, national origin, and other criteria of invidious discrimination. It took a long time to develop a commitment to this principle. We should not compromise the principle of equal protection for the sake of short-term gains.

For Affirmative Action 1: Affirmative action is defensible as a way of compensating traditionally disadvantaged groups for past discrimination.

Against Affirmative Action 2: In response to the above argument, benign discrimination does not compensate the particular individuals who suffered discrimination in the past and it does not compensate equally all members of the group who suffered in the past. It benefits only individual members of the disadvantaged group—namely the students or contractors who can qualify today for the special treatment—and therefore unfairly benefits an elite within the disadvantaged group as well as discriminates against those with equal qualifications who are outside the disadvantaged group.

For Affirmative Action 2: There is nothing wrong with the majority imposing burdens on itself in the interest of furthering the interests of the society as a whole. This gift of the majority to the minority is compatible with democratic principles. In contrast, invidious discrimination imposes burdens on "discrete and insular minorities"[37] who are powerless to defend themselves in the democratic process.

Against Affirmative Action 3: The difficulty with the argument based on a breakdown in the democratic process is that affirmative action must always be understood as a gift from the majority to a minority. It implies that if, say, African Americans gained control over a city government or a state government, they could not enact an affirmative action program as compensation for past discrimination. The validity of the legislation depends not only on the benign motive but on who is in power. If affirmative action is right under principles of egalitarian justice, then it should be constitutional, regardless of who is in power.

For Affirmative Action 3: The benefits of life in the United States should be distributed in roughly equal proportion among the various groups that constitute the population. The rationale for this principle of distribution could be that the groups themselves have rights, or, alternatively, that equal distribution and representation serve the common good. The latter holds with particular poignancy in educational institutions. Diversity is a desirable goal in itself, for a student body that is diverse—geographically, religiously, racially, in gender, and in other respects—enhances the value of the educational experience.

These six arguments represent the basic moves in the debate. Working one's way through this thicket is by no means easy, and therefore it is no surprise that in its first set of decisions the Court could not reach a consensus. Justice Stevens's role in this debate has been unique. He has been the only justice to approach the problem of affirmative action by pondering the implications of the Great Maxim. His fidelity to the words of the Secret Constitution and his openness of mind and spirit have led, after several false starts, to a sophisticated defense of affirmative action.

The debate about affirmative action was heating up as Stevens joined the Court in 1975. In the famous *Bakke* case, a white student sued to overturn the admission criteria used by a state medical school on the ground that if he had been black he would have qualified under the school's policy of setting aside a number of slots for minority applicants. The Court was deeply divided. Bakke got his court order requiring his admission to medical school, but the opinions of the justices were hopelessly fractured.[38] Justice Stevens wrote an opinion, joined by three other justices, supporting, in effect, Bakke's claim, but on the basis not of the equal protection clause but rather on the antidiscrimination provisions of the Civil Rights Act of 1964.

Two years later the Court was again divided, this time about the permissibility of set-asides in federal contracts for contractors for "minority group members," defined as people belonging to one of six specified groups.[39] A coalition of diverse views supported a finding that the set-asides were acceptable. Stevens wrote a stinging dissent attacking even benign racial quotas as a policy conditioning benefits on the accident of birth.[40] He quoted the passage above from his dissent on "illegitimate children" and, as in the former opinion, grounded his position not only in the Declaration of Independence but also in the provision of the 1787 Constitution that prohibits the state and the federal governments from granting titles of nobility.[41] Invoking the provision on aristocratic titles is significant, for these accidents of birth were hardly disadvantageous. The implication was that whether the accidents of birth are rewarded with a title of nobility or stigmatized as inferior, these arbitrary benefits and burdens are unconstitutional.

The opinion brought together a number of different arguments against affirmative action. Stevens rejected the set-asides as deserved compensation for past discrimination because there was no connection between the people who suffered the wrong and the entrepreneurs who would receive the benefit: "A random distribution to a favored few is a poor form of compensation for an injury shared by many."[42] He also suspected a measure of self-serving political lobbying. The black caucus in Congress negotiated a piece of the action.[43] The opinion communicated deep disgust at the very idea of inquiring about the racial characteristics of the people who would supposedly benefit from the set-asides.[44]

The succeeding six years of resolving cases brought Justice Stevens to a new understanding of the political maxim of equal creation and equal dignity. His thinking took a new course or perhaps just a deeper course. He began to refine the evil represented by adding to the burdens of those born under the stigma of social discrimination. The problem was not simply distributing benefits and burdens according to the accidents of birth but of burdening those who already face a pattern of social bias that clearly violated the proposition "All men are created equal." In short, the evil was not simply attending to birth but reinforcing the wrong represented by prejudiced social attitudes.

The specific problem confronting the Court was whether a school board could permissibly agree to a teacher lay-off plan that sidestepped the rule of seniority and required the dismissal of white teachers if necessary to preserve the racial balance of the teaching staff.[45] Again there was no consensus, though a coalition of five votes came together to declare the layoff plan unconstitutional as a violation of the equal protection clause. Justice Stevens dissented, drawing the critical distinction between "inclusionary" and "exclusionary" decisions:

> That persons of different races do, indeed, have differently colored skin, may give rise to a belief that there is some significant difference between such persons. The inclusion of minority teachers in the educational process inevitably tends to dispel that illusion whereas their exclusion could only tend to foster it. The inclusionary decision is consistent with the principle that all men are created equal; the exclusionary decision is at war with that principle. . . . Thus, consideration of whether the consciousness of race is exclusionary or inclusionary plainly distinguishes the Board's valid purpose in this case from a race-conscious decision that would reinforce assumptions of inequality.[46]

This is not quite the language of benign discrimination, but it is getting close. The critical point is the revision of the evil that Stevens so wonderfully formulated in dissenting against the government's "add[ing] to the burdens that illegitimate children inevitably acquire at birth. . . . We are committed to the proposition that all persons are created equal."[47] As adapted to the policy of retaining racial balance among teachers in the local schools, the argument would read:

> The reason is radiantly clear why the state government should not add to the burdens that children acquire at birth by virtue of assumptions of inequality. We are committed to the proposition that all persons are created equal.

That is, if children are likely to suffer because of antiegalitarian attitudes tendered by the rest of society, then the government is flatly prohibited from imposing additional burdens on the children. But if, on the

contrary, the policy of the state is to counteract these prejudices by providing the broadening experience of a multiracial teaching staff, then
the policy of the state actually serves the value of equal dignity at birth.

A major transitional case leading to this argument in favor of inclusionary and opposed to exclusionary thinking came one year earlier.
The dispute turned on whether a municipality could enact a zoning regulation prohibiting mentally retarded people from establishing a home
in a residential neighborhood. Stevens joined the majority of the Court
in holding the zoning to be unconstitutionally discriminatory against
the mentally retarded. As an aside, the justice let the following line drop
in his opinion:

> An impartial lawmaker—indeed, even a member of a class of
> persons defined as mentally retarded—could rationally vote in
> favor of a law providing funds for special education and special
> treatment for the mentally retarded. A mentally retarded per-
> son could also recognize that he is a member of a class that
> might need special supervision in some situations, both to pro-
> tect himself and to protect others.[48]

This sentence overflows with philosophical wisdom and significance.
First, by bringing the hypothetical "impartial lawmaker" front and center, Justice Stevens provides us with a test of what it means to call legislation rational and nondiscriminatory. And then he recognizes that
sometimes rationality consists in legislation designed to help a particular group. In effect, he was willing to endorse benign discrimination, if
it could be shown to serve a rational purpose.

The transformation of John Paul Stevens from an advocate of a
color-blind Constitution to a champion of affirmative action, properly
construed, was nearly complete. The final step would come in another
case of racially based set-asides in awarding government construction
contracts.[49] The party who submitted the lowest bid sued because the
subcontract went to another company whose owner qualified, by virtue
of his Hispanic surname, as a "socially deprived individual." Recall that
the first time this issue came up, a splintered Court scraped together five
votes to uphold the racial set-asides. Stevens dissented. Now, with several new justices on the Court, the majority went the other way. Again

Stevens dissented, this time joined by the newly appointed Justice Ginsburg. This opinion, at odds with his earlier stance, would be the occasion to develop a clear philosophical view of the difference between invidious and benign discrimination. Citing the language quoted above about inclusionary decisions as compatible with the principle of equal dignity in creation,[50] he reformulated the evil that he had been trying to define for two decades:

> There is no moral or constitutional equivalence between a policy that is designed to *perpetuate a caste system* and one that seeks to eradicate racial subordination. Invidious discrimination is an engine of oppression, subjugating a disfavored group to enhance or maintain the power of the majority. Remedial race-based preferences reflect the opposite impulse: a desire to foster equality in society.[51]

Thus, a clear philosophical position presents itself: One of the purposes of the equal protection clause is to prevent the creation of a caste system in the United States.[52] A "caste" is a group of people who by virtue of birth or other characteristics think of themselves and are taken by others to be inherently superior or inferior to others. Castes arise as a result of religious beliefs and popular attitudes. They can be reinforced by governmental programs, such as granting titles of nobility. They can also be perpetuated, in my view, by discriminatory plans of school financing that give advantaged children greater opportunities than children economically disadvantaged at birth. There is no single idea more at odds with the Great Maxim. The duty to "provide equal protection of the laws" means above all: resist and fight the creation of castes.

This principle as formulated, finally, by Justice Stevens yields a general approach to equal protection of the laws. The system is not one that Justice Stevens himself has formulated but it follows directly from his position, expressed elsewhere,[53] that the various standards of review are unnecessary. The single question of rationality relative to the purpose of the legislation should be sufficient to resolve all attacks against state legislation. It follows that all cases of classification in commercial and economic legislation must meet the test of rationality or, as the Court often says, reasonableness. The same would be true of cases of affirmative action or benign discrimination. There would be only one exception. The actions of a state that reinforce existing castes should be treated, as lawyers say, as per se irrational. The rule should be a prohibition flat out—no inquiry about whether a compelling state interest permits the confinement of Japanese in wartime[54] or whether some interest of the state permits discriminatory legislation that subjects men to duties not imposed on women.[55]

Of course, there are some who argue that benign discrimination reinforces the caste system in the United States. Many African Americans who have benefited from affirmative action detest the tendency of others to think that they have arrived at their station in life only because of special allowances made for their supposedly poorer qualifications.[56] This is a subtle issue and it makes clear that invoking the word "caste" hardly solves all of our problems, but at least the concept provides some guidance in thinking about benign versus caste-affirming discrimination.

Nor does the invocation of the Great Maxim lead necessarily to Justice Stevens's interpretation of equal protection. Now Justice Thomas also invokes the words of the Declaration of Independence in order to argue in favor of a color-blind Constitution.[57] He makes the perfectly respectable argument that benign discrimination represents a kind of governmental paternalism, which is at odds with the principle that "all men are created equal."[58]

Words alone are rarely decisive. If they were, we could not have given lip service for so long to the language of the Gettysburg Address without grasping its implications for the problem of affirmative action. The words are always with us. The problem is whether we grasp the potential of the language to give us wisdom and lead us through the morass of today's conflicts in the theory of equality under law.

It is fair to say that the Great Maxim, however interpreted, has finally begun to play a major role in the thinking of the Supreme Court. We have traced the influence of "all men are created equal" in equal protection cases, but the same idea has cropped up in other disputes as well. One of the most notable is in the freedom of religion cases. In 1991, Justice Blackmun coined this marvelous turn of phrase: "A government cannot be premised on the belief that all persons are created equal when it asserts that God prefers some."[59] From this premise of equality among religious groups, the opinion infers that a state high

school could not authorize a nonsectarian prayer at its graduation ceremonies. Doing so was a violation of the First Amendment's prohibition
against the establishment of religion. In a more recent and very complicated dispute about public school teachers providing remedial instruc-
tion in religious schools, Justice Souter dissented against what he took to
be an excessive entanglement of state and religion. In the tradition of
the dissenters of recent years, he invoked the ideal of equal dignity, re-
stated in Blackmun's well-crafted sentence, to argue that any practice
that furthered the establishment of religion violated the equality of all
religions in the sight of God.[60] I confess that I do not find this reasoning
terribly persuasive. It makes sense only if we consider atheism to be a
religion to be considered equal in the sight of God—an unlikely position for God to take.

The important point in this study of Justice Stevens's and others' decisions in the field of equal protection law is to demonstrate the revival
of an idea that lies at the foundation of the Secret Constitution. The
idea was stated in the Declaration of Independence, reformulated in the
Gettysburg Address, quiescent for many years, misused in Justice
Brewer's rhetoric favoring free enterprise, and finally emergent in recent years to argue against the caste system in American society. As the
law stands today, the Great Maxim appeals primarily to dissenting Justices. But it may soon triumph as the creed of the Court. Great ideas
never die. Nor do they fade away. They may remain dormant and secret
for many years. But then, when our sensibilities are ripe, they flower
again; they return laden with an ancient wisdom that, for too long, we
failed to see.

CHAPTER 9

THE SECRET
CONSTITUTION RESURGENT

> "The great cycle of the ages is renewed . . . returns
> the Golden Age: a new generation now descends
> from Heaven."
>
> —*Virgil*

In recent years, the Secret Constitution has come to assert itself in the opinions, particularly the dissenting opinions, of the Supreme Court. If we are to understand the impact of our implicit postbellum commitment to the ideas of nationhood, democracy, and equality, we cannot limit ourselves to the jurisprudence of the nine justices who happen to sit on the Court in Washington. The Secret Constitution has, in fact, a much deeper grounding in American political and legal culture, and it has come to express itself in diverse arenas. It spontaneously percolates through civil society. It shapes the process of constitutional amendment; indeed, virtually every constitutional amendment enacted since the Civil War expresses, in one way or another, the values of the Secret Constitution. This is true as well of the two leading proposed constitutional amendments that have gained a large political following in the last decade: the proposal to protect the flag against "desecration" and the movement to protect victims of crime. The values of the Secret Constitution have also found their way into subconstitutional federal legislation based, as a technical matter, on the Interstate Commerce Clause, granting Congress authority to regulate commerce "among the states."[1] The earlier defeat in the Supreme

Court of the Civil Rights Act of 1866 meant that Congress had to find other means of bringing to bear the same set of values in the pursuit of equal treatment in public facilities and in the workplace. In order to see the resurgence of the three great ideas of the Secret Constitution—nationhood, democracy, and equality—we have to look afield, away from the courts, to these diverse areas that give birth to legal trends and define the bedrock of the American Constitution.[2]

CONSTITUTIONAL AMENDMENTS

Of all the arenas in which the Secret Constitution has come to the fore, none is more impressive than the process of constitutional amendment. All of the amendments adopted and ratified over the last 135 years reveal the traces of a shared understanding, an unconscious plan, of what American government should be like. This is a remarkable thesis, for the general tendency is to assume that the amendments consist in a hodgepodge of special responses to unrelated problems.

The dominant theme is the spread of the franchise and the fine-tuning of the system of democratic representation. But there are other strains from the Secret Constitution as well. As we work our way through the amendments, from the Thirteenth to the Twenty-Seventh, we shall also see a countervailing principle at work. Democracy stresses the responsibility of the people for their self-governance. The offsetting principle is that the government must be strong, well financed, and act with a sense of compassion for the weak and defenseless. Our postbellum commitment to democracy is well known. Less well appreciated is the deep American sense of concern for those who are not able to fend for themselves. The final implication, then, of the Secret Constitution is the commitment of government to the dignity and self-esteem of all its citizens.

If we think of the Civil War as a moral drama, we cannot but perceive a government at work that is committed to the dignity of all. The drama can be narrowly understood as an enormous sacrifice of human life to liberate people held in the most demeaning condition imaginable. The war snuffed out one life, one being created in the image of God, for every seven slaves freed. There might have been a less costly way of solving the problem. Simply waiting and negotiating, we might have seen the market itself render the keeping of slaves too costly an enterprise. Industrialization spreading South might have made "free labor" a more appealing alternative for those who profited from the system of slave labor. The end of plantation capitalism might have come as safely as the demise of communism in Europe. But these possible scenarios are beside the point. The sacrifice did occur. And we thought it was necessary, as Lincoln preached, to cleanse us of our "offences" and to give the nation a "new birth of freedom." We could not have survived this drama with anything but a sense that government was capable of a great moral undertaking. Government was no longer instituted simply to keep the peace, deliver the mail, and protect us from foreign enemies but also to ensure that we not descend into the kind of evil that seared the soul of the first American Republic. The period of the Civil War witnessed legislative measures that had never been seen before in the United States—the beginning of a national banking system, the issuance of a national currency, a homestead act that distributed 160 acres to each settler, and land grants for building universities. We incorporated this new understanding of government into the Thirteenth Amendment, which declared boldly that the particular kind of evil that had led to war would never again exist in the United States. To prevent this reoccurrence, the federal government would have to be strong and vigilant. It would have to observe the transactions that occurred in the marketplace to ensure that they did not approach the danger zone of "involuntary servitude." The war itself and this consequent postbellum policy of necessary vigilance laid the foundation for the later expressions of compassion for the weak and defenseless.

From the Thirteenth to the Fifteenth Amendment, however, from 1865 to 1870, we can sense a sharp decline in the moral energy of government. Section 1 of the Fourteenth Amendment contains, of course, the invocations of "privileges and immunities," "due process," and "equal protection" that have engaged the Supreme Court and its academic commentators. But implicit in this 1868 amendment is the resurgence of the states' responsibility for the events that occur within their borders. And Sections 2, 3, and 4 of the amendment contain time-specific provisions designed to penalize the disloyal states and rebel soldiers and officials. These vengeful provisions have caused much mischief, as we have seen, by providing fodder today for those who prefer denying the franchise to convicted felons.[5] Still, the equal protection clause was a breakthrough and supplied the anchor for a cardinal principle of the postbellum legal order. And the due process clause would prove to be the umbrella that would enable the Supreme Court, in the last half-century, to develop a jurisprudence of human rights that applies to the entire country.

The framing of the Fifteenth Amendment suffered from the loss of moral ambition. Congress could have drafted the amendment simply to require the franchise for all persons above the age of 21. But that would have required a clear rationale for the democratic franchise, a clear principle telling us who should vote and why. At the most, we had a vague commitment to the new idea of democracy for the entire nation of Americans. The women's suffrage movement had begun but it had little support. And it was not at all clear that emancipated slaves would receive the vote. Democrats were naturally fearful that the newly enfranchised blacks would vote for the party that promoted their liberation. Republicans in Congress pressed both for the vote for former slaves and for the disenfranchisement of disloyal members of the Confederacy. A new coalition, they hoped, would break the power of the landed élite and bring about a social revolution in the South. President Johnson himself identified with the class of small white farmers in Tennessee, who felt threatened by the potential rise of black political power in the South.

These political considerations played themselves out against ambivalent sentiments about who constituted the "people" in "government of the people, by the people, for the people." Yet, we should not underappreciate the radical step of granting the franchise to emancipated slaves on the same terms as it was available to the rest of the population. This transformation of a slave population was unique in the history of revolutionary wars. The concept of popular democracy was beginning to take root. We should not forget that despite pretensions of a democratic founding in 1787, the idea that more than a dominant élite should vote was as foreign to the mind of the late eighteenth century as were the terms "American nation" and "equality." Rule by the *demos* or the nation was, like equality, still unfolding as a way of life. It had no guiding theory—no rationale and no historical model. It was not at all obvious that the uneducated, propertyless masses should govern the country.

The entire constitutional structure drafted in 1787 needed revamping but, without a compelling theory to guide them, the political powers in Congress settled for the modest demand in the Fifteenth Amendment that the states not deny the franchise "on account of race, color, or previous condition of servitude." It is hard to imagine a lesser demand on the states, consistent with the policy of treating the emancipated slaves as members of the nation with equal political rights.

The ensuing amendments also pursue the principles latent in the Secret Constitution. The Sixteenth Amendment, ratified after a lapse of forty-five years, recognized the legitimacy of the income tax. The government had already experimented with the income tax during the Civil War, and enacted another tax in the 1890s. The Supreme Court initially upheld the imposition of an income tax,[4] but then in 1895, the Court vetoed, five votes to four, the new aspirations of the federal government.[5] The rationale for the Court's intervention was an obscure provision on "direct" and "indirect" taxes in the Constitution of 1787 that had gotten in the way of the new vision of government.[6]

The Seventeenth Amendment brings us back to the process of developing a democratic system of government. Henceforth, senators would have to be elected not by state legislatures but directly by the people. The tone of the amendment remains deferential to the states' control of the electoral process, even for national office. The text does not tell us that all people over the age of twenty-one should be entitled to vote but leaves it up to each state to decide who shall be able to vote "for the most numerous branch of the state legislature." Whatever that standard happens to be will prevail as well for elections to the United States Senate.

The Eighteenth Amendment is the most significant of the lot, for once again we witness in action a government solicitous of the welfare of its people. The structure of this amendment is exactly the same as the Thirteenth. As the latter declares that a certain form of private relationship of subordination shall not exist in the United States, the Eighteenth Amendment tells us, analogously, that another private relationship shall not occur: "the manufacture, sale, or transportation of intoxicating liquors within . . . the United States . . . is hereby prohibited." This much misunderstood amendment, ratified in 1919, expressed a collective concern for the dignity and welfare of all those whose lives were destroyed by drink. Of course, we know that it did not work, but the sentiment expressed was a noble one. It reflects a politics of mutual responsibility in a single nation, a concern for those who could easily get lost in the rough and tumble of capitalist America.

We encounter this noble motive at work and see its failure in our current policy toward the sale and use of narcotics. We deploy vast sums and personnel in an effort to halt the spread of drug usage, although it is hard to see any tangible payoff from our investment. The reason is simple. It is not easy for government to interdict the pleasures of those who can satisfy them through purely private transactions. The level of vigilance required exceeds the capacity of government in a society that also seeks to protect privacy and civil liberties.

In the case of liquor, in particular, Prohibition had the effect of making consumption tantalizing and exciting. The speak-easy, the drink on the sly, the home brew—all these brought extra pleasure to those who imbibed. The effect of Prohibition was much the same as in the case of flag burning. The law's forbidding the act makes it more thrilling. The effect is just the opposite of that intended.

Therein lies a message for the politics of governmental intervention. There are times when we must rely on civil society to achieve our goals—sometimes with a slight nudge from government. Witness the turnaround that has occurred in the United States with regard to cigarette smoking. The government posted health warnings on cigarette packs, required airlines and governmental buildings to ban smoking, but did not try to follow the model of Prohibition or the drug laws. The policy of deferring to voluntary initiative has been more effective. A revolution in attitudes toward smoking has occurred, largely because people were free, in effect, to decide for themselves in their homes, offices, and other spheres of influence. They did not need the coercive force of government behind them.

For many, the limitations on governmental power represent a trivial and self-evident proposition. But those who believe in the power of government, as I do, should pay heed. And conservatives, who are generally skeptical of the power of government, would do well to ponder the analogies between Prohibition and the drive for prayer in the schools or the criminalization of flag burning. Of course, there are some areas, such as the protection of the victims of crime, where only the government can act. Of that problem there will be more to say later.

Allow me to take the Twenty-First Amendment out of order. After a decade of Prohibition, the country realized in 1933 that the government simply could not act upon its noble motives. The Constitution had to be amended once more, this time to countermand the Eighteenth Amendment. Some states, for example, Mississippi, retained Prohibition for many more years. As a colleague from ostensibly dry Mississippi once jibed, "Prohibition is better than no liquor at all." The country as a whole finally decided, however, that a little liquor was more desirable than the costs to freedom in trying to achieve Prohibition.

The rest of the amendments, beginning with the Nineteenth, are all directed to the process of spreading the franchise and refining the mechanism of democratic representation. The Nineteenth (1920), the Twenty-Fourth (1964), and the Twenty-Sixth Amendments (1971) all serve the purpose of extending the franchise. The drafting style follows the Fifteenth Amendment by specifying the criterion on account of which the states may not limit or abridge the right to vote. By using this negative formulation, the first of the series finally extends suffrage to women, the second to those who have not paid a poll tax or any other tax required to vote, and the third, to all men and women over the age of 18. Also in this group is the Twenty-Third Amendment, which extends the right to vote for the president and vice president to citizens otherwise qualified in the District of Columbia.

These amendments bespeak the philosophical principles of the Secret Constitution. A clear commitment to a universal right to vote finally takes hold. The franchise attaches not to those with qualifications, education, wealth, age, or even the supposed superiority that, according to the attitudes of 1920, men enjoyed in practical affairs. The franchise belongs to all Americans and even to resident noncitizens who are capable of knowing, in the minimal theory of democratic voting, when "the shoe pinches."[7] Lincoln's vision of government "by all the people" was becoming the law of the land.

Also, elections for the presidency begin to take on the quality of a national referendum in place of a compilation of preferences by the individual states. People started voting and expressing themselves as the voice of the nation. Thus, it came to be obvious that citizens of the country who did not reside in the states (namely, those in the federal district) must also have the right to vote for national offices. The Constitution nominally retained the electoral college as a way of giving lip service to the states, but it is clear that the popular vote expresses the will of the nation. This became clear in the presidential election of 2000, discussed in detail in the Afterword. On the basis of the results certified on November 26, Governor George W. Bush acquired a one vote majority in the electoral college. Vice President Gore's persistent legal challenge to the certified result depended, in part, on the sense of legitimacy he acquired from winning the confidence of the nation in the popular vote.

The remaining constitutional amendments fine-tune the workings of Congress and the presidency. The Twentieth shortens the lameduck period between the November election and the change of leadership in the following year. Previously the inauguration was prescribed for the beginning of March, but the amendment moved up the date to January 3 for Congress and January 20 for the presidency. Although this amendment appears simply to address matters of the calendar, it came into play recently in the dispute about whether an outgoing lameduck House of Representatives could, in the period between election and going out of office, constitutionally impeach President Clinton. Bruce Ackerman shocked the Capital by testifying before the House that the newly seated Senate could not constitutionally try the president on an impeachment passed by the outgoing House.[8] The amendment also authorizes Congress to prescribe a mode of succession to the presidency between elections.

The Twenty-Second Amendment (1951) limits the term of office of the president to two four-year terms plus a maximum of two years inherited from a predecessor unable to complete his term. And the Twenty-Fifth (1967) regulates in detail the problem of transition when the president is still alive but incapable of executing the office. The last amendment, the Twenty-Seventh, prohibits congressionally legislated pay raises from taking effect until another national election has taken place, and a new Congress is sworn in. This last revision of the national charter also testifies to the theme of improving the workings of popular democracy: the people must be consulted before their elected representatives should be allowed to raise their own salaries. The curious twist in this last addition to the Constitution is that although it was finally ratified by three-fourths of the states in 1993, it was originally proposed by James Madison two hundred years earlier. Its formal roots lie in the original Constitution of 1787.

The amendments to the original Constitution all bespeak the same pattern of realizing the implicit postbellum commitment to nationhood, democracy, and equality. The realization of these values in the amendments bespeaks the resurgence of the Secret Constitution.

COMPASSION FOR VICTIMS

The structure of our basic rights favors those who act—those who speak, assemble, worship, carry guns, keep their homes private, or stretch their liberties to the point that the state charges them with criminal offenses. The attention paid to the rights of criminal defendants in the Bill of Rights is extraordinary. The Fourth, Fifth, Sixth, and Eighth Amendments address the rights of suspects, defendants, and those convicted of crime. Noticeably absent in this catalogue of rights is due regard for those who suffer from the constitutionally protected actions of others. Our liberties entail costs, but for some reason the human beings who bear these costs are left outside of the constitutional equation. The victims have no rights. They are mentioned nowhere.

Indifference toward the victim began to change with the Thirteenth Amendment. For the first time, the people who must bear the cross of involuntary servitude became the focus of attention. They shall no longer suffer in the United States. The federal government has the duty to protect them. The government also asserted its duty to protect the weak in the Prohibition Amendment, but, alas, the duty to help others is not always easily realized. Yet, the idea that the government should protect the weak, that it should tender compassion for victims, became a mainstay of the Secret Constitution.

Of course, no one is constitutionally protected in the action of committing a crime. The rights attach to those suspected of crime. The purpose of the amendments is to insure both that innocent persons will not be convicted but just as critically to protect the dignity of every suspect as he or she falls under the investigative and prosecuting power of the state. For example, the privilege against self-incrimination goes beyond the protection of the innocent to speak to the dignity of the suspect who may remain silent. Similarly, the protection of the home and private papers often deters the efficiency of law enforcement, but only for the sake of promoting personal privacy. So long as we recognize that the constitutional provisions are interlaced with dignity concerns, then we cannot properly disregard the claims of victims to be treated in the same way. The victims' rights movement focuses, therefore, on increasing the participation of victims in various stages of the process. Participation itself helps enhance the dignity of the victim by allowing him or her to be heard and to feel respected as a citizen.

The most common problem faced by victims is that they are not allowed to attend the trials of those who have allegedly assaulted or raped them or killed members of their families. The trial of Timothy McVeigh for bombing the Murrah Federal Building in Oklahoma City in 1995 and killing 168 people provides dramatic proof of indifference to discrimination against the interests of victims. First, federal Judge Richard Matsch changed the venue of the trial from Oklahoma City to Denver, which of course made it much more difficult for the murdered victims' families to attend the trial. The nominal reason for the change of venue was that McVeigh was more likely to receive an unbiased jury in a city several hundred miles away. The likelihood of finding potential jurors, in Denver or anywhere else in the United States, unaffected by the intensive media coverage of the bombing was thought to be minimal. The other factor influencing the judge's decision to relocate the trial in Denver was the politely undiscussed fact that he owned a ranch outside of Denver. It suited his personal interests to be close to home.

If the change of venue was not bad enough, Judge Matsch also banned the victims who braved the journey from sitting in the courtroom during the trial. Many courts require witnesses to wait outside if they are likely to be called later in the trial, but in this case the defense prevailed on the judge to bar the victims' families on the ground that their very presence might induce an emotional response in the jury. This decision, we might say, represented the nadir of compassion for victims in the United States. Finally, Congress intervened to guarantee victims who have suffered direct physical, emotional, or financial harm the right to observe the trial by closed circuit television.[9]

A more compassionate approach to victims' rights became evident in the famous O. J. Simpson case, which held the country's rapt attention for more than a year in 1996 and 1997. In the pretrial skirmishes, the defense objected to the families of the two victims, Nicole Brown Simpson and Ron Goldman, remaining in the courtroom if they might later be called as witnesses. Marcia Clark won the argument in the name of the Brown and Goldman families, actually with some help from a book I had just published on victims' rights. Whether his words did the trick or not, the author could not help but enjoy hearing them enter into the deliberations. As Clark read them in the debate: "The minimal task of the criminal trial is to stand by victims, to restore their dignity, to find a way for them to think of themselves, once again, as men and women equal to all others."[10] Judge Ito made the right decision to let the families stay in court. If they were later called as witnesses, the defense could adequately protect itself by cross-examining the witnesses about testimony previously heard.

European courts are also chary of allowing potential witnesses to hear the testimony of other witnesses before they testify (they put less faith in cross-examination), but they take strong measures to protect the interests of victims at trial. The typical pattern is to allow the victim to join the proceedings either as a civil plaintiff suing simultaneously for tort damages or as a coprosecutor arguing and presenting the case alongside the state prosecutor. American reformers want to improve the position of the victim at trial, but none of them dares go so far as to suggest reforms comparable to accepted practice on the Continent.

The American movement favoring compassion for victims of crime has found expression in a variety of low-visibility measures. The constitutional amendment, sponsored by Senators Jon Kyl of Arizona and Diane Feinstein of California, sought to introduce the following rights:

To be notified of the proceedings
To attend all public proceedings
To be heard at certain crucial stages in the process
To be notified of the offender's release or escape
To consideration for a trial free from unreasonable delay
To an order of restitution
To have the safety of the victim considered in determining a
    release from custody
To be notified of these rights and to have standing to enforce them

So far as it goes, the proposed amendment makes sense. It expresses the spirit of compassion rooted in the Secret Constitution. It expresses the same sentiments that led to other initiatives to protect the weak and defenseless. Although each of the constitutional efforts to intervene on behalf of the powerless has a different impulse and a different agenda, they all spring from a root concern for those who are not strong enough to act for themselves. This is the common thread that begins in the Thirteenth Amendment, peaks, perhaps wrongly, in Prohibition, and issues today into the movement "to stand by victims, to restore their dignity, to find a way for them to think of themselves, once again, as men and women equal to all others."

The opposition to victims' rights stems from both prosecutors and defense counsel. The former do not want victims complicating the trial. They are surely opposed to my proposal that victims be able to veto plea bargains and insist on going to trial to vindicate their charges.[11] Prosecutors generally like to have victims around at the sentencing phase. The suffering and rage of the victims, when expressed in court, tends to spike the punishment. Defense counsel are opposed for other reasons. They are afraid that empowering victims will distract from the rights of criminal defendants, but this is not necessarily the case.[12] The victim's interest is primarily in participating in the trial. He or she may communicate a desire for conviction but that parochial sentiment of interest will be readily discounted by the commonsense responses of the jury. The fact is that it is possible to strengthen the participatory rights of victims without unduly complicating the procedure or compromising the traditional rights of the defense.

CIVIL SOCIETY

The central question in any movement of compassion is whether the government is the best agency of reform. There are obviously some areas where we must rely on the government or on no one. Only the federal government could have waged the Civil War and emancipated the powerless. Only the federal government could secure the franchise to those who had no power on the local level. Only the federal courts can secure equal protection of the laws when the states decide to disfavor some of their citizens. But in other areas of life, the government can further its ends by staying its hand.

The U.S. government has sought to maintain the religious sensibility that brought forth the Declaration of Independence but was abandoned in the secular Constitution of 1787. Americans have become and remained one of the most religious nations on earth, and largely because the state has evolved toward a rigorous policy of symbolic support for religion, at the same time insisting that the religious culture either thrive or die on its own. The symbolic gestures include printing "IN GOD WE TRUST" on our money, celebrating two Christian holidays as national holidays, and using the Bible in oath-taking ceremonies. These are significant public gestures in a society that rigorously forbids the state's spending money to support religious education. Amusingly, the Court even quotes the Great Maxim from the Secret Constitution—all men are created equal—to support the separation of Church and State.[13] These postures seem to be the mirror opposite of European practices, where the state readily provides subsidies for religious schools, but would not consider using religious symbols on its money or even using the Bible in court to administer the oath to "tell the truth, the whole truth, and nothing but the truth." Whether these differences in practice are determinative or not, it is clear that the United States has remained a more deeply religious country than Germany, France, or even Italy. For religious faith to remain strong, it might be better for the state to keep its distance.

The same could be said of devotion to the nation. The state must engage in some elementary gestures of national pride. It must define and disseminate a flag, a national anthem, and celebrate holidays such as the Fourth of July, Veterans' Day, and the birthdays of great national leaders. Nations that fail to do these things have trouble melding their people into a single culture of national identity. A good example is Israel, which has yet to find a holiday that Jews and Arabs can celebrate together. We live in a time of national disintegration—witness Czechoslovakia, the Soviet Union, and the near-misses in Canada—and, therefore, the state is properly advised to cultivate a common identity and a sense of shared history and destiny.

Since the Civil War, the United States has hardly lacked a strong sense of national patriotism. But the state has had to do little to further it. In the 1890s, the Pledge of Allegiance, our secular prayer to the flag, spontaneously spread across the country and became a standard part of the socialization process for all American children. There was little national hesitation about our wars of national aggrandizement against militarily weak opponents in Cuba and Panama. And the country joined enthusiastically in sending our doughboys overseas, in President Wilson's words, "to make the world safe for democracy." The generation that fought and won World War II is still with us, infusing in both blacks and whites a strong sense of a national mission well executed. The war in Vietnam was undoubtedly a setback for the spirit of patriotism. A whole generation—my friends and students—became skeptical about the use of military power. Yet, to my surprise and somewhat to my chagrin,[14] a new cohort took up the sentiments of their grandparents and enthusiastically supported the questionable goals of the government in the Gulf War. As we were bombing Iraq, the country erupted again in a spontaneous display of unity and patriotic enthusiasm. Yellow ribbons appeared everywhere. It reminded one of the pledge that burst out a hundred years earlier, a paean to the flag in school houses around the country.

Civil society is a powerful medium, and when the public takes up the cause either of religion or of patriotism, its strength overshadows the feeble efforts of government to manipulate its opinions. Yet, in both fields—religion and patriotism—we face a constant challenge from those who are unsatisfied with the successes of civil society. They want government to join the action. Nowhere is this more evident than in the politics of schooling. We worry constantly, perhaps with good reason, that the young in America are growing up with the wrong values. They supposedly suffer from all the mistakes of their elders who promote violence on television and have permitted the country to be flooded with guns, which, as everyone knows, enable teenagers who go on rampages to gain a few hours of prime time news coverage. One wonders, however, whether it is an effective response for government to require, as suggested in one Republican initiative, schools to post the Ten Commandments on schoolhouse walls. This drive toward governmental intervention in the field of value formation has been nowhere more evident—and questionable—than the recently revived push for a constitutional amendment to protect the flag against protestors who want to burn it.

The commitment to the flag has surely been one of the stable and recognized provisions of our *sub rosa* constitution. We do well to cultivate reverence toward the flag, which coupled with national rituals like the pledge, instills sentiments of national loyalty in our children. Although patriotic sentiments toward the flag antedate the Civil War, we begin to find, in the early twentieth century, a duty of reverence toward the stars and stripes formulated as a legal issue. In 1907, the Supreme Court upheld the conviction for flag desecration of a beer manufacturer who printed the flag on his cans. Appropriating the flag for commercial purposes was considered disrespectful.[15]

Our attitudes toward the flag were then so obeisant that we adopted religious language to describe acts of disrespect toward Old Glory. It would be difficult to say that piece of cloth on which the stars and stripes were printed was ever "consecrated" so that it could be "desecrated." These terms imply the ritual use of an object exclusively for worshiping God. Despite the inappropriate use of religious language, the Supreme Court upheld this crime as a sensible expression of government's instinct to protect the symbols of the nation.

But then the commitment to national pride ran into a contrary trend in American thought that had been in the process of emergence for over a century. The impulse to protect the flag against desecration confronted the rising devotion to the cardinal American value of free speech. Since World War I and the dissenting opinion of Justices Holmes and Brandeis,[16] the American recognition of the primacy of free speech has been on an upward trajectory. The Supreme Court, including its most conservative justices, has consistently favored the primacy of speech over the interests of victims injured or offended by the rough and ready rumble of the "marketplace of ideas."[17]

The collision was inevitable. Two American ideas — protecting the flag and celebrating freedom of speech — would eventually come into focus as contradictory ways of being American. It was a close battle, but in two sharply divided votes of the 1990s, the Supreme Court decided that freedom of expression must prevail.[18] But this was hardly a defeat for the politics of national sentiment. Those who loved the flag still had recourse to civil society.[19] The proponents of patriotic rituals, such as honoring the flag, could learn from the history of religious sensibility in the United States. The government cannot coerce religious observance without, as John Locke argued in his first Letter Concerning Toleration (1689), corrupting the act of faith into an empty gesture of external compliance. The opposite effect occurs when the government seeks to punish those who burn the flag. The punitive sanction enhances the

communicative sting of flag burning. The simple act of destroying a
piece of cloth becomes a major event watched closely by the police and
the media. The subsequent trial of the flag burner gives him or her a
platform for broadcasting the political views expressed in the illegal act.
At one time, burning the flag was something like wearing a jacket in the
courthouse blazoned with the words "Fuck the Draft."[20] But when flag
burning becomes an acceptable and potentially routine event, it draws no
more attention than the use of four-letter words at cocktail parties.

There is no doubt that free speech has its victims, and in most European societies and in Canada, the courts rush in to protect the victims
against being offended. A good example is the way every major jurisdiction outside the United States treats Holocaust denial. Someone pub-
lishes a book saying that Auschwitz never happened, that it is a lie
propagated by the Jews. This is a punishable act in Germany, France, Israel, the Netherlands, Canada—just about everywhere where people
believe that the government must intervene in order to protect those
who might be disturbed and offended by the obscene lie. By intervening
and putting the Holocaust denier on trial, of course, they only broadcast
the lie to a larger audience, and they convert the mad dissident into a
martyr in his own circle.

The Supreme Court has remained remarkably unaffected by the academic swing toward support for hate speech legislation. In the *R.A.V.*
case, for example, the Court struck down a municipal ordinance that
punished the display of a symbol that one knows or has reason to know
"arouses anger, alarm or resentment in others on the basis of race, color,
creed, religion or gender."[21] Academic critics of the decision stress the
value of regulating speech that has the effect, it is argued, of silencing
minorities.[22] The overriding value, they claim, is the equality of those
affected by hate speech. Only by restricting intimidating speech, the argument goes, can all potential participants in the democratic dialogue
feel free to speak and to make their opinions known. In the courts, however, the *ancien* principles still reign. The primary value is not equality
but freedom.

But the government's staying its hand does not mean that hate
speech goes unsanctioned. Civil society has it own spontaneous means of
chastising those who veer too far from the acceptable range of discourse.
The best remedy against the "Auschwitz lie," as the Germans call it, is

to ignore it. Deborah Lipstadt, in her book *Denying the Holocaust*, wrote that we should not publicly debate unacceptable as well as obviously false claims, and thus she advanced a remedy as powerful as governmental censorship. When civil society turns a deaf ear, crazy ideas lose their edge. The remedy disturbed one historian labeled a "denier" so much that in late 1999 he unsuccessfully sued Lipstadt for libel, primarily to force her to confront his claims.[23]

In other areas, where racist and sexist speech wounds, the spontaneous order of American society has been uncannily effective in changing patterns of speech. Consider the careful choice of words in this book. I do not write "Negro" or "colored," as people were wont to do not long ago. "Black" and "African American" have become the norm, and it all happened without government's uttering a sound. When governmental officials try to tell people how to talk, they look slightly ridiculous. Witness the French trying to outlaw the use of the word "cheeseburger" and other insidious harbingers of American culture. However strong the value of preserving the French language in all its purity, the task is not one for government. At a certain point we have to trust the unplanned, powerful forces of civil society.

HUMAN DIGNITY

But civil society is not always to be trusted. Witness the drive toward a constitutional amendment to protect the flag against physical desecration. The amendment actually passed the House of Representatives in the summer of 1999, but it is not expected to command the necessary two-thirds vote in the Senate. When speech induces a sense of victimization in minorities and women, many academics in the United States and even more lawmakers abroad reach for the arsenal of legal remedies to show their compassion for victims. Two basic strategies present themselves. One technique trades heavily on the values of the Secret Constitution and the other, characteristic of German thought, relies heavily on the Kantian concept of human dignity. The general principle of equal treatment, as we have elaborated it, lends itself to the argument for limiting freedom of speech. The claim is that obscenity degrades women and, thus, fails to treat them equally with the men who are interested in consuming the obscene material. Similarly, hate speech systematically degrades its targets and, therefore, treats them as unworthy of equal status in society. These are good arguments that draw on a long tradition of concern in the theory of equality for protecting the weak and defenseless.

The alternative mode of compassionate jurisprudence relies on the concept of human dignity, elaborated in Article 1 of the German Basic Law of 1949. The term "human dignity" is not defined in the Basic Law and, therefore, the courts must rely on the basic Kantian principles that human dignity expresses the ultimate personhood of each individual. In my view, although we have never expressed a principle of human dignity in American constitutional law, the same principle underlies our commitment to the Great Maxim. Our notion of equality-in-creation derives from the view that we are all of ultimate value, an idea that can be expressed either by going back to the biblical idea of creation in the image of God or taking the secular alternative of human dignity beyond all price, as articulated in Kant's moral theory.[24]

To see how the notion of human dignity operates in practice, let us take a look at the well-known Peep Show case decided in 1981 by the Federal Administrative Court [*Bundesverwaltungsgericht*] in Germany.[25] The operators of a peep show were denied a business permit because their show supposedly violated the morals of the community. Their show displayed a naked woman on a circulating round stage, viewed by men in private booths equipped with one-way windows. The women could not see the men who were gawking at their genitalia and the men could not see each other. The Federal Administrative Court upheld the denial of the license on the ground that the show violated the "human dignity" of the women who chose to participate. That participation was voluntary was irrelevant, for the state had an absolute duty under Article 1 to "protect human dignity" whether the victims wanted the help or not.

The court's rationale for the decision traded heavily on the Kantian principle that no one should ever use another person exclusively as a means to an end.[26] The judges had no objection to strip-tease performances, which they regarded as a variation on dancing in front of an interactive public. But the one-way nature of the viewing in this case disturbed the court:

By contrast with a strip tease, the women in the peep show are subjected to a humiliating objectifying role, brought about by a number of factors: the automatic way in which the viewers pay for the opening of the "peep" window, in which the viewing of the naked woman resembles buying a product from a vending machine, the one-way windows that leave the women, without eye contact, as the isolated objects of salacious desire and the voyeurs relegated to their secret cabins.[27]

One has to think twice before rejecting this argument. This is not simple prudery. The fact is that the entire enterprise does degrade the participating women into mere objects, and though one could imagine a woman enjoying doing a strip-tease to an appreciative bunch of unruly sailors, the anonymity of private sexual gratification could leave one with a sense of humanity abandoned. Yet, there is obviously another point of view. The self-exposure of the woman on the rotating stage is not that much different from doing a strip-tease before a television camera. The audience is invisible; each viewer is in his little cubicle, called a living room. The danger in the argument of human dignity is that it carries the risk of dogmatism. In the face of the conviction that the peep show violates the dignity of the women who choose to participate, there is little one can say.

At least one German feminist favors the American approach of treating the problem in the Peep Show case as one of equality rather than human dignity.[28] The participation of the woman may seem voluntary on the surface. But the mandate of equal justice for men and women requires that we inquire whether in light of the existing power structure, the participation of the women is really voluntary. Appearances deceive. The argument of dignity begins and ends with the question whether the work reduces women to the status of objects. The perspective of equality, by contrast, encourages a broader political inquiry into the relations between women and men in the arenas of sex and money. The feminist assumption, apparently, is that in a state of true equality, no one would agree to engage in this kind of self-humiliation for pay. To be sure, however, that the work is so degrading, we must make implicit judgments about the kinds of activities that allow our sense of humanity to flourish. We are invariably drawn back to the Kantian theory of human dignity.

Whether we approach the problem of sexual exploitation as a problem of dignity or of equality, we can see the politics of compassion at work. The society as a whole undertakes to protect the self-worth of those who fall prey to superior forces. We have made the transition from governmental intervention to prevent slavery to a collective responsibility for the welfare of each. Perhaps Americans would not interfere with the appearance of autonomy in the peep show. But we took aggressive measures during Prohibition to protect individuals against the self-degradation of alcoholism, and we intervene today in a mammoth and seemingly unproductive campaign to protect people against drug abuse.

The paradox of the American approach toward equality is that though we trail European societies in our concern about economic equality and wealth discrimination, we lead the world in other areas of egalitarian thinking. The Secret Constitution has emerged, with vigor, in our collective effort to curtail sexual harassment and discrimination against women in the work place. The movement has occurred at the level of federal law, particularly in the interpretation of Title VII of the 1964 Civil Rights Act.[29] The public often forgets that the expansion of sexual harassment law is grounded in the simple commitment to overcome gender inequality in the workplace. The law has moved so quickly in this arena that most men and women no longer know when and how they can approach a coworker and make a compliment or request a date. President Clinton even paid a ransom of $850,000 to avoid an appeal in a sexual harassment dispute in which the law and the lower court judgment seemed clearly on his side.[30] Whatever the merits of this body of law, there is little doubt that Americans stand responsible for exporting this vision of sexual equality on the job and even for the creation of a new vocabulary of *sexuelle Belästigung* and *harcèlement sexuel* necessary to discuss the problem.

The redress of sexual harassment should be understood, in part, as an expression of the egalitarian aspirations of the Secret Constitution. Yet, as a symptom of the times, sexual harassment also represents a new vision of government; it has developed against the background of growing skepticism about whether things really are what they seem.

EQUALITY FOR BELIEVERS
AND NONBELIEVERS

The values of the second constitution continue to collide with those of the first. The egalitarian approach toward freedom of religion dictates a leveling of two conflicting clauses in the First Amendment on freedom of religion. One clause prescribes "establishment of religion"; the other mandates "the free exercise of religion." For the past thirty years or so, the tendency has been to read these two clauses together to prohibit both the state financing of religious activities and the state's favoring one religion by granting to believers special exemptions from the laws applicable to everyone.[31] The opposition claims that religious reasons warrant exceptional treatment, say, for refusing to work on one's personal Sabbath,[32] for using hallucinatory drugs,[33] or for keeping one's children out of school in violation of truancy laws.[34] Again the conflict is between equality and freedom. Equality requires that all be treated alike—no exceptions for those motivated by fear of God. The faithful object and insist on the teaching found in Matthew 22:21: "Render therefore, unto Caesar the things which are Caesar's; and unto God, the things that are God's."[35] The constitutional right to "freedom of religion," they argue, requires special exemptions for those who dissent, as a matter of conscience, from the laws applicable to others.

While the judicial proponents of freedom continue to hold the upper hand on free speech, the reigning approach to freedom of religion underscores the even-handedness of the law—the same rules should apply to religious and nonreligious alike. In 1990, in Oregon v. Smith, the majority of the Court held that this egalitarian approach to religion should govern the cases of some Native Americans who claimed the right to use peyote in their religious services. Their good-faith claim for exceptional treatment did not prevail in the face of the general prohibition against peyote as a drug perceived to be dangerous.[36] In order to reach this conclusion, the Court had to push aside a line of precedents recognizing a policy of deference to any who refused, as a matter of religious conscience, to comply with the laws of the state.[37]

Congress responded to *Smith*'s egalitarian treatment of religion by enacting the Religious Freedom Restoration Act of 1993.[38] The purpose was to restore the earlier jurisprudence of the Court and "to provide a claim or defense to persons whose religious exercise is substantially burdened by government."[39] The supposed ground for Congress's overruling a constitutional decision of the Supreme Court was Section 5 of the Fourteenth Amendment.[40] The proponents of the statute thus relied upon a provision of the second constitution to defend a conception of freedom rooted in the First Amendment and the first Constitution. When the case reached the Supreme Court, six justices found that Congress had exceeded its authority under the Fourteenth Amendment.[41] The spirit of the decision dovetails well with the Court's decision in 1883 to overturn the first civil rights acts as an excessive claim of congressional authority.

The decision reflects a general tendency of the Supreme Court to suppress the independent significance of the second constitution. If the postbellum constitutional order were taken seriously, as an independent source of constitutional law, its legislative provisions would be construed as liberally as the grants of legislative authority under the "interstate commerce" clause and the other provisions of Article I defining the power of Congress in the old Constitution. Yet, the Court's attitude toward legislative authority under the Fourteenth Amendment begins on the assumption of fear. Congress should be able to implement the "due process" and "equal protection" clauses but not engage in imaginative interpretations of what these clauses should mean in practice. In defense of the current Supreme Court, however, we should note the extraordinary claim that Congress should have the authority—wherever it might be located—explicitly to overrule a constitutional decision of the Supreme Court. Recognizing congressional authority for this purpose would destabilize the structure of judicial review, as it has evolved since the early nineteenth century, and therefore the conservative inclination of the Court has much to commend it.

One cannot but be impressed by the "postmodern" style of the Court's resolution of this constitutional crisis about freedom of religion. The Supreme Court relies on egalitarian thinking—a value drawn from the second constitution—to develop an approach to the conflicting clauses on religion in the First Amendment. Congress seeks to return to an interpretation of religious liberty attributed to the first Constitution, but grounds its authority in the Fourteenth Amendment, the cornerstone of the second constitution. The Court parries in the name of equality by cabining and curtailing the legislative authority that could be used to further the egalitarian values of the Fourteenth Amendment.

CHAPTER 10

GOVERNMENT AS
PARTNER AGAINST
THE PAST

"Liberty . . . is indeed little else than a name,
where the Government is too feeble to . . . confine each member of the Society within the limits
prescribed by the laws and to maintain all in the
secure and tranquil enjoyment of the rights of
persons and property."

—George Washington

66 A specter is haunting Europe," Karl Marx and Frederick Engels wrote in 1848, as the first sentence of *The
Communist Manifesto*. The specter they had in mind
eventually became a political movement that came to dominate nearly
half the world in the twentieth century. Behind this movement, however, lay an even more powerful idea that Marx had inspired—a Marxist conception of reality. The marketplace of economic relationships is
not what it seems to be. Workers enter into seemingly voluntary contracts with employers, but underlying this system of apparent cooperation is a vast system of exploitation. Those who hold capital reap profits
off the backs of those whom they hire as their laborers. This generates a
dynamic of history that should, according to the theory, eventually produce a revolution by the exploited class of laborers. This theory failed to
recognize the just contribution of capital in generating the opportunity
to work, and the political incarnation of Marxism turned out to be historically more transient than expected. Nonetheless, the insight remains
with us that relationships of employment—indeed all forms of relationship—require more than nominal consent to be legitimate. Behind

the appearance of voluntary interaction there lurks the ever-present possibility of unjust exploitation.

The Marxist challenge was but the beginning of a continuing critique of the idea of freedom, so revered at the close of the eighteenth century. Behind the nominal appearance of freedom lies a structure of influence, a set of conditions that influences people to make the choices they do. Sometimes these influences are morally desirable. Peer group and family pressure can lead people to finish their university degree or to stay in difficult marriages or to remain loyal when tempted to act in self-interest. Looking back, individuals who make these choices under social influence are often grateful for the external inducement to do the right thing. Yet, economic and social conditions can also lead people to enter into socially and economically oppressive relationships, abusive marriages, and postures of dependence on drugs and alcohol. They can be induced to undress and prostrate themselves on stages in front of booths with one-way windows. The fact that people are influenced by others or their economic and emotional needs is, in itself, morally neutral, but the results can vary widely.

THE PARADOX OF FREEDOM

This is the paradox of freedom in modern times. We still believe that freedom is the great contribution of American democracy to the culture of the West. "Freedom" was our rallying cry in the decades-long battle against the political enemy that Ronald Reagan labeled the "evil empire." Although Martin Luther King, Jr. dreamed of a society committed to the proposition that would realize the American vision of equality under law, the word that would sound from the mountaintops would not be "equality" but "freedom." "Let freedom ring," King reminds us in the memorable refrain of his dream. In his choice of words, King harks back to Lincoln, who recognized our commitment to the proposition that all men are created equal but hoped that the emancipation would generate "a new birth of freedom."

We may be willing to die in the name of freedom, but we can no longer pretend that we live in the uncomplicated moral world of the eighteenth century. In a post-Marxist world, we know that freedom requires more than the experience of choosing. We cannot escape our recognition that nominal freedom leads, sometimes, to exploitation and oppression.

The late eighteenth century was indeed a marvelously simplistic time. Adam Smith could write, in the same year as the Declaration of Independence, of the wonders of a free market, based on the voluntary cooperation of producers and consumers, and its invisible hand that would produce the maximum possible welfare for humankind.[1] Immanuel Kant could glorify freedom in his theory of law, published in 1795, a theory based on the absolute right to enter into any contract that one chooses to make.[2] And, of course, the great monuments to the eighteenth-century understanding of freedom are the Constitution and the Bill of Rights. These documents are revered because they are designed to protect the individual sphere of freedom from a presumptively aggressive and overreaching central government. The basic freedoms protected in the first Ten Amendments, ratified in 1791, include freedom of speech and the press, freedom of religion, the right to bear arms, the right to privacy against state intrusion in one's home and papers, and a plethora of rights designed to protect suspects of crime against the federal government's power to investigate and prosecute. All of these freedoms or rights are understood to be a matter of opposition of the individual against the government. They imagine a dyadic conception of government—the individual pitted against the state.

The significant feature of our basic freedoms—apart from the franchise and those that arise in the criminal process—is that we can imagine enjoying all of them in a state of nature. We do not need government in order to exercise our freedom of speech or religion, to bear arms or to be free of state intrusion in our homes. As these rights are formulated, government acquires the image of the interloper, the enemy, the potential violator of our freedom to do as we please.

And who do we fear will invade and intrude upon our island of freedom? At the time of the revolution, the fear was directed toward King George III and his colonial governors. In the newly established Republic, the fear was redirected toward the federal government. This dyadic opposition between individual and state underlies most constitutional thinking to this day. The fear of the federal government has grown into distrust toward all government. According to the official doctrine, the Bill of Rights only applies to limit "state action" encroaching upon individual liberty.

As Akhil Amar recently formulated the idea, officials of the state are likely to act for their own benefit rather than the benefit of its citizens.[3] Therefore, we must be eternally watchful against overreaching by the state. The purpose of the Constitution is to arm us with the legal means to check the tendency of the state—federal government and indeed all forms of government—to limit our natural freedom.

But there is another model of thinking that recognizes the paradox of freedom. If freedom can generate exploitation, then the task of the state should be to intervene to protect the individual against the exploitation by other private individuals. The paradigm of the exploitative, oppressive relationship in the American experience is, of course, slavery, and therefore in 1865, as the first task of the new constitutional order, we banned the very possibility of private relationships of slavery, established either by force or by consensual agreement between master and slave. The Thirteenth Amendment charges the federal government with the responsibility to make sure that neither "slavery" nor "involuntary servitude" shall come to exist in the United States. The amendment does not say that the *state* may not create relationships of subordination or slavery. It says simply that these private relationships, however they might come about, "shall not exist." The important point about this formulation is not merely that it dispenses with the requirement of "state action." It does that and more.

The Thirteenth Amendment betokens an entirely new way of thinking about government—not as an ever-threatening enemy, but as a necessary partner in the building of a society free of interpersonal exploitation. The focus of the Thirteenth Amendment is not on the potential evils of government but on the wrongs committed by private parties. Unjust private relationships do not cease existing just because one declares them not to exist. They can arise spontaneously, and in a state of nature some people would inevitably come to dominate others. The passive voice of "Neither slavery nor involuntary servitude shall exist" means that the government must be ever watchful, lest relationships of exploitation come into being.

The new function of government departs radically from the dyadic structure—the individual pitted against the state—underlying the Bill of Rights. The relationship of government to private individuals becomes triadic or three-cornered. The relationship arises between two private parties: slave owner and slave, dominator and subordinate, aggressor and victim. The third pole is the government, which must intervene to insure that the incipient relationship of "involuntary servitude" shall not exist.

A triadic relationship between two people and the government represents an entirely new kind of constitutional order. A dyadic focus takes the government to be the enemy. The triadic orientation accepts the government as a partner in conquering evil. The dyadic picture assumes that the desired form of liberty exists in a state of nature and it treats the transition to government as a threat to liberty. The triadic conception recognizes the evil of domination inherent in a state of nature and treats government not only as necessary to rid us of that evil but as a welcome partner in the effort to build a civilized society.

This difference in the attitude toward government parallels a different understanding of freedom and how it comes into being. The freedom celebrated by the Bill of Rights resembles an island of solitude, a retreat from society. Its ideal is the individual in the state of nature, intimated by Henry David Thoreau's retreat to Walden Pond.[4] The individual stands alone, fearful that a far-off agent called government will aggress against him and limit his freedom. But the liberty that comes to the fore in the intended postbellum constitutional order and under the Secret Constitution requires the intervention of government. Liberty is born in the state's assertion of responsibility to oversee and prevent relationships of oppression. The relationship between rights and freedom is thus turned on its head. Those who identify with the Bill of Rights and the mentality of 1791 think of both rights and freedom as islands of autonomy protected by the walls of the law against the threat of government. The view that comes to the fore in the Secret Constitution recognizes that freedom as well as rights depend on the proper interaction with government. Government is not the enemy of freedom but rather the mechanism by which freedom is secured in a society that tends toward domination and oppression.

The assertion of a triadic conception of government brought us into line with the middle European conception of freedom as the privilege that arises from living in a matrix of protective state regulations. It is not nature but the law that makes us free. Freedom is realized not by the state's absence but from the construction of a network of laws that liberate the individual from the oppression that would otherwise occur. Compulsory temperance and drug laws generate freedom for those who are able to stay clean. Prohibitions against sexual self-degradation and peep shows strengthen the inner freedom of our human selves.

This is the European conception of constitutional freedom. When the German Basic Law of 1949 declares human dignity to be the foundational value of the constitution, the implications run through all relationships that may come into being. This "third-party effect" means that private individuals are bound to respect the human dignity in each other, precisely as they are bound not to subject each other to relationships of involuntary servitude or, during Prohibition, not to sell each other alcoholic beverages. Today, men and women must avoid sexual harassment on the job, even though in this case the "third-party" effect arises not directly from the Constitution but from federal legislation.

An activist tripartite conception of government requires funding. Fighting a major military campaign to suppress the Southern insurrection required a stronger financial base than the government had needed up to that time. The war drove up spending from the customary 2 percent of the gross national product to 15 percent. (By comparison, in the early 1990s, government spending represented 20 percent of the GNP.)[5] With no place left to turn, a Republican Congress approved the first income tax in 1862. By 1865, the income tax generated over 20 percent of federal revenue, the balance coming from tariffs and reintroduced excise taxes.

The Civil War income tax lapsed in 1872, and when the direct tax against income returned to the national agenda in the 1890s, the times were different. The disputes took on the tones of class struggle. This time, it was the Democrats who favored the tax as a measure of social justice. Many of the wealthy who were affected by the modest 2 percent tax denounced the measure as socialist. Almost immediately after the tax's introduction, a challenge under the original Constitution made its way to the Supreme Court, where five of the nine justices were convinced that any form of income tax violated the prohibition against direct taxes not in proportion to the census.[6] Progressive politics as well as the government's demand for revenue generated a coalition that supported a constitutional amendment to reverse the decision of the Supreme Court. By 1913, the Sixteenth Amendment found the necessary three-fourths vote for ratification, and the income tax became a basic tool of modern state finance.

The origin of the income tax in the Civil War has largely symbolic meaning. It testifies to the government's beginning to conceive of itself as an aggressive agent charged not only with winning a total war against states in insurrection but also with taking charge of the postbellum constitutional order that would be based on different premises from the social order of freedom and fear of government.

In the second founding of the United States, thirty-seven states constituted themselves as a single nation "conceived in liberty and dedicated to the proposition that all men are created equal." The government would assume the task of supervising relationships in the commercial and private spheres to assay whether they were impermissible relationships of domination—relationships morally equivalent to "involuntary servitude." The government was newly envisioned as a triadic structure powered by an activist, well-financed government. Unfortunately, the Supreme Court did not clearly get the message.

TWO CONCEPTIONS OF GOVERNMENT

The tension between two conceptions of government—bipartite and tripartite—came to a head in a classic decision of the Supreme Court in 1905. The State of New York had enacted legislation designed to protect workers in the bakery trade. Among other provisions, the legislation limited the permissible hours of work to ten per day and sixty per week. The legislation was based rather clearly on the assumption that employees are at a serious bargaining disadvantage and cannot protect their interests adequately simply by negotiating the number of hours they want to work. The state was reaching out to the worker, motivated by compassion for those who lacked the bargaining leverage to limit their hours of employment.

The defendant, Lochner, was prosecuted under a provision of the statute that made it a misdemeanor to employ someone in excess of the limit. The Supreme Court concluded by a large majority that the statute violated the liberty of the employer and presumably of the employees as well—although the latter were not complaining about being prohibited from working too many hours.[7] A majority of five on the Court read the notion of liberty in the due process clause ("no person shall be deprived of life, liberty, or property without due process of law") as including freedom of contract. The dyadic structure prevailed. A similar analysis in the Peep Show case would have led to the conclusion that the women and their employers had the right to contract any form of self-exhibition they thought desirable. Any other result supposedly implies paternalism. Autonomy (if not dignity) requires freedom of contract as a basic right.

The alternative view of the case, winning support from four justices, including Oliver Wendell Holmes, Jr. and John Marshall Harlan, was that limiting hours of employment was a legitimate way for the state to exercise its responsibility to protect the health of those who chose to work as bakers. The dissent, written by Justice Harlan, explicitly addressed the problem of unequal bargaining power between owners and bakers:

> It may be that the statute had its origin, in part, in the belief that employers and employees in such establishments were not upon an equal footing, and that the necessities of the latter often compelled them to submit to such exactions as unduly taxed their strength.[8]

Justice Holmes had the same point in mind when he wrote, apodictically, "The Fourteenth Amendment does not enact Mr. Herbert Spencer's Social Statics."[9] In other words, the principles of the free market economy need not be entrenched as a dimension of constitutionally protected liberty.

Lochner ranks among the more widely scorned decisions of the Supreme Court. The general complaint is that the Court ignored the interest of the state in furthering the health and welfare of its citizens. To put this objection in other terms, the opinion ignored the ascendancy of the tripartite conception of government. The issue remains with us—if only in a slightly different guise. Since the late 1930s, the principle of freedom of contract has given way to the propriety of the state and federal measures to protect working people on the job. Yet, the question of liberty and its potential abuse in an oppressive relationship remains a flash point of debate. Although the concept is not mentioned in the Constitution, the freedom to say "yes" or "no" to particular commercial relationships has become an essential dimension of personhood. It is as much a part of the basic liberty protected under the due process clause as the right to be free from unjustified physical restraint.

Freedom of contract enables individuals to express their personhood, but it also facilitates relationships of oppression, including "slavery and involuntary servitude." After all, it is possible to choose to enter into a contract of slavery. The book of Exodus permits the purchase of a Hebrew slave, but after six years of service "he shall go out free, for nothing."[10] Yet, there are people, the Bible recognizes, who prefer the condition of servitude:

> And if the servant shall plainly say, I love my master . . . I will not go out free, then his master shall bring him . . . to the door or to the door post, and his master shall bore his ear through with an awl and he shall serve him Forever.[11]

In this example, the servant chooses the condition of servitude. We know from the fate of many long-term prisoners that after a certain period they choose a life of dependence, free of the responsibility of caring for themselves. It is not impossible that someone might actually prefer the secure life of the slave to the anxious life of the free person who must care for himself.

There are two distinct grounds on which the law might sensibly prohibit the possibility recognized in Exodus. First, the claim might be that freedom and its blessings represent a great gift that no individual "made in God's image" should be able to forfeit as though it were a disposable piece of property. Alternatively, the argument might be that in principle people have the right to choose to forego their freedom, but that in reality these choices are always influenced by personal necessities that becloud the choice actually made. This is especially true under market conditions, where the need for sustenance can drive people into relationships that they would not choose in and of themselves. It is clear that even the choice of the Hebrew slave discussed in Exodus can never be shown to be completely free. The legal arrangements also stipulate in the same passage that if during his period of servitude the slave acquired a wife or children, then he must leave them behind when he leaves his master's service. Some purchased servants might decide to opt for permanent servitude simply because they cannot bear to live without their wives and family. The full text in the quoted passage reads: "I love my master, my wife, and my children, I will not go out free."[12] The cruelty of subjecting him to the choice between freedom and leaving his family obviously means that his choice is not free in any meaningful sense.

Under modern capitalism there are many conditions that render choices less than fully free. Material necessity is the most obvious. But, as we have learned from the history of alcohol and cigarette consumption, advertising and peer group influence can lead people to develop habits that they later regret. The same is true of heroin consumption, which may readily develop into a condition of dependency in which the addict may enjoy the illusion of freely choosing not a hole bored in his ear but rather numerous telltale holes bored in his veins.

The question of exploitation and manipulation of consent has shifted from the economic to the sexual arena. That is why the peep show case so beautifully captures our concerns about equality and human dignity. The right to enter the romantic and sexual relationship of one's choosing is surely an important dimension of freedom. It includes the right to marry the person of one's choice, to choose and act upon a sexual orientation, gay or straight, to enjoy (within appropriate limits) reproductive freedom, and to say "no" to sex if one is so inclined.

The law of rape has become a major battleground of American law. The central question has become whether nominal consent to sexual relations constitutes actual consent, deep agreement in the heart. As in the economic context, power tends toward exploitation. The problem is particularly acute when the party seeking sexual favors—usually a man—is in a position of authority over his desired partner. The most hotly debated cases are spun from skepticism about whether nominal consent actually generates the kind of voluntary relationship that should be regarded as an expression of freedom rather than of exploitation. The same is true of regulation of sexual harassment on the job. If the boss promises advancement or threatens disadvantaged treatment on the job, the appearance of complete and voluntary participation is readily undermined. So far, in the name of equality, we are willing to tolerate rather intrusive regulation of dating practices in corporate or university settings, but one can sense a coming backlash favoring the principle that students old enough to vote should be old enough to make a responsible decision about their sexual lives.[13] Making it a crime or private action for damages for coworkers or costudents to have sexual relations would surely violate the right to sexual autonomy now recognized as an aspect of liberty protected by the due process clause.[14]

The problem of exploitation in apparently voluntary sexual relations has long been with us. In the late nineteenth century, the problem was whether the Mormon practice of polygamy should be regarded as protected as liberty and the free expression of religious conviction. Those who defended the institution, as provided in the accepted Mormon religious doctrines of the time, cited its social benefit of caring for all the women and children in a society in which the available men had fallen victim to the hardships of settlement and warfare. The critics, by contrast, claimed that the choice of the women in these cases is not really free and voluntary. John Stuart Mill, a great advocate of liberty, sided with the critics of polygamy.[15] Western governments have had no qualms about prohibiting the practice, sometimes for parochial religious reasons, sometimes out of solicitude for women who are subjected to an institution that arguably diminishes their status. The Mormons sued, thinking they had the kind of argument that eventually prevailed in the *Lochner* case. In 1878, the Supreme Court upheld the conventional view that the prohibition represents permissible intervention by the state to protect the weak against entering into exploitative relationships.[16] Many voices today argue that this decision was wrong. The freedom to choose any form of domestic arrangement one wants should prevail against the state's concern to protect people against their own potentially bad choices.

The same problem recurs in the current debate over physician-assisted suicide. The argument for freedom and autonomy holds that individuals should be able to choose when and how to end their lives. If they need the assistance of a physician to be able to die with dignity, they should have that right. The contrary view stresses the dangers of manipulated consent. Once the possibility of voluntary euthanasia is recognized, the danger presents itself that terminal patients will encounter social and economic pressure to consent to an early and painless death. Again, the problem is whether choices are as free as they seem on the surface, or whether they represent the subtle pressures that lead us to think that the government should intervene to protect people from manipulation and exploitation.

The anchor for this new conception of government—a government that intervenes in private choices in order to protect individuals from exploitation—lies in the Thirteenth Amendment. Yet, it seems very ambitious to derive all of this from a black-letter prohibition against private arrangements of "slavery and involuntary servitude." The fact is that we are not entirely sure how far we should extend the prohibition against unjust relationships of domination. At the time the amendment was enacted, it was fairly clear that the drafters and the public had a broad construction in mind, for the Thirteenth Amendment became the constitutional foundation in 1866 for the first Civil Rights Act—indeed, the Act that is still used today to prosecute those who, like the police who beat up Rodney King, engage in racially motivated deprivations of civil rights.[17] Because the deprivations of civil rights were understood to be an instantiation of relationships of unjust domination, it is clear that the framers envisioned a new constitutional order much broader than merely business as usual, just without slavery.

Academic writers have found the Thirteenth Amendment a rich source for constitutional speculation. Some have claimed that the amendment goes so far as to require the government to be watchful and intervene against child abuse.[18] Others have argued that the amendment offers convincing grounds for recognizing abortion rights. Requiring a mother to carry a child to term arguably amounts to an oppressive form of involuntary servitude.[19] A third voice holds, much in line with the argument of this book, that the potential ambit of "involuntary servitude" includes all forms of employment and labor that are unjust and oppressive.[20] These are imaginative readings, and others are possible.[21]

Some restraint is necessary. We have to be mindful of the prospect that the values of the Secret Constitution might play themselves out more effectively as the informal restraints of civil society rather than as binding rules of law. As we have seen, our impulse to promote religion, love for the nation, and "politically correct" speech seems to yield greater results when the state holds back and limits itself to a gentle nudge in the right direction. But, more significantly, we have to recognize that we are locked in ongoing contradiction between the values of our first and our second constitutions.

The first Constitution commits itself to freedom and the second builds both on a preference for equality and the recognition that freedom is often an illusion. The lovers of freedom want the government to keep its hands off, lest Big Brother's intermeddling do more harm than good. The skeptics of the Secret Constitution place their trust not in the natural mechanisms of social interaction but in the judgment of a vigilant hierarchy.

The first Constitution plays on the theme of distrust in government. We must secure our freedoms against potentially abusive officials seeking "rents" by pursuing their own bureaucratic interests.[22] The second constitution presupposes trust in an aggressive government, a watchdog of transactions that might slide into the forbidden territory of "involuntary servitude." In this regard, public opinion seems to be at odds with the de facto tolerance of Americans for governmental action that is becoming ever more intrusive. The public supposedly suffers from declining trust in government.[23] Yet, in fact, the average person tolerates actions by government that can make sense only on the assumption that those potentially affected by governmental abuse see Washington officials as their allies in a common struggle. A good example is the census and the popular reaction. The census form for the year 2000, like several before it, poses probing questions about racial and ethnic identity. The government wants to know how many blacks and other minorities live in particular sections of the country. The questionnaire imposes a detailed grid of racial variations on people who might otherwise simply have thought of themselves as Americans or perhaps as "minorities." This information becomes relevant, it is said, to Justice Department officials monitoring the distribution of voting power in congressional districts.[24]

Americans would not cooperate in answering these questions if they did not trust the government not to misuse the collected information. There was a time when the government sought indirectly to find out how many Jews still spoke Yiddish at home. One can be sure that the purposes of early twentieth-century officials, ever concerned about swelling immigration patterns, were not benign. And yet, today the common assumption is that our officials may be trusted with a precise racial and ethnic map of the American nation. Popular attitudes even go beyond tolerance for the intrusion into our personal identities. Many people of multiracial backgrounds prefer to identify themselves as "black," on the theory that it enhances the interests of the African-

American population to appear as numerous as possible.[25] For the government to serve as the vanguard of a new constitutional order, the people must trust officials in Washington with additional powers and run the risk of governmental abuse.

This trust makes sense—despite the surveys in which people report distrust—on the assumption that the nation chooses to cooperate in the ascendancy of the government as the watchdog of equality and popular democracy. The breach of equal treatment need not be feared, and information on the distribution of potential voting blocks serves the cause of securing fair representation of all major groups in American society.

Yet, the very effort to secure this fair representation of all voting groups threatens both the sense of common nationhood in the United States and calls into question the integrity of individual decision making in democratic elections. Encouraging people to identify themselves as hyphenated Americans encourages multicultural consciousness and generates a growing sense of puzzlement about what it means to say that all Americans are of a single nation. Also, the assumption that black candidates can be elected only by black voters places us on a path that we cannot pursue to a logical conclusion. It would hardly be consistent with the premises of popular democracy to consider—even as a thought-experiment—voting districts that consisted primarily of women or gays. The notion that particular groups are entitled to congressional representation merely as groups eventually runs squarely into the principle that in a democratic system individuals vote not as representatives of groups but solely as individuals. They have no duty to a hyphenated consciousness.

Yet, a trusted government can do much to remedy past discrimination and eliminate the badges of slavery. A new conception of government might yet emerge to realize the ambitions of Gettysburg, to ensure equality of all those "created equal" as it simultaneously promotes a "new birth of freedom." It is as though nothing has been resolved. When the pursuit of equality begins to encroach upon our basic freedoms we are unsure where to turn.

CHAPTER 11

NEITHER BLUE
NOR GRAY

"A foolish consistency is the hobgoblin of little
minds, adored by little statesmen, philosophers,
and divines."

—Ralph Waldo Emerson

The Civil War may have achieved unity of the nation, but it left our minds in ideological tatters. The great dichotomies that drove brothers to fight and die would no longer animate the American psyche. True, slavery was gone, but it did not follow that, in practice, all men were to be treated equal. True, the Union survived, but Webster's rhetoric of "Union now and forever" lost its currency as a meaningful slogan. Washington gained confidence and power in having fielded and managed the world's greatest army in its time, but in defeat the states of the Confederacy unceasingly pressed for their autonomy and their rights. A new constitutional order was born, but the *ancien* system of individual rights survived. The idea that the country would have to choose between these conflicting ideals rapidly became anathema.

A distinctively American school of philosophy called "pragmatism" generated a way of thinking that gave Americans hope that they would not have to choose between the ideological opposites that drove the Civil War. As developed by Charles Peirce and William James a generation after the war, the pragmatic way of thinking has many different meanings and applications, and many of them have nothing to do with working out a middle way between the demands of our two constitutions.[1] Yet, the central metaphor of pragmatism—the problem of rebuilding a ship at sea—has a direct bearing on the idea of legal revolutions and the effort to construct an entirely new constitutional order.

If you are at sea and you seek to rebuild your vessel, you cannot pull up all the floorboards, you cannot start from scratch, you have got to stand somewhere. The same is true of Lincoln at Gettysburg and the postbellum Supreme Court. Presidents and judges cannot rip out the old Constitution for the sake of a new one, for then they themselves would loose the grounding for their own offices. Their legitimacy turns on the very system of laws that they may, in their hearts, reject.

The great spokesman for pragmatism in legal thought was himself wounded three times in the Civil War. According to one story, Oliver Wendell Holmes, Jr. once saw a tall figure on the battlements and yelled out, "Get down, you damn fool, before you get shot."[2] The endangered man turned out to be Abe Lincoln. Holmes survived this and other battles to become one of the great jurists of American law. Sixteen years after the war, he wrote a book on the common law that sets forth, in phrases that still echo in classrooms around the country, a philosophy of law that rejects the absolutes both of "higher law" and of "legalism." One senses in these words a yearning for a mode of reaching consensus that would never again require brothers to go to war:

> The life of the law has not been logic: it has been experience. The felt necessities of the time, the prevalent moral and political theories, intuitions of public policy, avowed or unconscious, even the prejudices which judges share with their fellow-men, have had a good deal more to do than the syllogism in determining the rules by which men should be governed. The law embodies the story of a nation's development through many centuries. . . .[3]

The absolute logic of abolition led one side to die for one ideal. The logic of independence and autonomy led the other side to lay down their lives for their vision. The nation's "experience" taught us that we could adhere too strongly on one ideal or other. The future would lie neither with higher law zeal nor legalistic resistance to the values embedded in the Declaration of Independence. The "felt necessities of the time" dictated recognition for the value of peoplehood as well as nationhood, freedom as well equality, republican élitism as well as popular democracy. The new constitutional order must live with the old. The outcome would be neither blue nor gray.

Pragmatism does not necessarily mean compromise, or finding the golden mean between the extremes, but it does imply that the extremes are dangerous. They represent the dictates of logic rather than the guidance of experience. Later appointed to the Supreme Court, Holmes reserved some of his best judicial barbs to attack the polar opposites of the conflicting constitutional orders. When it looked like "freedom of contract" was becoming an absolute that stood in the way of the protective social legislation, he quipped in dissent, "The Fourteenth Amendment does not enact Mr. Herbert Spencer's Social Statics."[4] But, if freedom had to give way to the felt necessities of the time, so did equality. Upholding a Virginia statute that provided for the sterilization of mental defectives, Holmes gave short shrift to argument that the statute discriminated unfairly by limiting its effect only to those who happened to be in mental institutions: "It is the usual last resort of constitutional arguments to point out shortcomings [inequalities] of this sort."[5] Holmes had no tolerance for orthodoxies of any stripe—on freedom, on equality, or on any other matter. This explains in large measure his becoming, along with Louis Brandeis, the Court's leading advocate of freedom of speech. The famous metaphor of the "marketplace of ideas," an idea coined in Holmes's dissenting opinion in *Abrams*, requires free and open debate of conflicting opinions.[6] Truth must win out—not with the aid of courts, not by the force of arms, but in the hearts of those who participate in the debate.

This, then, is the way Americans have come to conceive of their redemption from the evils that generated the killings at Gettysburg and all the fields stained by the blood of the zealous. The Holmesian instinct to avoid dangers of ideological extremes carries, alas, its own dangers. In the face of evil, we might not be prepared to act. We might settle for the reasonable when we should be fighting for the right.[7] And, yet, the legacy of the American struggle with evil is certain skepticism about whether we can know the devil when we see him.

The European response to the mid-nineteenth-century wars of national unification took a turn different from the American embrace of pragmatic thinking. In response to the newly unified Italian government's seizure of church lands, Pope Pio Nono (Pius IX) retreated within the walls of the Vatican and in 1870 his council declared the infallibility of his office on matters of faith and morals.[8] This declaration that we can know absolute truth became a model for all the ideological extremists who followed on the right and on the left. As the concepts of nationhood, equality, and democracy appealed to postbellum American constitutionalists, they also seduced anticonstitutionalist European zealots. For those on the right, the concept of the "nation" or *Volk* became sacred; for those on the left, the Enlightenment values of equality and democracy found new distortions of meaning. Either way, as the Americans were groping for the felt necessities of the time, the Europeans suffered from the consequences of thinking that they had found a new set of political absolutes.

In seeking to overcome the self-imposed miseries of the twentieth century, Europeans, in their postbellum period, have developed their own brand of legal pragmatism. In the last fifty years, as they seek redemption from the recurrent warfare of European brother against brother, they have found their own way of rebuilding without pulling up the historical planks on which they stand. They may censor speech more quickly than would Americans, for they are ever fearful of the right's rising again. For the same reason, they may be hasty to censure Austria for accepting within its coalition government a party and a politician, Jörg Haider, who reminds them too much of the dangers they must avoid. And, further, the felt necessities of economic competition require less governmental spending, and the celebrated egalitarian social policies of many European governments have come under additional scrutiny. The multilingual Europeans seek union, but without giving up nationhood. In the politics of the postbellum Continent, the point is simple: The truth lies in what works, in the validation of experiences, not in the abstract requirements of ideological logic.

This, then, is redemption by law in the Western world. The resolution comes neither with resignation nor with passion. The virtue of law is a quiet one, a patient hearing of both sides, of accommodation and staking out the range of the reasonable. The purpose is to seek justice, but with the humility of knowing that absolute justice is always beyond our reach. The evils of the past—slavery, aggressive war, genocide—

mark the domain of the unreasonable and the unjust. The center of diverse possibilities holds. As an East German politician said after unification with the West in 1990: "We sought justice and we got the rule of law." We hold to the rule of law, for we fear the zealots who believe they know justice and seek to impose it on us at all costs.

The "pragmatic" legal mind rushes to reject moral extremes in favor of some vague standard of what is good for everybody, all things considered.[9] Yet, the extremes can be rejected for the wrong reasons. The higher law thinking of the abolitionists points to an ideal that we should not abandon or postpone without good reason. And the argument of autonomy and "states' rights" reminds us that any social and legal arrangement requires a heavy dose of tolerance.

The rule of law dictates an ongoing quest for reconciliation. The Secret Constitution will ever challenge us to find the right way of reconciling the commitments of our historical nation with the choices of a freely associating people, the requirements of equality with the opportunities of freedom, the will of the many with the wisdom of the few. We sought a Constitution and we found that we had two. And with two constitutions in constant tension, we are redeemed from the dogmatism of those who believe they have the last word.

ELECTION BLUES
2000

"Instead of the Blue vs. the Gray, we have a
scorched-earth war between two prescription-
drug plans."

—Frank Rich,
commenting on the presidential election of 2000

The movement toward popular democracy has, since the Civil
War, remained constant and ascendant. The Secret Constitution and its principles of organic nationhood, equality, and
popular democracy have progressively won the upper hand against the
1787 values of voluntary association, freedom, and republican élitism.
Yet there has been one holdout, one major exception, to the thrust toward trusting the popular vote. The gap in the populist pattern has been
the electoral college.

The original Constitution provides for a system of election by "presidential electors" who shall be "equal to the whole Number of Senators
and Representatives to which the State may be entitled in the Congress."[1] These electors are "appointed" by the state. The same clause,
which I shall call the electoral college provision, informs us further that
the legislature of each state shall "direct" the manner in which the
state appoints its electors. The Twelfth Amendment, ratified in 1803,
clarified the procedures by which this group of state-appointed electors
chooses the president of the United States.[2] The electoral college must
vote separately, on two lists, for the president and vice president. The
electors vote in their home states and transmit their votes to Congress,

where the vice president, sitting as president of the Senate, opens
the certified votes in the presence of both houses of Congress. A federal statute mandates a process of non-partisan counting of the ballots. The Twelfth Amendment continues that the candidate receiving
the majority of the "whole number of Electors appointed" shall be
president.

The general view supporting the creation of the electoral college is
that it was an institution of republican élitism. It was designed to inter-
pose a layer of good judgment between the voters and the actual process
of decision. The closest analogy in our structure of government is the
trial jury, which interposes the judgment of common people as a restraint on the official application of the law. Yet the electoral college has
an anti-populist thrust, while the jury enthrones the judgment and
common sense of the average person.

Also, more profoundly, juries deliberate; they meet and talk and leaving their loyalties aside, they typically seek a unanimous verdict based
on the evidence and the law. Electors do not deliberate. They never sit
down and discuss the candidates with other electors. They are chosen
precisely because they are loyal to their parties. They are expected to
vote as their party dictates.

The electoral college has undergone a transformation comparable to
the evolution of the electoral system in general. At the outset, in the
late eighteenth century, the candidates ran as individuals, not as representatives of parties. In 1796, when John Adams was elected president
his opponent Thomas Jefferson became vice president. This "cohabita-
tion" of diverse political orientations was possible because the Constitution of 1787 prescribed that regardless of party, the candidate who
received the second largest number of votes should be named vice president. So long as candidates were running as individuals, their electors
were also chosen as individuals.

The Twelfth Amendment, ratified in 1803, implicitly recognized the
growing influence of political parties in the race for the presidency. By
requiring separate votes for the presidency and vice-presidency, the
amendment was designed specifically to avoid the outcome in 1800,
when Jefferson and his running mate Aaron Burr tied in electoral votes
for the presidency. The notion of the party presidential "ticket" eventually became the norm, and along with the rise of parties, the electors lost

their individuality and became agents of particular parties pledged to elect the candidates who were victorious in the popular election. If the electors were originally supposed to vote as the "wise men" of the Republic, this surely was not their task after ratification of the Twelfth Amendment.

As the electoral college has evolved over history, other features of the electoral system have come to be entrenched as constitutional practice. There is nothing in the original Constitution or in the Twelfth Amendment that requires the popular election of slates consisting of electors representing political parties. They could be appointed by the legislature, in the same way that Senators were selected by the state legislators until the ratification of the Seventeenth Amendment in 1913.[3] Originally, most state legislatures did appoint the electors; but now by virtue of binding customary principles, all states require popular election of the "presidential electors."[4]

It has also become the customary constitutional rule that electors must—at least in the normal case—execute the pledge that they make when they are nominated to represent a particular political party. If electors violate their pledge, we cannot do anything to them (or at least nothing major), and in this limited way, the actions of "faithless" electors resemble the decisions by jurors to act contrary to the judge's instructions as applied to the perceived facts. The analogy with jury nullification can, however, mislead. When it works right, jury nullification expresses higher principles of law and justice, principles that trump the judge's overly restrictive instructions on the law. True, the electors might switch their votes in the name of a higher value as well, namely the good of the country. If, for example, it were shown that one of the candidates had committed fraud against the electorate or had a serious health problem, the electors might exercise their residual discretion to decide for themselves what the welfare of the country required. Yet the rise of popular democracy is hardly compatible with the electors' bearing the charge of promoting national welfare. It cannot be the case both that the people decide what that welfare requires and that they are second-guessed by a college of electors.

There is a deep tension between the popular vote in each state and of the entire nation. The rise of a strong national consciousness gives the popular vote of the nation as a whole great legitimacy. It is after all the nation—not a collection of states—that the president represents. At

Gettysburg Lincoln spoke for the nation, those dead and those unborn. Yet it is the popular votes of the states in a series of 51 winner-take-all contests that determines the votes of the rigidly bound electoral college.

In the aftermath of the contest between Vice President Al Gore and Governor George W. Bush in November 2000, a number of constitutional law scholars committed themselves to the view that the electors should be free to cast their votes for the candidate who won the popular vote.[5] That respectable scholars would take this position testifies to the extent that the relentless push toward popular democracy has discredited the electoral college. It is now thinkable—at least for many—that electors would break ranks with their party in order to elect the candidate with the greater moral legitimacy—namely the candidate who commands a majority or a plurality verging on majority, in the popular vote.

Prior to election day, November 7, 2000, the media pundits expected that Bush might win the popular vote, and Gore, the electoral vote. The polls showed Bush consistently ahead by a few percentage points. The surprise was that though Gore carried the nation by over 330,000 votes, in the weeks after election day there was a breakdown in determining the winner of the electoral vote. The stumbling block was Florida, which turned out to be too closely divided to allocate either to Gore's or Bush's column. Without Florida, Gore was leading Bush in the electoral totals 267 to 246. If Bush could eventually secure Florida on his side, he would jump ahead and pass the threshold of 270 votes—the majority of the total of 538 "appointed" electors.

The remaining weeks of November and early December 2000 turned into a major political and legal fight about the meaning of popular democracy at both the national and state levels. No single incident demonstrated how torn our psyches were between the procedures laid down in 1787 and modified in 1803 and the new principles of democracy that were born in the Gettysburg Address and anchored in the Secret Constitution.

In part of our minds, in some moments, we made peace with the electoral college and its series of 51 independent contests for the presidency. In other moments, however, we regarded the whole practice as illegitimate, as a frustration of the general will of Americans as expressed in the popular vote. The Republicans and Democrats used these conflicting loyalties to their respective advantage. The Republicans devoted all their energy to the legitimacy conferred by the official counting of the popular vote in the decisive state of Florida. The Democrats relied on the ultimate will of the people as expressed in the popular vote of the nation and in the presumed preferences of uncounted ballots in Florida.

Our split-consciousness tracks the tension between our two constitutional orders. Our sense of tradition warms us to the old order of playing by the rules in place at the founding in 1787, but our sense of moral principle makes us gravitate toward the new order of national democracy. The last time we witnessed dissonance between the electoral college and the popular vote was in the late nineteenth century, the period when popular democracy was aborning. The problem today is whether we can still tolerate this relic of the original Constitution and its anti-democratic bias.

THE ELECTION OF 1876

Of the three historical precedents for divergence between the popular and electoral votes, two are clearly unrelated to the quandary of 2000. In 1888, Grover Cleveland, then sitting as president, outpolled Benjamin Harrison by 90,000 votes but he lost several key states by small margins, which meant that Harrison carried the electoral votes by an impressively large majority. The electoral college may have been creaky but the result for Harrison was clear and firm. In 1824, Andrew Jackson led in the popular vote, but in a three-way race with John Quincy Adams and Henry Clay no one received a majority in the electoral college. In the constitutionally prescribed procedure, the House of Representatives eventually chose Adams. Neither of these races raised the deep doubts about the electoral college that were generated by the stalemate between Bush and Gore in 2000.

The closest historical analogue to the standoff in Florida was the fight between Republican Rutherford B. Hayes and Democrat Samuel B. Tilden in 1876. This disputed election bears many structural resemblances to the confrontation of Bush and Gore, and it turns out to have been a critical event leading to the end of the military-supported Reconstruction and the political analogue to the judicial burying of Lincoln's intended postbellum legal order.

Florida was one of the few contested states in 1876 as it was in 2000. The Florida Supreme Court played a key role by siding with Republican candidate Rutherford B. Hayes, declaring him the winner of the state's electoral votes. At the same time it confirmed the election of Democratic Governor Frank Drew, who promptly intervened in the presidential election by replacing the canvassing boards and authorizing a recount of the ballots. Not surprisingly, the recount produced a victory for Samuel B. Tilden. Two slates of electors sent their ballots to the Senate, to be opened and counted for the state of Florida. The same confusion and conflict affected the voting in Louisiana, South Carolina, and Oregon. Out of a total of 371 electoral votes at the time, 22 were subject to dispute.

Tilden had a commanding lead in the popular vote—about a quarter million votes out of ten million cast. That the Democrat Tilden, with support across the entire South, could take the presidency rekindled still latent regional animosities. As November bled into December and then Congress reconvened in January, the country was on the verge of taking up arms once more. Many newspapers blared the headline "Tilden or War." It was, after all, only eleven years after Lee had delivered his sword to Grant. The muskets had hardly grown rusty. For the South, this was the critical opportunity to send the carpetbaggers home. They rallied against the North's use of troops to prop up the black-supported populist state governments in the former Confederacy.

The rallying cry for the South was that they should "redeem" their governments from occupation. The rebellious legislature in South Carolina was dubbed the "Redeemer" legislature.[6] The language of redemption thus entered both sides of the debates. It came to stand, as the first chapter of this book argues, for reclaiming the true American self, the American creed as expressed in the Declaration of Independence. It came as well to stand for the more immediate goal of reclaiming "self-governance" in the South, where autonomous government was thought possible only without Northern intervention.

Tilden's Democrats supported the withdrawal of federal troops from the South. For one thing, the U.S. government now had other concerns. In June of 1876, the Sioux and Cheyenne slaughtered Lieutenant Colonel George Custer and his cavalry at the Little Bighorn in Montana. The ambush and total defeat are still described as one of the "worst American military disasters ever."[7] Driving the Indians back into reservations became more important than the effort to remake the South in the vision of a new egalitarian and democratic order. In the centennial year of the Declaration of Independence, the federal government yearned for retreat from Lincoln's aspiration for a nation "committed to the proposition that all men are created equal." The Democrats led the way but the Republicans too were wavering.

For his part, Hayes was convinced that if the freedmen had been allowed to vote he would have won the popular vote. While the votes were being counted, he wrote in his diary,

> History will hold that the Republicans were by fraud, violence, and intimidation, by a nullification of the Fifteenth Amendment, deprived of the victory which they fairly won.[8]

Because he felt the election was rightfully his, Hayes fought for all 22 disputed electoral votes. If Tilden had gotten just one of them he would have prevailed in the final count. But Congress was too divided to permit an impartial count of the disputed electoral ballots. The Republican Senate supported Hayes; the Democratic House, Tilden. To resolve the dispute, Congress improvised. They appointed a special commission of five Representatives, five Senators, and five justices of the Supreme Court. The decisive vote was supposed to be in the hands of independent Justice David Davis. At the last minute, however, the Illinois legislature appointed Davis to the Senate. There were no other resolute independents on the Court, and therefore the power to decide the election fell to Justice Joseph P. Bradley. Five years earlier Bradley had distinguished himself as a leading voice in the *Slaughterhouse* dissent. That opinion favoring federal intervention against state power could not generate an accurate prediction about how he would vote in the controversy between Tilden and Hayes. He eventually assigned all 22 disputed electoral votes into the Republican column, thus settling the election. Bradley may have had the sense of acting in the name of principle,[9] but behind the scenes machinations made the election of Hayes politically acceptable.

In the tension-filled days of February 1877 (the inauguration was then in early March), the Democrats sought a concession to protect their interests. Their primary goal was securing the withdrawal of federal troops; Hayes and the Republicans were willing to give assurances that this would happen. The Democrats then gracefully conceded. It was a disastrous deal for African Americans, but there were new items on the national agenda.

A political élite had taken upon itself the power of choosing the president in a make-shift electoral system. The élite expressed itself in the unprecedented and constitutionally dubious procedure of authorizing a special presidential commission as the arbiter of the election. And finally, the candidates themselves resolved the matter by making a private deal to withdraw federal troops. The locus of power was hardly in the people. The power brokers ruled. This was the political prologue to the Supreme Court's abandoning the quest for civil rights for blacks in 1883. As a few politicians decided to bring an end to Reconstruction, a few men in black robes decided that Congress did not have the authority to enact a civil rights law to end the vestiges and badges of slavery. Politics and law, in tandem, drove the intended postbellum legal order underground.

The history of the Secret Constitution is framed, then, by two disputed elections—the elections of 1876 and 2000. The election of 1876 spelled the end of Reconstruction, the suppression of the values of equality and democracy, and the vindication of élitist decision-making. The election of 2000 appeared at the outset to vindicate our democratic commitments but in the end the resolution bore many resemblances to the high-handed intervention of the power-brokers in 1876.

NATIONHOOD AND
DEMOCRACY REVISITED

The sense of nationhood was stronger in 2000 than it had been in the course of the 1980s and 1990s, as the nation witnessed extended commentary about multiculturalism, the racial divide, the gender gap, and other assumed divisions in the American collective. The fact is that as the country observed the seemingly endless counting and recounting of the Florida ballots, the American people approached the impasse with extraordinary tolerance and understanding. There were critical divisions in the popular vote. Men voted heavily for Bush (53%) and women for Gore (54%). Blacks and Hispanics voted overwhelmingly for Gore

(90% and 62%) and whites favored Bush (54%). The larger cities voted predominantly for Gore, and the smaller towns for Bush. And yet no one claimed that their advantage in a subdivision of the electorate gave them an edge in legitimacy.

In most countries of the world, the dominant group would claim that having won within its own sector of the electorate, it was entitled to win the whole election. For example, in Quebec's periodic votes for secession, it is not uncommon to hear the argument that those of French descent— the real Québecois—favor secession, as though those who identified with France had some special entitlement to decide the issue. Similarly, in the contest between Benjamin Netanyahu and Simon Perez in 1996, the billboards and posters proclaimed that Jews favored Netanyahu—as though the Jewish vote counted more than the Israeli-Arab vote. In Hungary, politicians have often insulted rural voters with the implicit claim that the more sophisticated voters in the cities are the bearers of democratic legitimacy.

Arguments of this stripe are not heard anymore in the United States, and this is a great achievement of nationhood, equality, and democracy. No one ever claimed that Bush deserved to win because he was the candidate of the whites, or of the men, or of the small towns that make up the "real" America. The America that expressed itself in the popular vote for Al Gore included everyone. And no one dared suggest otherwise.

Popular democracy cannot work simply as a random collection of blocs. The idea requires a strong sense of nationhood. France, Germany, and England can vote on a nationwide basis and treat the outcome as the voice of the nation as a whole. But the countries of the European Union have not yet reached the point in the evolution of consciousness where they can contemplate a popular vote for the officers of the Union. Joschka Fischer, the Foreign Minister of Germany, dreams of a single European president on the American model. But national loyalties are still too strong. An overwhelming majority in one large country like Germany or France would determine the outcome, thus drowning out the voices of the smaller nations. Because the Europeans are not yet a single nation, they cannot accord to a fraction of the German or Italian vote the same weight that is due to the entire voting population in Ireland or Denmark.

Those who support the electoral college might think the same way about the United States. We are supposedly still a collection of states or, at best, a union of regions. We see these regions in the electoral map of 2000. The South and Midwest voted solidly for Bush. The Northeast, the region of the Great Lakes, and the Far West, for Gore. If we had a nationwide popular election, we would take the risk that an overwhelming majority in New York or California could determine the outcome whenever the candidate could poll a respectable percentage in the rest of the country. In our present system, a super-majority in one state is for nought. This forces the candidate out of their home states and home regions and requires them to engage the undecided electorate all across the country.

The downside of the electoral college is that it violates the principle of one person, one vote. A vote by someone in the Gore majority in California or New York did not carry as much weight in the election as the run of the mill vote in Florida or Oregon or New Mexico—all closely divided states. In fact, under the system of winner take all, all votes in excess of the one necessary to create a majority are superfluous.

Also, because each state starts with a base of three electoral votes—regardless of its population, the allocation of electoral votes is skewed toward the smaller states. The electoral college incorporates the principle of representation in the Senate, which treats each state as though it were a separate nation entitled to an equal voice with all others. Although regionalism remains alive in the United States, it is hard to take seriously the idea that each state stands for a distinctive culture entitled to representation in its own right. At one time we tolerated a similar representation of counties in the upper houses of state legislatures, but the Supreme Court declared this mode of representation unconstitutional in violation of the principle "one person, one vote."[10] The Courts dismissed the idea that geographical units per se were entitled to representation. Yet the text of the Constitution itself prevents the logical extension of this critique to the Senate and the electoral college.

The power that the Senate and electoral college gives to the smaller states ensures that they will both survive.[11] Three-fourths of the states would have to ratify a constitutional amendment, and the smaller states are unlikely to vote to surrender their relative influence. Yet some reform might be possible. For example, it should be possible to gain acceptance of an amendment that would apportion electoral votes according to the popular vote in each state.

The continuing control of the states over the electoral process is one of the remarkable features of our system that became painfully apparent to observers of the deadlock in Florida in November 2000. It is hard to believe that the election of the president of the United States would be governed by a series of fifty-one independent state (and District of Columbia) laws. One could understand how and why state elections would proceed according to the preferences and the law of the local electorate. But why should a national office representing the nation as a whole follow the same rules? The only answer is history.

In the original conception of the Constitution, the public—the nation—had no independent existence. All residual power was reserved to the states. The states chose their senators. They chose their electors for the electoral college. Even elections for the House of Representatives were to be governed by the rules for electing members of the "most numerous branch of the state legislature."[12] State law was supreme—even in shaping the federal government.

All of this should have changed after the Civil War. As the Fourteenth Amendment defined national citizenship, the Fifteenth Amendment should have approached the problem of voting rights for emancipated blacks as a federal matter. Instead, the Fifteenth and all subsequent amendments on voting rights took the approach of prohibiting state discrimination on the basis of certain criteria—race, gender, age, etc. The emphasis on discrimination as the nexus of federal law has meant that state authority of elections has survived—despite the growing sentiment that the American nation has a palpable reality and has indeed become the touchstone of legitimacy in elections of the president.

Not only did Florida think itself sovereign over elections within its borders, but specific counties within Florida exercised extraordinary local control over the process. The Palm Beach County Board of Elections could design the ballot that would be used in their county and not elsewhere. The Dade County Canvassing Board could decide, on its own, to go forward with a recount of the votes by hand, as authorized by the state Supreme Court. And the feature of the election that was most disturbing was the authority of each county to adopt their own criteria for fathoming the voter's intention in cases of imperfect ballots. Thus, a ruckus erupted about how to treat a "dimpled" or "hanging" chad. The word "chad" was generally unknown on election day, but the subsequent disputes about counting the votes brought home to everyone following the news the meaning of this term for the piece of paper punched out of a ballot.

This degree of localism in the United States must come as a great shock to observers unaccustomed to American practices and traditions. We noted the same phenomenon in the approach toward school financing. According to the *Rodriguez* decision, equality of financing is not required at either the national or state level. All that the equal protection clause demands is equality at the level of the individual school district.[13] Localism is difficult to comprehend when the stakes are the education of local schoolchildren and harder to grasp as a system for electing the national president; county control over the design of the ballot and the criteria for counting votes seems only to invite unnecessary confusion and dissonance.

FLORIDA AND THE STATE OF DEMOCRACY IN 2000

There has probably never been an election in American history that has undergone the media scrutiny that focused on Florida in the days and weeks after the voting on November 7. Perhaps any election, when exposed to this kind of detailed inspection, would reveal fissures and faults. Florida's process certainly disturbed many people.

There were the roughly 4000, largely elderly, voters in Palm Beach County who misread the "butterfly" ballot and voted, by mistake, for right-wing conservative Pat Buchanan. They punched the second hole on the left-hand page in order to vote for Gore whose name appeared second on the page. They did not realize that the second hole correlated with the first name on the right-hand page, namely Buchanan. Then there were the 19,000 citizens in the same county who punched two holes, presumably to make sure that despite the confusion they voted for Gore. The ballot-reading machines threw out the doubly-punched cards. In Miami-Dade County there were at least 9,000 ballots that the machine failed to read. They were supposed to be counted by hand in a procedure authorized by the state Supreme Court on November 21.[14] But for reasons that historians have yet to clarify, the local canvassing board decided not to proceed with the manual recount.

In Broward and Palm Beach Counties, where a hand count was un-
derway in the week before November 26, there was considerable disagreement about the criteria for assessing the voters' true intentions in
cases where the ballot punch did not dislodge the chad at the center. In
some counties the bipartisan teams of hand counters were instructed to
look at the ballot as a whole to assay the voters' true intentions.

Most of the disputes about the recount seemed to redound to the advantage of Al Gore, who was behind by several hundred votes in the
machine count. But the Republicans had their complaints too. There
were the potential Bush voters in the long Western panhandle of the
state who were arguably deterred from voting because the networks
called the election for Gore while the polls were still open in their counties. And then there were the absentee ballots from the military that
were thrown out because they bore no postmark, even though a postmark was unattainable under the circumstances.

As they debated the Florida recount, both sides gravitated toward the
word "disenfranchisement." All those whose votes did not count were disenfranchised. The accidental Buchanan voters, the double-punchers, the
military without a postmark—all were deprived of their voice. A certain
hypocrisy ran through this debate, for virtually no one mentioned the
greatest group of disenfranchised of all—the more than one half-million
Florida residents who could not vote because they had been convicted of a
felony. Florida is one of the eleven states that still disenfranchise convicted felons for life. The impact on African-American voters is astound-
ing. Twenty-four percent of the black male adults in Florida are unable to
vote. If they had been able to vote, there is little doubt about who would
have won the election (90% of blacks voted for Gore in 2000).

The continuing disenfranchisement of felons is one of those scandals
that is so deep and so obvious it can hardly be discussed. On April 1,
1999, the Constitutional Court of South Africa held that inmates were
entitled to vote because "the vote of each and every citizen is a badge of
dignity and personhood." And yet, apparently, Americans love to hate
their criminals. In a Massachusetts initiative in the 2000 election, 65
percent of the state's voters approved of a proposal to disqualify inmates
in prison from voting. It is hard to understand this reactionary attitude
in the context of growing support for popular democracy.

Because so many blacks could not vote, the total count in Florida
suffered from the the same shortcoming that led Hayes to question the

legitimacy of the Florida vote in 1876. In those days, the forces of racism used intimidation, poll taxes, and literacy tests to keep blacks from the polls. Today our hatred for criminals leads to the same pattern of disenfranchisement.

The debate about the 22,000 or 23,000 citizens in Palm Beach County who misread the "butterfly" ballot (by punching the hole for Buchanan or two holes to be sure) carried a special poignancy. The reaction of many was intolerant. There was talk of third graders following the instructions correctly. The claim was that the confusion of those who lost their vote was their own fault. Those who felt the wrong to run deep— to the core of our democratic values—expressed an important theme of the Secret Constitution. It is our duty in a democracy to protect the weak and elderly from the risk of their own mistakes. We have the burden of designing a system of voting that extends the franchise even to those who have difficulty following instructions. This is what it means to take every voter as equal in his or her right to vote.

The image of democracy in Florida could not survive unless we turned a blind eye toward all the disenfranchised. This was a tragedy, a betrayal of egalitarian, populist values, but the quest for stability required us to act *as if* the electorate had gone to the polls and cast their votes. All sides agreed that every vote counted—at least among those who could vote and chose to vote. The guiding rhetorical principle was that the will of the people should be probed by counting the ballots as precisely as possible. Yet there were many, including Florida Secretary of State Katherine Harris, who put the value of finality and her understanding of the rule of law ahead of a free-ranging probe of the voters' expressed preferences. In its well-reasoned opinion of November 21, the Florida Supreme Court ruled that Harris had abused her discretion by imposing a deadline that ruled out a hand recount of the disputed ballots.[15] The principle underlying the rules laid down in the Florida Election Code had a single rationale: to assess the will of the people.

Yet there are obvious limits in assessing the will of the electorate. The Palm Beach voters who mistakenly punched the hole for Pat Buchanan did not have their will registered in the election. Though many proposals for correcting the mistake were forthcoming, it seemed beyond the capacity of the system to provide a remedy. Some critics thought that Palm Beach voters should have a chance to vote once

again. But there was no way to recreate the situation that existed on November 7, with all its temptations to vote for Buchanan or Ralph Nader.
Others thought that both Buchanan and Gore should receive the votes
of the doubly-punched ballots or that the votes should be apportioned
according to the general pattern of voting in other counties,[16] but that
remedy would have generated problems with regard to other doubly-
punched ballots that were declared invalid. There are some wrongs in
life for which the law has no plausible remedy, and the disenfranchisement of the Palm Beach voters—including the 19,000 who punched
two holes—appeared, unfortunately, to be one of them.

The relevant standard, therefore, is not simply the will of the voters,
but the will of voters as expressed in their actions. The action of punching the wrong hole precludes a further inquiry into intention. But what
about a partial punch of some hole—not knowing whether the voter
really wanted to punch it out or not? There are so many different ways
that a vote can appear to be different from the standard vote that people
began to wonder whether an accurate count of the votes was possible. A
mathematician put it this way:

> No mountaineer would climb Mount Everest, scratch a quarter
> inch of ice off its summit and then claim that it was now only
> 29,027 feet, 11 3/4 inches high. After all, everyone realizes that
> its height is just an estimate—and that the margin of error is
> much greater than a quarter of an inch.[17]

Supposedly the same is true of the vote count in Florida. A difference
of 500 votes is essentially a tie. But if so, who should win? We naturally
resist the idea that the true majority is unknowable. Columbia Law
School recently claimed that it added its one-millionth volume to the library. Did they mean one million-plus-or-minus-a-hundred? Can't they
count the number of books they have? Can't the canvassing boards count
the number of votes for each candidate? It seems that we should be able
to control for fraud and count the votes cast, patiently and precisely.

Maybe not. In Florida's case there were human problems of recounting the ballots that evoked Heisenberg's uncertainty principle. The han-
dling of the ballots changed them, sometimes by dislodging a
"hanging" chad. Observers of the hand count saw little pieces of white

paper collecting on the floor. The mere fact of trying to observe changed the thing being observed.[18]

The dispute about counting the votes in Florida brought to the fore two different conceptions of the rule of law, and the conflict of these conceptions recapitulated the positions taken before the Civil War between the advocates of higher law and the legalists. The Democrats sided with the same school of higher law and moral principle that motivated the abolitionists before the Civil War and the Republicans, with the conservative line taken by the South. The Democrats used the law as a sword to pursue the "truth" about the will of the electorate. They were willing to accept the subjective judgments of election officials in reading "dimpled chads." They had the persistence and passion that comes with taking the moral high ground. Of course, their principles also served their political interests.

The Republicans invoked the value of legal regularity in order to protect their lead in the machine count. They rejected an open and flexible set of criteria for fathoming the voter's intention. They favored the blind judgment of machine counts to the more discriminating but possibly flawed judgment of human ballot readers.

The general attitude of the American public in the aftermath of election 2000 was that the situation was so surreal that you could not write a credible novel with all the twists and turns that we then experienced. I wonder whether this is so. The refinement of polling technique, the use of focus groups, and the constant monitoring of potential voter response has converted politics into the science of wooing undecided voters. That two effective campaigns would end up splitting the uncommitted votes in the middle should come as no great surprise.

The more basic question is why politics has degenerated into a form of marketing without regard to ideological commitment. Perhaps this is a consequence of good fortune—the end of the cold war, the strongest economy in history, and the gradual taming of social conflict. In the campaign of 2000, it seemed that neither the American public nor their candidates had any serious disagreements, except perhaps whether one debating style was preferable to another. When the decision comes down to vanilla versus strawberry, it is not surprising the voters would be evenly split. The legacy of postbellum pragmatism in the year 2000 was an evenly divided public in a campaign without serious issues and an electoral machinery that did not accurately register the votes.

THE INTERVENTION OF THE SUPREME COURT

When nothing else worked, Americans kept their faith in the United States Supreme Court. The country might be evenly divided, the courts and Secretary of State in Florida might be at loggerheads, but the nine justices in Washington could be counted on to provide a source of calm deliberation. They would remain grounded in reason and tradition. The Supreme Court had never decided an election before, but since the days of Hayes and Tilden—when the country relied on a Congressionally-appointed commission—the Court had grown in influence and self-confidence. The idea of resolving the election was tempting. The better part of wisdom would surely have been to stay out of the political thicket. The justices could only alienate half the country by appearing to favor one side over another. Hayes's commission knew that after a politically motivated decision, it could disband. But the Supreme Court lives on to face the political consequences of its decisions.

When Bush first indicated that he would appeal to the U.S. Supreme Court, the experts and pundits responded dismissively. There was no apparent "federal question," no dispute about the interpretation and application of either a federal statute or the Constitution. How, then, could the justices possibly intervene?

Well, they did. The first tentative strike came on December 4 (*Bush I*), a second hit stayed the manual recount on December 9 (*Bush II*), and the final blow gave the election to Bush on December 12 (*Bush III*). In *Bush I* the justices maintained a united front in asserting that there were federal questions in the case that centered primarily on language of the electoral college provision.[19] This decision was relatively harmless, for Florida could still carry out its manual recount in four specified counties if it could avoid running afoul of federal law. Four days later, the Florida Supreme Court decided, four votes to three, that the canvassing boards must tabulate not only the uncounted ballots in Miami-Dade County but also the remaining "undercounts" in all of the counties in the state.[20] In *Bush II*, a five-vote majority crystallized to prevent the "irreparable harm" to the petitioner George Bush that would occur if a final count of the ballots revealed that Gore had won the Florida election, even though the Court might subsequently decide that the recount was illegal.[21] Then, in *Bush III*, the same five votes concluded first that there was a federal question in the case, that it was sufficiently grave to require the Court's intervention, and that there was no time left for the Florida courts to repair the defect.[22] The election was over. Bush was, in effect, declared the winner.

There are many sources of embarrassment for the five-vote majority. They were seen as overtly partisan. They appeared to be confused in their own convictions because they could not agree on reasons for favoring this drastic intervention in an election run by Florida officials under Florida law. Three votes (the so-called judicial conservatives: Justices Antonin Scalia, William Rehnquist, and Clarence Thomas) reasoned that Florida had run afoul of the electoral college provision of the federal Constitution. The two swing votes (Justices Anthony Kennedy, Sandra Day O'Conner) joined them in shutting down the federal election but were willing only to support the argument that the recount procedures in Florida raised "problems" under the equal protection clause of the Fourteenth Amendment.

The dissenters were also divided. Two of the four (Justices Souter and Breyer) agreed in principle that there was a problem of equality under law, but they would have allowed Florida to correct the problem and finish the recount. The other two (Justices Stevens and Ginsburg) concluded that there was no federal question in the case and that the Court had no basis for interfering in the election.

If you did not believe that the Supreme Court was driven by politics before the decisions in *Bush II* and *Bush III*, you would certainly believe so afterwards. The semblance of a biased decision unfortunately validated the assumptions of television commentators, who emphasized that seven of the nine justices were appointed by Republican presidents. They appeared to have returned the favor and chosen a Republican president. This kind of symbiotic bond between the Court and the Chief Executive represents, to many, a serious threat to American democracy.

Yet every decision by an appellate court has two faces. One face looks to the parties and their specific dispute. The other face turns toward the future. The opinions provide language and argument that live potentially forever. The reasoning of the three *Bush* decisions will be cited back to the Court for decades and, let us hope, centuries to come. Perhaps the decisions were wrong, politically motivated, and an abuse of the nation's trust, but the arguments delivered by the Court have a life of their own.

The opinions in the three cases raise serious jurisprudential problems—problems that would be worthy of a book in their own right. There is the conundrum of distinguishing between interpretation by courts and legislating new law. There is a deep question about whether the federal Constitution grants power to the states or merely recognizes and relies on power that already exists. And there is an important distinction between federal legislation that imposes duties on the states and legislation that merely confers an optional power that might be exercised or not. The disagreements between the Court's majority and the dissenters turn largely on these philosophical issues, and there will be many occasions to address them in the future.

For our purposes in this study of the Secret Constitution, however, the most salient aspects of *Bush I*, *Bush II*, and *Bush III* are those that bear on the values of nationhood, equality, and democracy. These three themes that run through this book provide our organizing structure for reviewing the justices' opinions.

The question of *nationhood* took the form in the Florida electoral dispute, as it has so often in American legal history, of debating the relationship between the states and the federal government. In *Bush I* the Court came forth with a new conception of the nature of both state court judges and state legislatures. The starting point for the Court's thinking was the language of the electoral college provision: "Each State shall appoint, in such Manner as the Legislature thereof may direct, a Number of Electors. . . ." These few words would echo and the meaning they carry would become the leitmotif of all the opinions of the Supreme Court in the tumultuous days of December 2000.

The remarkable assertion of *Bush I* is that when a state legislature directs that the people shall elect slates of electors for president and vice-president, they are acting "by virtue of a direct grant of authority made under" the electoral college provision of the 1787 Constitution. There is some truth to this view, but the phrase "grant of authority" obscures a fundamental conceptual distinction.

The traditional view of a state legislature is that its legitimacy depends on the authority conferred on it by its state constitution.[23] Its decisions are *recognized* as carrying weight at the federal level. Under the majority's innovative view, the federal "grant of authority" to the state legislature means that the U.S. Constitution creates the authority in state legislatures to act in the way necessary to select electors in a presidential race.

To see the difference very clearly, think about the language in Article V requiring that amendments proposed by Congress be "ratified by Legislatures of three fourths of the several States, or by Convention in three fourths thereof." This provision *recognizes* the authority of the legislatures to say yes or no to an amendment, but it does not *confer* authority on the legislature to take a stand on the proposed amendment. There would be something disturbingly circular about a system in which the agency charged with amending the Constitution acquired all its authority from the Constitution itself. If there is anything fundamental in our constitutional structure, both before the Civil War and after, it is that the source of all authority is "We the People" or, in the postbellum phrase, the "American nation."

Yet in *Bush I* the Supreme Court actually seemed to endorse the view that when a state legislature defines a manner of presidential election, the legislature's authority derives not from the people of the state but from the federal Constitution itself. In order words, their authority flows not from the bottom up but from the top down. This is probably the most radical reinterpretation of states' rights ever proposed, more radical than anything accomplished in the Civil War. The idea had always been that the states elected the president and vice president by virtue of their intrinsic authority, the same authority that makes the states capable of ratifying and amending the Constitution and makes them, together with the people under the Tenth Amendment, the ultimate bearers of all powers "not delegated to the United States by the Constitution, nor prohibited" to them by the Constitution.

There are many references in the Constitution to matters prohibited to the states, but nowhere does the Constitution *grant* authority to the states. The very idea that the states or a state legislature would acquire authority from the Constitution violates the structure of constitutional authority that flows from the people, to the states, and finally to the federal government, including the Supreme Court. And yet the Supreme Court now proposes to turn this structure on its head and treat the federal Constitution as the source legitimating the states' appointing presidential electors.

If this were merely a jurisprudential nicety, we need not worry about it. But in fact vast consequences follow from a theory of what a state legislature is. The inference drawn by the Court in *Bush I* is that the state legislatures—in effect, as agents of the federal government—may direct the manner for the state to appoint its electors. The opinion of the Court found fault with the Florida Supreme Court's implicitly referring to the state constitution as a factor bearing on its decision. This means, apparently, that for purposes of federal elections, the state legislature should act under one and only one constitution—namely the federal Constitution.

There is no authority for these radical views about the nature of state legislatures. And that explains why the supposedly ardent conservatives on the Court—Justices Rehnquist, Scalia, and Thomas—shifted in *Bush III* to another version of this argument about the status of states in federal elections. As formulated in an opinion by Justice Rehnquist, the claim is even more radical than the suggestion that state legislatures are not bound by state constitutions. Because state legislatures are supposed to prescribe the manner for selecting presidential electors, it follows, the three justices claimed, that "the text of the election law itself . . . takes on independent significance."[24] Any significant judicial "departure from the legislative scheme for appointing Presidential electors, [therefore] presents a federal constitutional question."[25] The Florida courts must, by implication, adhere very closely to an election statute. If they do not, they run afoul of federal law.

The problem is that no one knows how close is close. The conventional way of talking about this problem is to distinguish, on a spectrum of possibilities, among various stages of interpretation. A court can simply read a statute word by word, it can give a gloss to a statute by explaining its overall meaning and purpose, it can seek an interpretation that reconciles its conflicting provisions, or it can reach beyond the words of the statute and ground its interpretation in the implicit intention of the legislature. All of these moves are within our conventional understanding of judicial interpretation. And yet, apparently, the Florida courts were not allowed to interpret their own election law in this way. And why not? The answer supplied by the Rehnquist opinion invoked another version of the argument that the Florida legislature was "their" legislature— that is, a legislature acting under the federal Constitution:

> This inquiry does not imply a disrespect for state courts but rather a respect for the constitutionally prescribed role of state

legislatures. To attach definitive weight to the pronouncement
of a state court, when the very question at issue is whether the
court has actually departed from the statutory meaning, would
be to abdicate our responsibility to enforce the explicit requirements of Article II [i.e. the electoral college provision].[26]

The reasoning, therefore, goes like this. For purposes of presidential
elections, state legislatures act, as the Court wrote in *Bush I*, "by virtue
of a direct grant of authority made under Art. II." It follows that the
state courts are not entitled to interfere with the legislative scheme as
"intended" by the state legislature. For these purposes, then, state law is
federal law, under the primary interpretative authority of the United
States Supreme Court.

Needless to say, the trio of so-called conservatives had no precedent
for this reading of the Constitution. They became a moving target by
constantly shifting the basis of their decision. In *Bush I*, they invoked an
obscure provision of federal law, 3 USC Sec. 5, that has no purpose other
than to guarantee the state-chosen electors a presumption of legitimacy
in the U.S. Congress ("safe harbor") if they are selected in a certain way.
In fact, the states cannot "violate" this provision. They can merely fail
to take advantage of it—something they might rationally choose to do.
Rehnquist argued that this provision in 3 USC informed his reading of
Article II but it is not clear how. Therefore, the argument shifted again,
this time to a few precedents decided during the confrontation between
the state and federal courts on the implementation of civil right legislation in the segregationist South. In a few cases, the Supreme Court did
conclude that the state courts of that era were acting in bad faith by resisting federal authority. To implement the federal civil rights policy,
the justices in Washington intervened with their own interpretation of
state law.

The conservatives' proposal in *Bush III* cuts much deeper into state
authority than an occasional overruling of an aberrant state court decision. If this theory prevails in the long run, no state will ever again have
authority to interpret its own election law in a presidential election. The
extent of this federal takeover of the state legislatures is revealed in the
way that the five-vote majority interpreted Florida law on the question
whether the Florida legislature would have wanted to have a complete

tally of its votes and name a slate of its electors even if this process would result in missing the deadline of December 12 and forfeiting the presumption of legitimacy under federal law. These are the lines in which the five-vote majority speaks to the option of remanding the case to continue the manual recount according to the instructions of the Florida Supreme Court:

> The scope and nature of the remedy ordered by the Florida Supreme Court jeopardizes the "legislative wish" to take advantage of the safe harbor provided by 3 U.S.C. Sec. 5[27] December 12, 2000, is the last date for a final determination of the Florida electors that will satisfy Sec. 5. . . . Surely when the Florida Legislature empowered the courts of the State to grant 'appropriate' relief, it must have meant relief that would have become final by the cut-off date of 3 U.S.C. Sec. 5.

Notice the language: The Florida legislature "must have meant" that the remedies possible were those that would permit a decision by December 12. Let us leave aside the fact that the U.S. Supreme Court itself, by granting the stay in *Bush II* on December 9 made relief by December 12 impossible. How did the "supposed" conservatives know that the Florida legislature would not regard the full execution of a manual count of ballots as more important than the presumption of legitimacy it might acquire under federal legislation? A rational legislature might well care more about the democratic value of counting the votes than about the "safe harbor" provision. The only basis for finding out what Floridians think is to ask them. That means, in the context of reading a complicated statute, relying upon the interpretation of the state supreme court. Instead of making this inquiry, the five-vote majority simply adopted the Rehnquist-Scalia-Thomas position that justices in Washington know better than the Florida Supreme Court what the Florida legislature "must have meant."

It is not easy to respond to arguments that are constantly moving from one set of premises to another. The four dissenting justices had a hard time training their rhetorical sights. For example, in his dissent in *Bush III*, Justice Stevens's opinion, joined by the other dissenters, attacked the argument made only in *Bush I* that for purposes of presidential elections, state legislatures should act unconstrained by their state constitutions: "[The Constitution] does not create state legislatures out of whole cloth, but rather takes them as they come—as creatures born of, and constrained by, their state constitutions."[28] This point is well taken but it came too late. The majority had already moved on to a different argument.

In their separate opinions, Justices Souter and Breyer tried patiently to dissect the "conservative" argument in Chief Justice Rehnquist's opinion that the decisions of the Florida Supreme Court deviated from the legislative plan to the point of violating federal law. They worked through various interpretative moves made by the Florida Supreme Court and, in the end, remained puzzled by the elementary question: How and why did the Florida courts exceed the permissible limits of interpretation?[29] Justice Ginsburg focuses on the systematic degradation of the state courts that follows from invoking the civil rights precedents for federal intervention in the interpretation of state law:

> The Florida Supreme Court concluded that counting every legal vote was the overriding concern of the Florida Legislature when it enacted the State's Election Code. The court surely should not be bracketed with state high courts of the Jim Crow South.[30]

Imperfect arguments—and the majority's arguments are undoubtedly wanting—can sometimes hint at sound impulses that the Court could not properly articulate. In this case the Court is obviously struggling with a felt imperative to treat presidential elections as a national question. Let us try to imagine how, if the five justices had more time to think about their position and they were completely forthright, their argument might go.

The first point is to recognize that the election of the president and vice president are unique issues in the structure of American government. The executive is the only branch of government that represents the nation as a whole. The Congress expresses the interests of states and districts, and the judiciary is supposed to be neutral—representing no one. The procedures for electing the president and the vice president must express values that speak, therefore, not to the interests

of the states but to the supremacy of the nation. We have reformed
other state-bound decisions by constitutional amendment; for example,
we have transformed the selection of senators by state legislatures into
the direct election of senators. And yet we are saddled with an antebellum provision on presidential electors that speaks in the idiom of states'
rights. This provision cannot be amended because the smaller states,
whose voice is amplified in the electoral college, will not agree. Therefore we must undertake to amend the Constitution by judicial construction. The way to do this is to begin to think of the state legislatures, for
purposes of electing the president, as fulfilling a mission delegated to
them by the federal Constitution. By making this assumption we can
develop a body of federal law that will avoid the breakdowns that occur
when each state manages its own federal elections.

Stated in this manner, the argument is too radical for general acceptance. But it is a way of looking at the Court's decision that makes sense
in light of the basic principles of the Secret Constitution. There are
times when the Court must act to insure the basic values of the American system. In the election of 2000, the argument of nationhood should
have strengthened Gore's hand because he won the popular vote by over
300,000 votes. An apology for the Court on the issue of nationhood requires, then, that we think not only about the contest between Gore and
Bush but about reform of the system in the long run. If the decision in
Bush III leads to an electoral system that more clearly recognizes the interests of the nation, then it might gain the approval of future judges,
lawyers, and scholars.

The Court's assertions in *Bush III* on the issue of equal protection are
even more dramatic than its implicit acceptance of the nation's importance in electing the chief executive. This argument, not even mentioned in *Bush I*, eventually carried the day. To use the conceptual
structure we developed in chapter 8, the focus of the argument in *Bush
III* was not the state's reinforcing caste discrimination against a particular group. The problem was rather the perceived arbitrariness of procedures adopted by the various counties for counting the disputed ballots.
The core of this felt arbitrariness was differing approaches to interpreting ballots that were only partially punctured, thus left with hanging or
dimpled chads. Everyone agreed that the relevant standard was the intent of the voter as expressed in physical marks on the ballot. But in

formulating criteria for assessing that intent, some counties went one way; others went the other way. Seven justices of the Supreme Court agreed that equality under law was a critical problem in the resolution of the Florida election.

That these ballot counting procedures became the central issue in *Bush III* provides dramatic confirmation of the way in which the principle of equality under law has matured since the enactment of the Fourteenth Amendment to become the cornerstone of our constitutional jurisprudence. The commitments of the Secret Constitution seem to be confirmed.

Yet it is not so clear the seven justices were really concerned about equal protection of the laws as that phrase has come to be understood. The analysis of an equal protection problem requires, first and foremost, the identification of a group that suffers unfavorable treatment under the application of the law. This is the group that has standing to sue on the ground of state-sponsored discrimination. Who is that group in *Bush III*? One of the questions before the Court was whether Miami-Dade county should count the 9000 "undervotes" that did not register in the machine recount. Does the petitioner George Bush suffer as the result of this recount? How do we know whether he would have gained or lost votes as a result of this procedure?

The victims of the recount would arguably be all voters whose ballots would have been counted by the application of less accurate criteria. But why would ballots so counted constitute a wrong to the voters? They would suffer an injustice only if the criteria applied in their case failed to gauge their true intentions. And there is no way of knowing which standard would be best suited to getting the voters' intentions right in the greatest number of cases. Suppose there are three possibilities: standard A (e.g., disregard ballots with dimpled chads), standard B (e.g., search for the voter's intent in the case of a dimpled chad), and the random application of sometimes A and sometimes B. Since we do not know whether A is always better than B, there is no way of knowing whether the random application of A and B would be a worse way of getting at the truth than either A or B standing alone.

Seven justices had an instinct of injustice that they termed the problem of equality under law, but the intuition that motivated them was not about equality in the ordinary sense. Their true concern was the rule of law. The view that triumphed finally in the minds of seven justices was that fluctuating and changing standards had substituted the rule of human beings—the canvassing boards—for governance by law. As we should recall, however, the rule of law lends itself to divergent interpretations. The higher law tradition favoring the pursuit of truth and justice stands in constant conflict with the view of law as a system requiring the regular and stable application of rules. The Democrats had urged the rule of law as an open-ended quest for the truth about the voters' intentions. The latter view of law as regular, predictable behavior triumphed and became anchored in an interpretation of the equal protection clause.

The rule of law requires, of course, courts that enjoy respect and legitimacy. If the courts are thought to be political and partisan, the rule of law loses its currency. Whether the decision in *Bush III* would damage the good name of American judges became the preoccupation of the dissenting justices. Justice Stevens wrote:

> Although we may never know with complete certainty the identity of the winner of this year's Presidential election, the identity of the loser is perfectly clear. It is the Nation's confidence in the judge as an impartial guardian of the rule of law.[31]

The other dissenting justices expressed similar views in their separate opinions, but the most significant harm wrought by *Bush III* was not to the prestige of the courts but to the institutions of popular democracy. The decision may have confirmed the first two planks of the Secret Constitution—nationhood and equality, but it did leave a deep wound in our understanding of the third principle, our commitment to "government of the people, for the people, and by the people."

There were two intentions at play in the debate—those of the Florida legislature and those of the Florida voters. In interpreting state law, the majority of the Supreme Court was willing to engage in imaginative arguments about what the Florida legislature "must have meant." But when it came to the voters' intentions, the majority made it clear that the people and their intentions were of subsidiary importance: "The factfinder [the ballot counter] confronts a thing, not a person."[32] This is true, as far as it goes. The statutes of the state of Florida are also things, but things that take on meaning and purpose because of the people that stand behind them.

The most disturbing line in the majority opinion expresses contempt for the institution of democracy as it has evolved since the Civil War:

> The individual citizen has no federal constitutional right to vote for electors for the President of the United States unless and until the state legislature chooses a statewide election as the means to implement its power to appoint members of the Electoral College.[33]

This seems true, if we just look at the words on the document of 1787. But as this entire book has argued, the historical truth has evolved. Democracy has become embedded in the very foundations of the federal Constitution. The vast array of constitutional amendments prohibiting discrimination in the franchise would make no sense if the states could simply abolish the right to vote across the board. The federal government is obligated to guarantee a "republican" form of government to the states,[34] and in our time, this would surely imply a recognition of the democratic franchise. The idea that the popular vote is a contingent matter, dependent on a choice by state legislatures, is hardly faithful to the legacy of Lincoln at Gettysburg.

Perhaps we should settle for a decision of the Supreme Court that affirms two principles of the Secret Constitution and slights the third. But "We the people" take our sovereignty seriously. The court and citizens of Florida care about whether Floridians should have been allowed to complete their electoral process without being told what their legislature "must have meant." The disenfranchised are properly bitter that they could not influence the outcome of the election in 2000. The election may have been settled, remarkably, without even a thought about taking up arms but the anger of the people will find other ways to express itself.

Allow me to end with a vision of another great awakening, akin to the early nineteenth-century surge of moral conscience that led to the abolition of slavery. We the American people will arise from our ideological slumber. We will realize that this Supreme Court has become an authoritarian institution that speaks in the name of the nation and equality but fails to credit the sovereignty of the people. We will experience a "new birth" of commitment to the great issues that define our

Secret Constitution. We will confront the problem of equality and explore its depths in a way that we have never done before. We will grasp the fate of the weak, the ill-educated, the disenfranchised, and the misfortunate left behind in the strongest economy on earth. We will refine our democratic institutions so that they conform to the rule of law. The nation will not only endure, it will become a nation that understands what it means to be "conceived in liberty and dedicated to the proposition that all men are created equal."

NOTES

INTRODUCTION

1. Noam Chomsky, *Syntactic Structures* (1978).

2. First Inaugural Address, March 4, 1861.

3. For the elaboration of this contrast between "higher law" thinking and "legalism" in the Civil War, see Robert Penn Warren, *The Legacy of the Civil War* (1961).

4. The heir to this position in contemporary American jurisprudence is Lon Fuller in his debate with H. L. A. Hart in the Harvard Law Review. See H. L. A. Hart, "Positivism and the Separation of Law and Morals," 71 Harv. L. Rev. 593 (1958); Lon L. Fuller, "Positivism and Fidelity to Law—A Reply to Professor Hart," 71 Harv. L. Rev. 630 (1958).

5. See Warren, supra note 3, at 26.

6. The higher law tradition in the United States has taken various forms. It is the foundation of judicial review. See Edward Corwin, "The Higher Law Background of the Constitution," 42 Harv. L. Rev. 365 (1928). It is also the basis for the contemporary assertion of a Constitution based in moral principles. See Ronald Dworkin, *Freedom's Law: The Moral Reading of the Constitution* (1996).

7. And indeed the Constitution of the Confederacy outlawed the international slave trade. See Constitution of the Confederacy, Art. I, Sec. 9.

8. See the discussion below in chapter 2.

9. See Bruce Ackerman, *We the People: Transformations* 8–11 (1998).

10. For a view more sympathetic to Lincoln, see Mark E. Neely, Jr., *The Fate of Liberty* 131 (1991) (arguing that the majority of those affected by Lincoln's suspension of the writ were deserters or draft evaders).

11. Warren, supra note 3.

12. See Michael Les Benedict, "Constitutional History and Constitutional Theory: Reflections on Ackerman, Reconstruction, and the Transformation of the American Constitution," 108 Yale L.J. 2011 (1999) (citing the "grasp of war" doctrine).

13. See Ackerman, supra note 9.

14. This theme is explored further in chapter 11.

15. For a full development of these themes, see chapter 6 infra.

16. Plessy v. Ferguson, 163 U.S. 537 (1896).

17. See Theda Skocpol, *Protecting Soldiers and Mothers: The Political Origins of Social Policy in the United States* (1992).

18. Mark Tushnet, *Taking the Constitution Away from the Courts* (1999).

19. Bruce Ackerman, *We the People: Foundations* (1991) and Bruce Ackerman, *We the People: Transformations* (1998).

20. Akhil Amar, *The Bill of Rights: Creation and Reconstruction* (1998).

21. Michael Sandel, *Democracy's Discontent* (1996).

22. Charles Black, *A New Birth of Freedom* (1997).

23. Eric Foner, *Reconstruction: America's Unfinished Revolution 1863–1877* (1988).

24. Garry Wills, *Lincoln at Gettysburg: The Words that Remade America* (1993).

25. James McPherson, *Abraham Lincoln and the Second American Revolution* (1992).

26. Two exceptions have come to my attention. Anders Stephanson, *Manifest Destiny* (1996); and Melina Lawson, *Patriot Fires: Loyalty and National Identity in the Civil War North* (Columbia Ph.D. dissertation 1997). I would be pleased to know that others have cultivated the same themes with as much clarity.

27. Robert Cover, "Nomos and Narrative," 97 Harv. L. Rev. 4 (1983).

CHAPTER ONE

1. David Daube, *Studies in Biblical Law* 122–23 (1947).

2. This line is quoted in Ken Burns's PBS series, *The Civil War* (episode 1).

3. On the role of law as the means of settling disagreements, see Jeremy Waldron, *Law and Disagreement* (1999).

4. Gustav Radbruch, *Rechtsphilosophie* 123 (8th ed. 1973) (*Recht ist die Wirklichkeit, die den Sinn hat, der Gerechtigkeit zu dienen*).

5. Compare Radbruch's response, id. at 345.

6. Translation by the author. The "inherent" does not appear in the original. It is added to make sense of the claim of the people's "constitutional authority" [*verfassungsgebende Gewalt*].

7. Decision of the German Constitutional Court, February 26, 1969, 25 BVerfGE 269.

8. Decision of the German Constitutional Court, February 25, 1975, 39 BVerfGE 1. For a later decision modifying the initially radical support for the "right to life," see Decision of the German Constitutional Court, May 28, 1993, 88 BVerfGE 203.

9. Decision of the German Constitutional Court, October 24, 1996, 95 BVerfGE 96, translation in 18 Human Rights L. J. 65 (1997). The most thoughtful commentary in English is Manfred Gabriel, "Coming to Terms with the East German Border Guard Cases," 38 Colum. J. Transnat'l L. 275 (1999).

10. Ken Burns, *The Civil War* (episode 3).

11. U.S. Constitution, Art. IV, Sec. 2, Cl. 1.

12. U.S. Constitution, Art. I, Sec. 10, Cl. 1.

13. The first four sections break down the contents of the Fourteenth Amendment, Sec. 1; the fifth section restates the content of the Thirteenth Amendment, Sec. 1; and the sixth replicates the Fifteenth Amendment, Sec. 1. The final section summarizes distinct provisions found in all three amendments.

14. It is not clear whether the original written version included the words "under God" or whether Lincoln added them spontaneously as he spoke. See Garry Wills, *Lincoln at Gettysburg* 192–98 (1992).

15. A less provocative way to formulate this thesis would be to think of law as a set of instructions to decision-makers. See Kent Greenawalt, *Statutory Interpretation: 20 Questions* (1999).

16. For a survey of the problem, see William E. Nelson, *The Fourteenth Amendment: From Political Principle to Judicial Doctrine* (1988). Also, for a good introduction to the field of equal protection, see Kenneth Karst, *Belonging to America: Equal Citizenship and the Constitution* (1989). For views on the significance of equal protection similar to my own, see David A. J. Richards, *Conscience and the Constitution: History, Theory and Law of the Reconstruction Amendments* (1993).

17. Michael Klarman argues that Brown v. Board of Education clearly departed from the original understanding of the Fourteenth Amendment. Michael Klarman, "An Interpretive History of Modern Equal Protection," 90 Mich. L. Rev. 213 (1991).

18. Babylonian Talmud, Baba Metzia 58b. The story concludes, in one version, with an encounter between Rabbi Nathan and the prophet Elijah. Rabbi Nathan asked, "What did God do at that moment when Rabbi Joshua proclaimed 'it is not in Heaven'?" Elijah answered, "God laughed and said: 'My children have defeated me, my children have defeated me.'"

19. See Jeremy Waldron, *The Law* 60 (1990).

20. The word count differs, depending on the draft used and the way of counting such words as "battle-field." Ken Burns claims 269 words. Ken Burns, *The Civil War* (episode 5).

CHAPTER TWO

1. Address in Independence Hall, Philadelphia, Pennsylvania, February 22, 1861.

2. The legality of the blockades was tested in the *Prize Cases*, 67 U.S. 635 (1862).

3. Ex parte Merryman, 17 Fed. Cas. 144 (C.C.D. Md. 1861) (No. 9,487).

4. Scott v. Sandford, 60 U.S. 393 (1856).

5. Message to Congress, July 4, 1861, *Complete Works of Abraham Lincoln*, vol. 6, 297, 309 (J. Nicolay and J. Hay, eds.).

6. See Garry Wills, *Lincoln at Gettysburg: The Words that Remade America* (1992).

7. According to the standard version and the usual counting, there are 268 words in the address. This treats "battle-field" as one word. "Nation" appears as the 16th word, which leaves 252 words remaining.

8. See Akhil Amar, "The Bill of Rights as a Constitution," 100 Yale L.J. 1131 (1991).

9. As I point out below, the use of the expression "Civil War" as opposed to "War Between the States" carries a partisan connotation.

10. See Arthur L. Goodhart, "Lincoln and the Law," in *Lincoln and the Gettysburg Address* 55 (A. Nevins, ed. 1964).

11. It was quite common to refer to slavery as the "peculiar institution" of the South. This euphemism was coined and popularized by John C. Calhoun in 1830. See Kenneth M. Stampp, *The Peculiar Institution: Slavery in the Ante-Bellum South* 2 (1961).

12. Second inaugural address, March 4, 1865.

13. See U.S. Constitution, Art. VI, Cl. 3: "no religious Test shall ever be required as a Qualification to any Office or public Trust under the United States."

14. On this dispute in the text of the address, see Wills, supra note 6.

15. Speech to the New Jersey State Legislature, February 21, 1861.

16. Psalms 19:10.

17. See Anders Stephanson, *Manifest Destiny* (1996).

18. U.S. Constitution, Art. I, Sec. 2, Cl. 3.

19. Theodore Parker, *The Slave Power* 250 (Hosmer, ed. year of publication not given) (emphasis added).

20. U.S. Constitution, Art. I Sec. 2, Cl. 1.

21. U.S. Constitution, Art. I, Sec. 3, Cl. 2.

22. U.S. Constitution, Art. II, Sec. 1, Cl. 2.

23. For details on these amendments, see chapter 10.

CHAPTER THREE

1. For further details on the process of constitutional amendment and the franchise, see chapter 10.

2. U.S. Constitution, Seventeenth Amendment.

3. The expression "bonds of memory" comes from the first inaugural address, March 4, 1861.

4. See, for example, the suggestive book title about the Confederate defeat at Gettysburg, Clifford Dowdey, *Death of a Nation: The Confederate Army at Gettysburg* (1986).

5. As quoted in Ken Burns, *The Civil War* (episode 1).

6. Walt Whitman, Leaves of Grass (1855) in Walt Whitman, *Collected Poetry and Prose* 5 (Justin Kaplan, ed. 1982).

7. Id. at 8.

8. Id. at 6.

9. Chishold v. Georgia, 2 U. S. 419, 455 (1793).

10. Lydia Maria Child, *An Appeal in Favor of That Class of Americans Called Africans* 123 (Carolyn L. Karcher, ed., rev. ed. 1996).

11. Second speech on Foot's Resolution, January 26, 1830.

12. Frederick Douglass, "The Present and Future of the Colored Race in America," in *The Life and Writings of Frederick Douglass*, vol. 3, 347, 352 (Philip S. Foner, ed. 1952).

13. Delivered at the Lincoln Memorial, August 28, 1963.

14. Congressional Globe, 40th Congress, 3rd Session, 982 (1869).

15. James Russell Lowell, "The President's Policy," North American Review, vol. 98, 222 (1864).

16. Orestes Augustus Brownson, The American Republic, *Collected Works of Orestes Brownson*, vol. 18, 30 (Henry F. Brownson, ed. 1966).

17. Id. at 74.

18. Id. at 23.

19. Id. at 43.

20. Id. at 7–8.

21. Id.

22. See my own efforts to elaborate the connection between loyalty and law in George P. Fletcher, *Loyalty: An Essay on the Morality of Relationships* (1993).

23. Brownson, supra note 16, at 29.

24. Id.

25. The document is entitled "Fragment on the Constitution and the Union." Apparently Alexander Stephens used the same metaphor in his letter to Lincoln on December 30, 1860.

26. Brownson, supra note 16, at 7–8.

27. Id. at 9–10.

28. For example, Brownson expressed very conservative views on the role of the family in structuring the nation. See id. at 14 (stressing the value of patriarchy).

29. On this historical development, see Telford Taylor, *The Anatomy of the Nuremberg Trials: A Personal Memoir* 8–11 (1992).

30. Reprinted in Francis Lieber, *Miscellaneous Writings*, vol. 2, 225 (1881).

31. Id.

32. Id. at 227.

33. Id.

34. Benedict Anderson, *Imagined Communities: Reflections on the Origin and Spread of Nationalism* (1991).

35. For details, see Geoffrey C. Ward, with Ric Burns and Ken Burns, *The Civil War* 246–53 (1990).

36. Lieber, supra note 30, at 227.

37. Id. at 228.

38. The recent French translation of Bruce Ackerman's *We the People* is entitled *Au Nom du peuple*.

39. Lieber, supra note 30, at 228.

40. Id. ("In the organic unity lies the chief difference between the words Nation and People.")

41. Id.

CHAPTER FOUR

1. U.S. Constitution, Art. III, Sec. 3, Cl. 1.

2. See 18 United States Code, Sec. 2381 (requiring "allegiance to the United States" as a condition for committing treason).

3. The *Prize Cases*, 67 U.S. 635 (1862).

4. D. P. O'Connell, *International Law*, vol. 2, 651 (2nd ed. 1970).

5. The Constitution does not say anything about the president's authority with regard to insurrections, but it does authorize Congress "to provide for calling forth the Militia to execute the Laws of the Union, suppress Insurrections and repel Invasions." U.S. Constitution, Art. I, Sec. 8, Cl. 15. The Justices also relied, in part, on Congress's subsequent ratification of the seizures.

6. 67 U.S. at 674.

7. Cummings v. Missouri, 71 U. S. 277 (1866).

8. Id.

9. Ex Parte Garland, 71 U.S. 333 (1866).

10. U.S. Constitution, Art. I, Sec. 10, Cl. 1.

11. Today we would sense a violation of the First Amendment "freedom of religion" clause in this prohibition, but at the time the clause did not apply to the states.

12. Cummings v. Missouri, 71 U.S. at 328–29.

13. See Bruce Ackerman, *We the People: Transformations* 8–11 (1998).

14. U.S. Constitution, Fourteenth Amendment, Sec. 3. ("No person shall be a Senator or Representative in Congress, or Elector of President and Vice-President, or hold any office, civil or military, under the United States, or under any State, who, having previously taken an oath, as a member of Congress, or as an officer of the United States, or as a member of any State legislature, or as an executive or judicial officer of any State, to support the Constitution of the United States, shall have engaged in insurrection or rebellion against the same, or given aid or comfort to the enemies thereof. But Congress may by a vote of two-thirds of each House, remove such disability.")

15. U.S. Constitution, Fourteenth Amendment, Sec. 4. ("The validity of the public debt of the United States, authorized by law, including debts incurred for payment of pensions and bounties for services in suppressing insurrection or rebellion, shall not be questioned. But neither the United States nor any State shall assume or pay any debt or obligation incurred in aid of insurrection or rebellion against the United States, or any claim for the loss or emancipation of any slaves; but all such debts, obligations, and claims shall be held illegal and void.")

16. U.S. Constitution, Fourteenth Amendment, Sec. 2. ("Representatives shall be apportioned among the several States according to their respective numbers, counting the whole number of persons in each State, excluding Indians not taxed. But when the right to vote at any election for the choice of electors for

President and Vice-President of the United States, Representatives in Congress, the Executive and Judicial officers of a State, or the members of the Legislature thereof, is denied to any of the male inhabitants of such State, being twenty-one years of age, and citizens of the United States, or in any way abridged, except for participation in rebellion, or other crime, the basis of representation therein shall be reduced in the proportion which the number of such male citizens shall bear to the whole number of male citizens twenty-one years of age in such State.").

17. For analysis of these political machinations, see Eric Foner, *Reconstruction: America's Unfinished Revolution 1863–1877,* at 183–85 (1988).

18. See the comment by Senator Welch, supra page 63.

19. Marquis Adolphe de Chambrun, *Impressions of Lincoln and the Civil War* (1952).

20. Id. at 84.

21. Id. at 105.

22. Id.

23. Id. at 109.

24. On the legal problems connected to adopting the Fourteenth Amendment, see Ackerman, supra note 13.

CHAPTER FIVE

1. Declaration of the Rights of Man 1789, Art. 1: *Les hommes naissent et demeurent libres, et égaux en droits.*

2. Bruce Ackerman, *Social Justice in the Liberal State* (1980).

3. John Rawls, *A Theory of Justice* (1971).

4. Id. at 56.

5. Jeremy Bentham, *An Introduction to the Principles of Morals and Legislation* (J. H. Burns and H. L. A. Hart, eds. 1970).

6. John Locke, *Second Treatise on Government,* chapter 2, section 6, lines 10–14 (1690).

7. This is one way to characterize John Rawls's intense commitment to human equality in Rawls, supra note 3.

8. U.S. Constitution, Art. I, Sec. 9, Cl. 8 (federal government); Art. I, Sec. 10, Cl. 1 (states).

9. For further details, see the discussion of the Supreme Court's jurisprudence in chapter 9 infra.

10. In the original: *Elle [la loi] droit être la meme pour tous, soit qu'elle protège, soit qu'elle punisse.*

11. Aristotle, *Nicomachean Ethics* 1155a–56b.

12. U.S. Constitution, Art. IV, Sec. 2, Cl. 1.

13. U.S. Constitution, Fifth Amendment.

14. Weimar Constitution, Art. 109(1).

15. German Basic Law, Art. 3(1).

16. Gerhard Leibholz, "Die Gleichheit von dem Gesetz und das Bonner Grundgesetz," 7 Deutsches Verwaltungsblatt 193 (1951).

17. For the details of this argument, see George P. Fletcher, "In God's Image: The Religious Roots of Equal Treatment under Law," 99 Colum. L. Rev. 1608 (1999).

18. William G. McLoughlin, *Revivals, Awakenings, and Reform* 105 (1978).

19. Second inaugural address, March 4, 1865.

20. Frederick Douglass, "An Antislavery Tocsin" speech in Rochester, New York, December 8, 1850, in John Blassinghame, ed., *The Frederick Douglass Papers*, vol. 2, 260–72, 262 (New Haven: Yale University Press, 1982).

21. Second inaugural address, March 4, 1865.

22. See Gary Wills, *Lincoln at Gettysburg: The Words that Remade America* 104 (1992).

23. Speech to the New Jersey State Legislature at Trenton, New Jersey, February 21, 1861.

24. This translation, with its engendered language, resembles any translation that would have been used in the mid-nineteenth century. My own view is that the passage is correctly rendered in English as "So God created the human being in God's own image, in the image of God created God it, male and female God created them." See Genesis 1:27 in the new translation, *The Five Books of Moses: A New Translation With Introductions, Commentary, and Notes* (Everett Fox, ed. 1997).

25. For a more careful analysis of the biblical text, see my recent article, supra note 17.

26. Immanuel Kant, *Fundamental Principles of the Metaphysics of Morals* 51 (Thomas Abbott, trans. 1949).

27. I am indebted to Robert Post for bringing this objection to my attention.

28. The Dred Scott Decision, Springfield, Illinois, June 26, 1857.

29. Genesis 1:27.

30. German Basic Law, Art. 1 (*Die Menschenwürde is unantastbar. Sie zu schützen und zu achten is Pflicht aller staatlichen Gewalt*).

31. For an elaboration of Kantian moral philosophy, see George P. Fletcher, "Law and Morality: A Kantian Perspective," 87 Colum. L. Rev. 533 (1987).

32. See, most recently, Charles Black, *A New Birth of Freedom: Human Rights, Named and Unnamed* (1997).

33. U.S. Constitution, Art. IV, Sec. 2, Cl. 1.

34. For a modest revival of interest in the privileges and immunities clause, see Saenz v. Roe, 526 U. S. 489 (1999)(right to travel upheld against a state residency requirement).

35. Bruce Ackerman, *We the People: Transformations* 8–11 (1997).

36. Akhil Amar, *The Bill of Rights: Creation and Reconstruction* (1998).

37. *Civil Rights Cases* (dissenting opinion) discussed below in chapter 6.

38. Carl von Clausewitz, *On War* (1832).

CHAPTER SIX

1. Robert Penn Warren, *The Legacy of the Civil War* 15 (1961).

2. U.S. Constitution, Fourteenth Amendment, Sec. 3.

3. See Eric Foner, "The Strange Career of the Reconstruction Amendments," 108 Yale L. J. 2003, 2005 (1999).

4. First inaugural address, March 4, 1861.

5. Nevada, the 36th State, was admitted in 1864.

6. Marbury v. Madison, 1 Cranch (5 U. S.) 137 (1803).

7. The most notable use of judicial review was the most disgraceful. See the *Dred Scott* decision, holding that the Missouri Compromise prohibiting slavery violated the due process clause of the Fifth Amendment. Scott v. Sandford, 60 U.S. 393 (1857).

8. See *Slaughterhouse I*, 83 U. S. 36 (1872).

9. Charles Black, *A New Birth of Freedom: Human Rights Named and Unnamed* 58 (1997).

10. *Slaughterhouse I* at 45.

11. Id.

12. 11 Coke's Reports 85 (Kings Bench 1602), reprinted in *The Selected Writings and Speeches of Sir Edward Coke,* vol. 1 (Steve Sheppard, ed. 2000).

13. 83 U.S. at 102.

14. Id. at 61.

15. See Dr. Bonham's Case, 77 Eng. Rep. 638, 652 (C. P. 1610).

16. 83 U.S. at 65.

17. For discussion of Justice Harlan's views, see pp. 133–37.

18. For example, it is mentioned in Corfield v. Coryell, 6 Fed. Cases 546 (No. 3230 E. Dist. Pa. 1823) as a factor in defining the "privileges and immunities" of state citizens.

19. On the history of the Pledge, see George P. Fletcher, *Loyalty: An Essay on the Morality of Relationships* 101–16 (1992).

20. U.S. Constitution, Art. III, Sec. 2, Cl. 1.

21. U.S. Constitution, Art. IV, Sec. 2, Cl. 1.

22. U.S. Constitution, Art I, Sec. 2, Cl. 2 (seven years citizenship required to run for House); Art. I, Sec. 3, Cl. 3 (nine years required for Senate); Art. II, Sec. 1, Cl. 4 (only "natural born citizens" may be President).

23. Scott v. Sandford, 60 U.S. 393 (1856).

24. U.S. Constitution, Art. IV, Sec. 2, Cl. 1.

25. The leading case is Corfield v. Coryell, 6 Fed. Cases 546 (No. 3230 E. Dist. Pa. 1823).

26. These and other minor restrictions on the states are listed in U.S. Constitution, Art. I, Sec. 10, Cl. 1.

27. 83 U.S. at 78.

28. Id. at 80.

29. 83 U.S. at 82.

30. Bradwell v. Illinois, 83 U.S. 130 (1872).

31. Minor v. Happersett, 88 U.S. 162 (1874).

32. Yick Wo v. Hopkins, 118 U.S. 356 (1886).

33. Ex parte Virginia, 100 U S. 339 (1880)

34. *Strauder*, 100 U.S. 303 (1880).

35. Civil Rights Bill originally passed April 9th, 1866, 14 Stat. 27, ch. 31, and re-enacted with some modifications in sections 16, 17, and 18 of the Enforcement Act, passed May 31st, 1870, 16 Stat. 140, Ch. 114.

36. 18 Stat. 335.

37. *Civil Rights Cases*, 109 U. S. 3 (1883).

38. 109 U.S. at 30.

39. Id.

40. U.S. Constitution, Art. I, Sec. 10, Cl. 1.

41. Granting this authority, thereafter, became common in constitutional amendments, particularly in those expanding the franchise, see, for example, U.S. Constitution, Nineteenth Amendment (women's suffrage), and Twenty-Third Amendment (presidential electors for the District of Columbia).

42. U.S. Constitution, Art. IV, Sec. 2, Cl. 3.

43. See Robert Cover, *Justice Accused* (1975).

44. U.S. Constitution, Art. I, Sec. 8, Cl. 3 (The Congress shall have the power "to regulate commerce with foreign nations, and among the several States, and with the Indian tribes."). But see United States v. Morrison, 529 U.S. 598 (2000) (upholding the reasoning of the *Civil Rights Cases*).

45. 109 U.S. at 41 (emphasis added).

46. Id. at 42 (emphasis added).

47. Id. at 46 (emphasis added).

48. Id. at 43–44.

49. Id. at 51.

50. Id. at 54.

51. Id. at 53 (emphasis added).

52. Id. at 28.

53. Plessy v. Ferguson, 163 U.S. 537 (1896).

54. See Walter Dean Burnham, "Constitutional Moments and Punctuated Equilibria: Political Scientist Confronts Bruce Ackerman's *We the People*," 108 Yale L. J. 2237 (1999).

55. On the difference between higher law thinking and legalism, see the discussion in the Introduction at page 6.

CHAPTER SEVEN

1. Eric Foner, *Reconstruction: America's Unfinished Revolution 1863–1877,* at 198–202 (1988).

2. On the Supreme Court's history of this legislation, see *Papachristou,* 405 U.S. 156, 161 (1972).

3. The definition of the ordinance struck down in *Papachristou* included as vagrants "persons wandering or strolling around from place to place without any lawful purpose or object, habitual loafers, disorderly persons, persons neglecting all lawful business and habitually spending their time by frequenting houses of ill fame, gaming houses, or places where alcoholic beverages are sold or served. . . . " Id. at 158, note 1.

4. For a review of some of the cases litigated at the time, see Peter Wallenstein, "Law and the Boundaries of Place and Race in Interracial Marriage: Interstate Comity, Racial Identity, and Miscegenation Laws in North Carolina, South Carolina, and Virginia, 1860s–1960s," 32 Akron L. Rev. 557 (1999).

5. See Foner, supra note 1.

6. O. W. Holmes, Jr., *The Common Law* 68 (1881), citing Lewis v. State, 35 Ala. 380 (1860).

7. See, for example, Screws v. United States, 325 U.S. 91 (1945) (holding the police brutality to be an action under "color of law" and therefore an expression of state action).

8. C. W. Harlow, *Profile of Jail Inmates 1996, Special Report, Bureau of Justice Statistics* (August 1998) to be found at http://www.ojp.usdoj.gov/bjs/jails.htm

9. P. Lewin and K. Wright, *Drug War Facts: March 1999* (Common Sense for Drug Policy Foundation).

10. Allen Beck and Christopher Mumola, *Prisoners in 1998*, U.S. Department of Justice, Bureau of Justice Statistics, August 1999.

11. Washington v. Davis, 426 U.S. 229 (1976).

12. Palmer v. Thompson, 403 U.S. 217 (1971).

13. *Strauder*, 100 U.S. 303 (1880).

14. Loving v. Virginia, 388 U.S. 1 (1967).

15. *Papachristou*, 405 U.S. 156 (1972).

16. The classic example is the beating of Rodney King discussed in detail in George P. Fletcher, *With Justice for Some: Victims' Rights in Criminal Cases* (1995).

17. See the trial of the Scottsboro boys reversed in Powell v. Alabama, 287 U.S. 45 (1932).

18. The active use of the civil rights remedy sought to overcome the problem of *impunidad* in Southern criminal justice.

19. See Foner, supra note 1, at 293–94.

20. U.S. Constitution, Nineteenth Amendment.

21. U.S. Constitution, Twenty-Fourth Amendment.

22. See the Voting Rights Act of 1965 as applied in Katzenbach v. Morgan, 384 U.S. 641 (1966).

23. See generally The Sentencing Project, Policy Report No. 9080, *Losing the Vote: The Impact of Felony Disenfranchisement Laws in the United States* (1998).

24. Id.

25. See German Criminal Code Sec. 45 (regulating the temporary loss of the right to hold office and the possible restriction on the right to vote).

26. See note 23 supra.

27. Hunter v. Underwood, 471 U.S. 222 (1985).

28. *Ramirez*, 418 U.S. 24 (1974).

29. See Michael Klarman, "An Interpretive History of Modern Equal Protection," 90 Mich. L. Rev. 213 (1991).

30. Compare the way the Court dismissed this problem in Minor v. Happersett, 88 U.S. 162 (1874).

31. It has to be recalled, however, that the Court did not apply the equal protection clause on behalf of women until the early 1970s. See, for example, Reed v. Reed, 404 U.S. 71 (1971) (held unconstitutional as violation of the equal protection clause, an Idaho statute providing that as between persons equally qualified to administer estates, males must be preferred over females).

32. See, for example, Dillenburg v. Kramer, 469 F. 2d 1222, 1224 (9th Cir. 1972); Washington v. State, 75 Ala. 582 (1884).

33. Convicted sex offenders are regarded as tainted for the rest of their lives. Under the rash of legislation dubbed Megan laws, they must register whenever they move into a new neighborhood. For a case upholding Megan's law, see, for example, Doe v. Pataki, 120 F. 3d 1263 (2d Cir. 1997).

34. Note, "The Disenfranchisement of Ex-felons: Citizenship, Criminality, and The Purity of the Ballot Box," 102 Harv. L. Rev. 1300 (1989) (arguing that ex-felons lack the virtue necessary under a republican approach to citizenship).

35. For a review of these constitutional arguments, see George P. Fletcher, "Disenfranchisement as Punishment: Reflections on the Racial Uses of *Infamia*," 46 UCLA L. Rev. 1895 (1999).

36. *Strauder*, 100 U.S. 303 (1880).

37. Batson v. Kentucky, 476 U.S. 79 (1986).

38. See note 31 supra.

39. Levy v. Louisiana, 391 U. S. 68 (1968) (violation of equal protection for Louisiana to deny "illegitimate" children the right to recover for the wrongful death of their mother).

40. Graham v. Richardson, 403 U S. 365 (1971) (violation of equal protection for states to condition welfare benefits on citizenship or to impose a residency requirement).

41. See John Coons, William Clune, and Stephen Sugarman, *Private Wealth and Public Education* (1970).

42. The leading case is Serrano v. Priest, 18 Cal. 3d 728, 557 P. 2d 929, 135 Cal. Rptr. 345 (1976), *cert. denied*, 432 U.S. 907.

43. San Antonio Independent School District v. Rodriguez, 411 U.S. 1 (1973).

44. Most of the academic criticism has chastised the Court for this decision, but there are some voices in favor. See Edward Foley, "*Rodriguez* Revisited: Constitutional Theory and School Finance," 32 Ga. L. Rev. 475 (1998). Foley's argument is that parents should have a right to purchase superior education for their children, precisely as they may use their resources to benefit their children in other ways. This way of looking at the problem shifts the focus from the rights of the children to the rights of the parents.

45. *Ramirez*, 418 U.S. 24 (1974).

46. Note the opening lines of the concurring opinion by Justice Stewart: "The method of financing public schools in Texas, as in almost every other State, has resulted in a system of public education that can fairly be described as chaotic and unjust. It does not follow, however, and I cannot find, that this system violates the Constitution of the United States." *Rodriguez*, 411 U.S. 1, 92 (1973).

47. Id.

48. Williamson v. Lee Optical, 348 U. S. 483 (1955). Compare the decision in the Slaughterhouse case upholding the commercial monopoly to the Crescent City Live-stock Landing and Slaughter-House Company. *Slaughterhouse Cases*, 83 U.S. 36 (1872).

49. See, for example, Mississippi University for Women v. Hogan, 458 U.S. 718 (1982) (excluding males from state nursing school violated the equal protection clause).

50. See the Court's summary of its own doctrine at *Rodriguez*, 411 U.S. 1, 95 (1973).

51. Id. at 46.

52. Shapiro v. Thompson, 394 U.S. 618 (1969).

53. The leading case is Serrano v. Priest, 487 P. 2d 1241 (Cal. 1971).

54. County of Santa Clara v. Southern Pac. R. R., 18 F. 385, 398–99 (1883); Railroad Tax Cases, 13 F. 722, 733 (1882).

55. *Rodriguez*, 411 U.S. 1, 68 (1973).

56. German Basic Law Article 3(1) provides: "All human beings are equal before the law." Article 3(2) adds a provision to foster affirmative action for women:

"Men and women have equal rights. The state shall further the realization of this equality between men and women and shall seek to neutralize the vestiges of inequality."

Article 3(3) adds a list of prohibited criteria for imposing legislative benefits and burdens:

"No one may be advantaged or disadvantaged on the basis of sex, descent, race, language, homeland or national origin, religion, or religious or political commitments. No one may be disadvantaged on the basis of a physical handicap."

57. Decision of the Constitutional Court, First Senate, November 23, 1976, 43 BVerfGE108.

58. German Basic Law, Art. 20(1).

59. David Johnston, "Gap Between Rich and Poor Found Substantially Wider," *New York Times*, September 5, 1999, p. 16. See Bruce Ackerman and Anne Alstott, *The Stakeholder Society* (1999) (claiming that the benefits of the current economic boom all go to the top 20 percent of rich Americans).

60. *Rodriguez*, 411 U.S. 1, 50 (1973).

61. For example, Griffin v. Illinois, 351 U. S. 12 (1956); Douglas v. California, 372 U.S. 353 (1963).

62. Harper v. Virginia Board of Elections, 383 U.S. 663 (1966).

63. John Ely, *Democracy and Distrust* (1980).

64. Buck v. Bell, 274 U.S. 200, 208 (1927).

CHAPTER EIGHT

1. German Basic Law, Art. 3(1).

2. This conclusion is based on a Lexis search in the English and Canadian databases.

3. Scott v. Sandford, 60 U.S. 393, 702–03 (1856).

4. 60 U.S. at 550.

5. *Slaughterhouse I*, 83 U S. 36, 146 (1872).

6. Bradwell v. Illinois, 83 U.S. 130 (1872).

7. *Slaughterhouse II*, 111 U.S. 746, 762 (1884).

8. This expression, no longer in use in constitutional argument, carries significant historical associations. In Dr. Bonham's Case, decided in 1610, Sir Edward Coke declared a statute of Parliament null and void because it violated "common right and reason." The notion of "common right" stands for the entrenched principles of the common law that are not subject to legislative change. Dr. Bonham's case is generally regarded as the precursor of judicial review, as recognized in Marbury v. Madison, 5 U.S. (1 Cranch) 137 (1807). The term survives in this case, both in Justice Bradley's opinion, as quoted in the text, and in the concluding lines of Justice Miller's opinion for the Court, *Slaughterhouse II*, 111 U.S. 746, 760.

9. Church of the Holy Trinity v. United States, 143 U.S. 457 (1892).

10. The opinion seems to interpret Christianity to include Judaism, as suggested by the following passage: "Suppose in the Congress that passed this act some member had offered a bill which in terms declared that, if any Roman Catholic church in this country should contract with Cardinal Manning to come to this country and enter into its service as pastor and priest . . . [after mentioning Protestant sects] any Jewish synagogue with some eminent Rabbi, such contract should be adjudged unlawful and void, and the church making it be subject to prosecution and punishment, can it be believed that it would have received a minute of approving thought or a single vote?" Id. at 472.

11. Id. at 467.

12. Gulf, Colorado and Santa Fe Railway Company v. Ellis, 165 U.S. 150 (1896).

13. *Yick Wo*, 118 U.S. 356.

14. Cotting v. Kansas City Stock Yards Company and the State of Kansas, 183 U.S. 79 (1901). Justice Brewer's opinion for the Court stresses both the issues of equal protection and the deprivation of property without due process of law. A separate concurring opinion, written by Justice Harlan and joined by five more Justices, argued that the equal protection issue alone was sufficient to overthrow the statute. Id. at 114.

15. Lochner v. New York, 198 U S. 45 (1905).

16. Plessy v. Ferguson, 163 U.S. 537 (1896).

17. See Laurence Tribe, *American Constitutional Law*, Sec. 16–6 (2nd ed. 1988).

18. City of New Orleans v. Dukes, 427 U.S. 297 (1976).

19. *Korematsu*, 323 U.S. 214.

20. See Herbert Wechsler, "Toward Neutral Principles of Constitutional Law," 73 Harv. L. Rev. 1 (1959).

21. Rostker v. Goldberg, 453 U.S. 57 (1981).

22. Michael M. v. Superior Court of Sonoma County, 450 U.S. 464 (1981).

23. With respect to children born out of wedlock, see Labine v. Vincent, 401 U.S. 532 (1971) (Louisiana could discriminate against "illegitimate" children in the area of inheritance).

24. See the cases above. On the conflict between opticians and optometrists, see Williamson v. Lee Optical, 348 U.S. 483 (1955).

25. Speech by Hubert H. Humphrey to the Democratic National Convention, July 14, 1948, published in *The Civil Rights Rhetoric of Hubert H. Humphrey 1948–1964* (P. Wilson, ed. 1966).

26. Brown v. Board of Education of Topeka, 347 U.S. 483 (1954).

27. Bell v. Maryland, 378 U.S. 226 (1964); School District of Abington Township v. Schempp, 83 S. Ct. 1560 (1963) (Clark, J. , for the Court). And see the dissenting opinions in McGowan v. Maryland, 366 U.S. 420 (1961) (Douglas, J., dissenting); In re Anastaplo, 366 U.S. 82 (1960); (Black. J., dissenting). The only opinion citing the Maxim between Brewer's last citation in 1901 and 1960 was Senn v. Tile Layers Protective Union 301 U.S. 468 (1937) (Butler, J., dissenting).

28. See Califano v. Goldfarb, 430 U.S. 199 (1977) (it was a violation of equal protection for widowers to be eligible for survivors' social security benefits only if they could prove that they received at least half of their support from their wives, while widows could receive the benefits without proof of dependence).

29. Mathews v. Lucas, 427 U.S. 495 (1976).

30. Id. at 516.

31. President Gerald Ford appointed John Paul Stevens to the Court in 1975. He replaced William O. Douglas, who dissented in *Rodriguez*, and therefore the appointment would not have changed the 5–4 vote in the case.

32. Bowers v. Hardwick, 478 U.S. 186 (1986)

33. Id. at 219.

34. Charter of Rights and Freedoms, Art. 15(2).

35. German Basic Law Art. 3(3).

36. German Basic Law Art. 3(2). For the full text of this provision, see chapter 8, note 56.

37. This famous phrase comes from footnote 4 in United States v. Carolene Prods. Co., 304 U.S. 144, 152–53 n. 4 (1938). It provides a rationale for the Court's acting contrary to the democratic preferences of the majority.

38. Regents of the University of California v. Bakke, 438 U.S. 265 (1978).

39. Fullilove v. Klutznick, 448 U.S. 448 (1980).

40. Id. at 532.

41. Id. at 533, note 1.

42. Id. at 539.

43. Id. at 542 ("The legislative history of the Act discloses that there is a group of legislators in Congress identified as the 'Black Caucus' and that members of that group argued that if the Federal Government was going to provide four billion dollars of new public contract business, their constituents were entitled to 'a piece of the action.'").

44. See the analogy to Nazi efforts to define who was a Jew. Id. at 535.

45. Wygant v. Jackson Board of Education, 476 U.S. 267 (1986).

46. Id. at 316–17.

47. Mathews v. Lucas, 427 U S. 495, 516 (1976).

48. City of Cleburne v. Cleburne Living Center, 473 U.S. 432, 454 (1985).

49. Adarand Constructors, Inc. v. Pena, 515 U.S. 200 (1995).

50. Id. at 249, note 6.

51. Id. at 243 (italics added).

52. This theme is explored in Cass Sunstein, "Word, Conduct, Cast," 60 U. Chi. L. Rev. 795 (1993), both with regard to "equal protection of the laws" and limitations on free speech.

53. *Cleburne*, 473 U.S. 432, 451 (1985).

54. As in *Korematsu*, 323 U.S. 214 (1944).

55. Note that Justice Stevens dissented from the holding in Michael M. v. Superior Court of Sonoma County, 450 U S. 464 (1981) that recognized the authority of the state to subject only men to crime of statutory rape.

56. Stephen Carter, *Confessions of an Affirmative Action Baby* (1992).

57. Adarand Constructors, Inc. v. Pena, 515 U.S. 200, 240 (1995).

58. Id.

59. Lee v. Weisman, 505 U.S. 577, 606 (1991).

60. Agostini v. Felton, 521 U.S. 203, 244 (1997) (Souter, J., dissenting).

CHAPTER NINE

1. U.S. Constitution, Art. I, Sec. 8, Cl. 3.

2. The general argument of looking more broadly for constitutional principles is expressed as well in Mark Tushnet, *Taking the Constitution Away from the Courts* (1999).

3. See the discussion in chapter 7 at notes 23–28 supra.

4. Springer v. United States, 102 U.S. 586 (1881).

5. Pollock v. Farmer's Loan & Trust Company, 158 U.S. 601 (1895).

6. U.S. Constitution, Art. I, Sec. 9, Cl. 4 ("No Capitation, or other direct, Tax shall be laid, unless in Proportion to the Census or Enumeration herein before directed to be taken").

7. See Kramer v. Union Free School District No. 15, 395 U.S. 621 (1969) (compatible with equal protection to limit voting in school board elections to those "primarily interested," defined by the local statute as those affected by school taxes and parents).

8. Bruce Ackerman, *The Case Against Lameduck Impeachment* (1999).

9. See Jo Thomas, "Court Weighs Limited Seats at Bomb Trial for Victims," *New York Times*, November 15, 1996, p. A30 (discussing impact of Anti-Terrorism and Effective Death Penalty Act on trial).

10. George P. Fletcher, *With Justice for Some: Victims' Rights in Criminal Trials* 6 (1995).

11. The proposal is articulated in id. at 247–48.

12. For a principled critique of victims' exercising their influence in the sentencing phase, see id. at 198–201.

13. See McGowan v. Maryland, 366 U.S. 420 (1961).

14. As I was discussing national loyalty in a seminar at the Columbia Law School in the early 1990s, the students, quite surprisingly, claimed that my generation had been "disloyal" during the Vietnam War.

15. Halter v. Nebraska, 205 U.S. 34 (1907).

16. Abrams v. United States, 250 U.S. 616, 621 (1919) (Holmes, J., dissenting).

17. Id. at 630 ("The best test of truth is the power of the thought to get accepted in the competition of the market.") For a good popular survey of the evolution of these ideas, see Anthony Lewis, *Make No Law: The Sullivan Case and the First Amendment* (1992).

18. Texas v. Johnson, 491 U.S. 397 (1989); United States v. Eichman, 496 U. S. 310 (1990).

19. I admit that I have moderated my views since my book *Loyalty: An Essay on the Morality of Relationships* (1992), in which I argue that the flag burning cases should have been decided the other way.

20. See Cohen v. California, 403 U.S. 15 (1971).

21. R. A. V. v. City of St. Paul, 505 U.S. 377 (1992).

22. See most notably the articles of Owen Fiss in *Liberalism Divided: Freedom of Speech and the Many Uses of State Power* (1996).

23. For a chronicle of the case, see D. D. Gutenplan, "The Holocaust on Trial," *Atlantic Monthly*, p. 45 (February 2000). The suit was dismissed in mid-April 2000. See Sarah Lyall, "Losing a Libel Case," *New York Times*, April 16, 2000, sec. 4, p. 2.

24. On the interaction between the "equality" and "dignity" arguments, see Susanne Baer, *Gleichheit oder Würde?* (1995).

25. Decision of December 15, 1981, 66 BVerwGE 274 (1982–83). The same result is reached, but without relying on the constitutional principle of human dignity, in Decision of January 30, 1990, 84 BVerwGE 314 (1990).

26. See I. Kant, *Foundations of the Metaphysics of Morals* (L. Beck, trans. 1969).

27. 66 BVerfGE at 278–79.

28. See Baer, supra note 24.

29. The first major case was Meritor Savings Bank v. Vinson, 477 U.S. 57 (1986).

30. Jones v. Clinton and Ferguson, 990 F. Supp. 657 (E. D. Ark. 1998) (granting the president's and the state trooper's motion for summary judgment).

31. One of the first articles to make this claim was Philip Kurland, "Of Church and State and the Supreme Court," 29 U. Chi. L. Rev. 1 (1961).

32. Sherbert v. Verner, 374 U.S. 398 (1963) (exception recognized).

33. Leary v. United States, 383 F. 2d 851 (1967) (exception denied).

34. Wisconsin v. Yoder, 406 U.S. 205 (1972) (exception recognized).

35. Analogous versions of this injunction are found in Mark 12:17 and Luke 20:25.

36. Department of Human Resources of Oregon v. Smith, 494 U.S. 872 (1990).

37. See cases cited in notes 32 and 34 supra.

38. 107 Stat. 1488, 42 USCS 2000bb et seq.

39. 42 USCS 2000bb(b).

40. On the grant of legislative authority in this provision, see the summary of the Secret Constitution in chapter 1.

41. City of Boerne v. Flores, 117 S. Ct. 2157 (1997).

CHAPTER TEN

1. Adam Smith, *The Wealth of Nations* (1776).

2. Immanuel Kant, *The Metaphysics of Morals* (Mary Gregor, trans. 1991).

3. Akhil Amar, *The Bill of Rights: Creation and Reconstruction* (1998).

4. Henry David Thoreau, *Walden Pond* (1854).

5. These figures are drawn from Elliot W. Brownlee, *Federal Taxation in America: A Short History* 21 (1996).

6. Pollock v. Farmers' Loan & Trust Co., 158 U.S. 601 (1895).

7. Lochner v. New York, 198 U.S. 45 (1905).

8. 198 U.S. at 69.

9. Id. at 75.

10. Exodus 21:2.

11. Exodus 21:5–6.

12. Exodus 21:5.

13. For example, the Harvard Law School Sexual Harassment Guidelines, adopted by the Faculty, April 1995, stresses that "both faculty and students must be presumed to be mature and responsible adults entitled to make personal decisions concerning intimate relationships."

14. Griswold v. Connecticut, 381 U.S. 479 (1965).

15. John Stuart Mill, *Saint Simonism in London* (1834).

16. Reynolds v. United States, 98 U.S. 145 (1878).

17. See my *With Justice For Some: Victims' Rights in Criminal Trials* 52–53 (1995).

18. Akhil Reed Amar and Daniel Widawsky, "Child Abuse as Slavery: A Thirteenth Amendment Response to *Deshaney*," 105 Harv. L. Rev. 1359 (1992). This article is a critique of Deshaney v. Winnebago County Department of Social Services, 489 U.S. 189 (1989) (holding that the state is not obligated to intervene to prevent child abuse even though its social workers should have known of the danger to the child).

19. Andrew Koppelman, "Forced Labor: A Thirteenth Amendment Defense of Abortion," 84 Nw. U. L. Rev. 480 (1990).

20. Lea S. Vandervelde, "The Labor Vision of the Thirteenth Amendment," 138 U. Pa. L. Rev. 437 (1989).

21. See, for example, Douglas L. Colbert, "Challenging the Challenge: Thirteenth Amendment as a Prohibition against the Racial Use of Peremptory Challenges," 76 Cornell L. Rev. 1 (1990).

22. On the use of rents in this context, see Akhil Amar, supra note 3, but see Amar taking a contrary line in favor of expansive governmental power, supra note 18.

23. See the series "The Politics of Mistrust: Why Don't Americans Mistrust the Government," *Washington Post*, January 29–February 4, 1996.

24. Shaw v. Reno, 509 U.S. 630 (1993).

25. See *New York Times*, February 13, 2000, p. 1.

CHAPTER ELEVEN

1. For a survey of the issues, see the article by H. S. Thayer, "Pragmatism," in *Encyclopedia of Philosophy*, vol. 6, 430 (1967).

2. The story is told in Shelby Foote, *The Civil War: A Narrative: Red River to Appomattox* 458–59 (1986).

3. Oliver Wendell Holmes, *The Common Law* 5 (Mark deWolfe Howe, ed. 1963).

4. Id. at 75.

5. Buck v. Bell, 274 U S. 200 (1927).

6. Abrams v. United States, 250 U.S. 616, 621 (1919).

7. For my earlier thinking on this theme, in which I express sympathy for the Continental preference for the absolute standard of Right, see my article, "The Right and the Reasonable," 98 Harv. L. Rev. 949 (1985).

8. See John Cornwell, *Hitler's Pope* (1999).

9. For a good example of this anti-intellectual bias in legal thinking, see Richard Posner, "Problematics of Moral and Legal Theory," 111 Harv. L. Rev. 1637 (1998). One of the better responses is Ronald Dworkin, "Philosophy and Monica Lewinsky," *New York Review of Books,* vol. 47, no. 4, 48 (March 9, 2000).

AFTERWORD

1. U.S. Constitution, Art. II, Sec. 1, Cl. 2.

2. The full text of the Twelfth Amendment:

> The Electors shall meet in their respective states, and vote by ballot for President and Vice-President, one of whom, at least, shall not be an inhabitant of the same state with themselves; they shall name in their ballots the person voted for as President, and in distinct ballots the person voted for as Vice-President, and they shall make distinct lists of all persons voted for as President, and of all persons voted for as Vice-President, and of the number of votes for each, which lists they shall sign and certify, and transmit sealed to the seat of the government of the United States, directed to the President of the Senate;—The President of the Senate shall, in the presence of the Senate and House of Representatives, open all the certificates and the votes shall then be counted;—The person having the greatest number of votes for President, shall be the President, if such number be a majority of the whole number of Electors appointed; and if no person have such majority, then from the persons having the highest numbers not exceeding three on the list of those voted for as President, the House of Representatives shall choose immediately, by ballot, the President. But in choosing the President, the votes shall be taken by states, the representa-

tion from each state having one vote; a quorum for this purpose shall consist of a member or members from two-thirds of the states, and a majority of all the states shall be necessary to a choice. [And if the House of Representatives shall not choose a President whenever the right of choice shall devolve upon them, before the fourth day of March next following, then the Vice-President shall act as President, as in the case of the death or other constitutional disability of the President.]The person having the greatest number of votes as Vice-President, shall be the Vice-President, if such number be a majority of the whole number of Electors appointed, and if no person have a majority, then from the two highest numbers on the list, the Senate shall choose the Vice-President; a quorum for the purpose shall consist of two-thirds of the whole number of Senators, and a majority of the whole number shall be necessary to a choice. But no person constitutionally ineligible to the office of President shall be eligible to that of Vice-President of the United States.

3. U.S. Constitution, Art. II, Sec. 1, Cl. 2 ("Each state shall appoint. . .").

4. Note that this common understanding of our Constitution and what it requires is challenged in *Bush III*, discussed below.

5. Mark Tushnet and Akhil Amar have expressed themselves in the media in line with this view.

6. See Eric Foner, *Reconstruction: The Unfinished American Revolution 1863–1877*, at 575–80 (1988).

7. See "The Battle of the Little Bighorn," http://www.ibiscom.com/custer.htm

8. Sunday, November 12, 1786, *The Diary and Letters of Rutherford B. Hayes, Nineteenth President of the United States* (Charles R. Williams, ed. 1922).

9. The history is retold with poignancy in Justice Breyer's dissenting opinion in the case that finally settled the 2000 election, Bush v. Gore, 2000 U.S. Lexis 8430 (2000).

10. Baker v. Carr, 369 U.S. 186 (1962).

11. See Daniel Lazare, *The Frozen Republic: How the Constitution is Paralyzing Democracy* (1996).

12. U.S. Constitution, Art. I, Sec. 2, Cl. 1.

13. For a discussion of the *Rodriguez* case, see chapter 6.

14. Palm Beach Canvassing Board v. Harris, 1000 Florida Lexis 2311 (November 21, 2000).

15. This decision was subsequently vacated by the Supreme Court in Bush v. Palm Beach Canvassing Board, 2000 Lexis 8087 (December 4, 2000)(*Bush I*). For reasons indicated below I do not regard the reasoning of the U.S.

Supreme Court as sufficiently persuasive for me to change my initial opinion that the Florida decision was "well-reasoned."

16. Thanks to Frank Lossy for this suggestion.

17. John Allen Paulos, *New York Times*, November 22, 2000.

18. Thanks to Russell Christopher for his analogy.

19. U.S. Constitution, Art. II, Sec. I, Cl. 2.

20. Gore v. Harris, 2000 Florida Lexis 2311 (December 8, 2000).

21. Bush v. Gore, 2000 U.S. Lexis 8277 (December 9, 2000)(Scalia, concurring).

22. Bush v. Gore, 2000 U.S. Lexis 8277 (December 12, 2000).

23. See McPherson v. Blacker, 146 U.S. 1 (1892). The opinion in *Bush I* cites *Blacker* incorrectly to support the view that legislatures are not bound by their constitutions in legislating voting procedures for national elections.

24. *Bush III* (Rehnquist, concurring).

25. Id.

26. Id.

27. Note that this "legislative wish" is entirely made up. It appears nowhere in sources attributable to the state of Florida. The origin of the phrase is in Scalia's opinion in *Bush I*.

28. *Bush III* (Stevens, dissenting).

29. Id. (Breyer, dissenting).

30. Id. (Ginsburg, dissenting).

31. Id. (Stevens, dissenting).

32. Id. (Per curiam opinion).

33. Id.

34. U.S. Constitution, Art. IV, Sec. 4.

INDEX